HOW TO THRIVE IN HARD TIMES

A Buddhist Manual

STEPHEN FULDER

WATKINS

First published and *What's Beyond Mindfulnes* 2019,
This edition first published in the UK and USA 2024 by
Watkins, an imprint of Watkins Media Limited

Unit 11, Shepperton House
89–93 Shepperton Road
London
N1 3DF
enquiries@watkinspublishing.com

1 3 5 7 9 10 8 6 4 2

Typeset by JCS Publishing Services Ltd

Printed and bound by CPI Group (UK) Ltd,
Croydon, CR0 4YY

A CIP record for this book is available from the British Library

ISBN:-978-1-91567-274-2 (Paperback)
978-1-78678-982-2 (ebook)

www.watkinspublishing.com

MIX
Paper | Supporting
responsible forestry
FSC® C171272
FSC
www.fsc.org

CONTENTS

"If we are to flourish during these times of global crises, we need to awaken the fullness of our natural wisdom and compassion. This illuminating book helps us remember the deepest truths and capacities of who we are, and invites us to inhabit our full aliveness, awareness and heart."

Tara Brach,
author of *Radical Compassion*

"The way I use the word 'mindfulness', there is nothing beyond it, because it is shorthand for deeply embodied wisdom and its myriad expressions in life. But in this deeply nurturing and illuminating book, Stephen Fulder unfurls the universe that gave birth to the most refined articulation of mindfulness on the planet, and how it can be understood and nurtured both from the more traditional Buddhist perspective, and from a more universal and inclusionary perspective, for the benefit of all. Stephen's life trajectory and choices are an embodiment of his fierce love of what is most sacred, and most easily missed."

Jon Kabat-Zinn, Professor Emeritus,
Creator of MBSR (Mindfulness Based Stress Reduction),
author of *Full Catastrophe Living* and *Falling Awake*

"Stephen Fulder has written a book that is at once deep, authentic and accessible. With clarity and heartfulness, *How To Thrive In Hard Times* helps us understand complex topics such as emptiness and liberation as well as how we can skillfully integrate that understanding into our daily lives while making a meaningful contribution to this world. This book is a gem."

James Baraz
co-author of *Awakening Joy: 10 Steps to a Happier Life*
and co-founding teacher of Spirit Rock Meditation Center

ABOUT THE AUTHOR

Stephen Fulder, PhD, is the founder of the Israel Insight Society (Tovana) and one of Israel's leading spiritual teachers. Drawing on 40 years of deep personal experience of vipassana/ mindfulness meditation and dharma practice, he has, over the last 20 years, guided thousands of people in exploring Buddhist teachings, practising meditation and rediscovering the magic of the moment.

He has also written 14 books on health-related subjects.

INTRODUCTION TO THE NEW EDITION

In 45 years of consistent spiritual practice and teaching, including endless retreats, it has been crystal clear that the field of transformation is right here and now, in this daily life, and not in some other place beyond. Heaven and Earth are right here on the tip of our finger. This is the reason I wrote this book. I first realised that the ordinary is the ground for the extraordinary when I met Eastern spirituality in Varanasi, in 1976. Half my time was spent with the spiritually intoxicated saddhus outside my front door on the banks of the Ganges. But the other half was spent in Banaras Hindu University where I was teaching biochemistry in the lab. And moving from one extreme to the other was not a problem if my own experience and definition of reality was wide and flexible enough to contain both.

This attitude has stayed with me. A prime example has been the years of peace work I have been doing in the Middle East. One program termed The Transformation of Suffering, involved bringing groups of Israelis and Palestinians together for weekends in the Palestinian city of Nablus. The methods used were straight out of the classic Buddhist teachings on practice. We started with exercises that helped create a sense of refuge and safety, as well as friendliness, and then worked on putting ourselves in each other's shoes using empathy, compassion and the mindfulness of deep listening. The core of the workshops was one hour of dialogue in pairs, each sharing their daily life suffering. It allowed participants to look at the other with new eyes and identify with the life of the other, and so peace was made. We also did a large number of peace walks throughout the region. Israelis and

Palestinians, Jews and Arabs, walked silently, slowly and mindfully and radiated loving-kindness ('metta' – the practice is described in the book) to all who watched us, whether they responded with encouragement or anger. The police who accompanied us said that, for them, it felt like a holiday.

We are living in hard times. The world that we have been used to seems to be crumbling away at the edges. Wherever we look, things seem more difficult day by day: whether it is the constant messages of environmental disaster looming on the horizon, or the level of conflict in the world and in our communities, or the general sense that we are getting poorer, or the unavailability of health care, or the incapacity of our leaders, or the general psychological insecurity of our times. It gets under our guard and eats away at the general level of hope and vibrant well-being. We can lose basic trust in life and in ourselves.

We all have our favourite ways of coping with such challenges. They may be wholesome, such as helping others, keeping fit and well, and ensuring a positive mindset. But often our strategies are reactive and automatic and may include smartphones, shopping and other diversions, denial, blaming others or letting ourselves get swept away by authority or unexamined beliefs. All too easily we may find ourselves shutting down and switching off, which can, unfortunately, slip into depression and despair. Do we sense that our default ways of coping don't really do the job anymore? If so, it can be wise to look somewhere else completely. Out of the box. This is the purpose of this book. It brings the full panoply of Buddhist methods, wisdom and insight to bear on the woes and wonders of our daily life.

The Buddhist teachings are arguably the most sophisticated and insightful ways of working with difficulty that are known on this planet. Indeed they have often been misconstrued as a teaching that is obsessed with suffering. This is a misunderstanding. The teachings simply acknowledge that life is just life, however once we are born into a body, we cannot avoid suffering at some point, and it is better to call things by their true name rather than get swept away by avoidance, blind faith and chasing rainbows.

A gift of these teachings is that they regard pain as a wake-up call, which propels us on a search for the way out, or better, a way through. If we feel that our life, or indeed our inner development would be fine, except for all the obstacles, these teachings regard the obstacles themselves as vehicles that carry us on our journey of renewal. So how do we put down the loads we are carrying through life? For a start, we need to fully realise that it is actually our minds that carry the loads, not life. For circumstances are constantly changing and not in our control, but how we face change is entirely up to us. We need to turn towards ourselves and take responsibility for what our minds and hearts are experiencing. However, meeting and shifting our minds is not easy. The loads seem to be permanently stuck to us. For this reason, the ability to turn to meet them directly and learn how to drop them is such a powerful switch in attitude that it has been described in the suttas, the early Buddhist canon of the discourses of the Buddha, as 'The Lion's Roar'!

This is where the great potential of mindfulness and the many other Buddhist inspired psychological and spiritual practices that are described in this book come it. They can help us to make a shift at the deepest level in the way we are with ourselves, with our experiences and with the world, moment by moment. This not only helps us look at the challenges and threats that appear in our life with new eyes. But in an extraordinary way we can discover that our very nature is peaceful, joyful and connected, though we could not see it because it was obscured by beliefs, stories, memories, narratives and habits that filled our consciousness with clouds and burdens. Once the clouds are seen as unreal and not solid, the sun shines out. And in its light our life is lived differently.

The book is grounded in Buddhist teachings, but it is not a Buddhist book. The Buddhist character of the text is inherent, lifting us up from underneath rather than pulling us from above. This is also loyal to the simple, direct, non-mystical and non-religious way the Buddha himself appeared to have taught. Thankfully this is how it has reached us today – intact, practical and direct and not covered over by layers of religious obscurations. We are in a new phase of acceptance and interest in Buddhist inspired teachings in the modern world and the West. In particular, mindfulness is extremely well known and written about intensively. It is having a major impact in Western culture. For example it has changed the face of psychology with the rise of CBT, and impacting health care, education, business practices and even politics. However, it is embedded in an extremely rich teaching. This book recruits the whole teaching and is way beyond just mindfulness. Though there are currently a large number of books on Buddhist teachings and mindfulness, this book may reflect the next generation of such literature. It is not about bringing new and Eastern teachings into the modern world, it is not even about the teachings. It embodies them. I have tried where possible to impart a taste of the experiences and states of mind that are discussed in the book. As if it does not just describe a horse and how to ride it, but shows that you are already riding it.

There are around 50 pieces in this book, all of which offer a fresh look at many aspects of our daily lives and show us how we can rise above or slide between the 'slings and arrows' that are thrown at us, as well as work with the pain of those that hit us. It goes further, and explores what our life might look like from a place of awakening. The chapters are like exploratory conversations that cherish insight. Each article is independent and deals with a specific topic, idea or question relating to our lives. Therefore, I would suggest that you read the articles in the form in which they were written – spontaneously. You are invited to choose the chapter that fits the needs of the moment.

The book is divided into three sections, which are titled according to the traditional 3 legs of the teachings. The first, entitled sila in the Pali language (how we live responsibly) is about how we act and function wisely and harmoniously in life. The articles look at a variety of life circumstances, such as sickness, work, moral sensitivity, energy, speech, simplicity, money, etc. The second part, entitled samadhi in Sanskrit (practice, serenity, meditation) deals with sources, methods and directions for our journey. What are the paths up the mountain and what should we take with us? The articles include working with difficult emotions, conflict, mindfulness, body awareness, memory, conditioning, unconscious potentials, etc. The third part, entitled pannya in Pali language (wisdom, realization, awareness), is the big view - how things look from up there. These pieces deal with presence, the divine, autonomy, self and non-self, wise social action, duality and non-duality, equanimity, liberation, karma, etc. Here we may discover that the mountain may be just a mound, that climbing may be just being, and the view is actually us. Though the third part seems more advanced than the others, all are needed all the time. If we strive spiritually without a base of beneficial and ethical action in life, we will be like rowing the boat while it is still tied to the shore, and if we just deal with the quality of our actions and not our inner life, we will be just circling the mountain trying to get things right all the time, and never glimpse the peak.

The pieces that make up this book are meant to be like lamps that are just bright enough and steady enough to dispel the total darkness of the night sky and light up the road. Or maps which we refer to as we navigate through our 24 hour daily life which is the field in which we ramble, explore, fall over, get up, and in the end dance with beauty and wild freedom. There can be no other field. It reminds me of the famous Zen story of a young monk who asked the head of the monastery, what is the highest form of practice. The Abbott answered, "meditation, of course". "But I never see you sitting in meditation", said the student. "You are doing the monastic accounts, cleaning, receiving visitors, solving problems, tending the garden, busy all day." "It's true," answered the Abbott, " I am doing the accounts, receiving visitors, cleaning, solving problems, teaching and occupied all day. But I never once stop meditating."

We have all experienced whispers from the beyond, beyond our life struggles and thinking habits; whispers that tell us about the forgotten places within us that we long to rediscover. They may arrive while walking in the hills, when gazing up into the space of the heavens, in moments of love that thrill us, in a touch of unexpected sanctity that lifts us, or in the mysterious unconscious sense that 'this is limitless' ... These are all reminders of our innate freedom that the book offers. They remind us of the possibilities of understanding our true potential and our true nature as human beings.

PART ONE
HOW TO LIVE

(How I Am is Who I Am)
(SILA)

CHAPTER 1
HAVE YOU FORGOTTEN?

Have you forgotten
How to do nothing
And watch nature not doing too?
The edges of leaves, the soft fur of cats
Myths in the shapes of clouds
The stillness of the moon, tones in the wind
Your own soft breath
Dissolving the boundary between you and the world.
Have you forgotten
That your troubled mind still loves stars,
And can see the pain behind another's eyes?
Can you allow yourself to love yourself
Just the way you are
And do the same
With every stranger on the road?
Come close, get comfortable, and let me remind you …

CHAPTER 2
MORAL SENSITIVITY AND INNER DEVELOPMENT

We tend to think of our personal growth and development as an inner path with the development of awareness as its heart. Millions of people practise hatha yoga, forgetting that *yam/niyam*, ethical behaviour and sensitivity, are the first steps in the eight limbs of yoga, before hatha yoga. At the beginning of vipassana workshops we hear about the five principles of moral behaviour, but soon we are instructed to focus on the "serious" issue of meditation practice and see this as the true spiritual work. We rightly assume that continuous practice of meditation will make us better human beings, and transform our behaviour in everyday life as a result, but forget that we also need to transform our behaviour beforehand.

Once, when I was in a Buddhist monastery for a short stay, I had a deep and subtle conversation with the abbot about consciousness. But at the end of the meeting, he looked directly into my eyes and said: "Never forget the importance of conduct." There is a pithy Arab maxim that says it well: "Believe in God, but don't forget to tie your camel!"

This is central: the essential basis of our development is the ongoing conversation between our insights, the choices we make every moment in our lives and their results. Our inner world and outer action mutually, continuously and seamlessly influence each other. Action shapes consciousness and consciousness directs action. Moral behaviour is therefore an inherent and necessary part of the spiritual path. Without awareness and constant sensitivity to the quality of our actions we will not be able to climb the mountain. Creating damage and distress with harmful words or deeds to ourselves or others is like a cable that ties a boat to the pier – even if we strenuously row the boat of spiritual practice, it will not budge.

In the words of the spiritual teacher Jiddu Krishnamurti: "First of all put your house in order." This means inner sweeping and cleaning, striving for a life of wholeness and harmony (Pali: *kusala*) that does not cause damage, and that is free of guilt, regret or jealousy. This housekeeping is the basis and the ground for every spiritual practice.

There are five moral guidelines or precepts in the Buddhist world that are regarded as basic and fundamental. But unlike the Ten Commandments, which are sometimes seen as a Judeo-Christian equivalent, they include "do" not only "do not". More importantly, they are regarded as a practice rather than a fixed set of rules that we have to take on board and by which we judge ourselves or others. The practice is the constant development and refinement of what feels right, harmonious and beneficial. We can outline the five precepts here as fundamental commitments to develop awareness of how we relate to the world. They are expressed below as personal intentions:

1. I will try to be more sensitive to the suffering caused by harming myself and others and I will cultivate compassion and learn ways to protect living beings. I will endeavour not to do harm, nor to condone acts of harming, in my thinking, and in my way of life.
2. I will try to be more sensitive to the suffering caused by exploitation, injustice, stealing and oppression, and I will endeavour to work for the well-being of living beings by sharing my time, energy and resources with others. I will endeavour to live modestly and not to take what is not freely given.
3. I will try to be more sensitive to the suffering caused by exploitative or abusive sexual energy and behaviour and I will endeavour to manage my sexual energy with care, awareness and harmony in relation to myself and others.

4. I will try to be more sensitive to the suffering caused by unmindful and hurtful speech and the inability to listen to others. I will endeavour to cultivate kind, truthful speech and deep listening in order to bring joy to others, and reduce conflict and discord.
5. I will try to be more sensitive to the suffering caused by unmindful eating, drinking and consuming. I will endeavour not to ingest intoxicants or toxins that damage the body and dull the mind, and to care for the health and well-being of body and mind.

If we can live in the light of these five guidelines, our lives and the life of our environment will change beyond recognition. But it is not easy. If we take this seriously, we will need to be constantly mindful of how we are in the world. Are we killing ants as we walk? Are we responding with sensitivity and care to the call of other sentient beings? We will find ourselves in constant deliberation. For example, at an international conference of vipassana teachers in which I participated, the question arose: "Is there such a thing as a just war?" The answers were varied and complex, reflecting the magnitude of the dilemma. Another example concerns lying. At the end of the 1980s, my youngest daughter didn't like her school and kept wanting to stay at home. At first, I was happy to write a note saying "She is sick today" when in fact she was happy as a skylark, playing in the garden. But as I continued to practise dharma, lying became painfully crude and unethical. So I wrote notes that didn't actually lie, but were not entirely true and authentic either: "She is unable to get to school today." Then as I continued my spiritual journey even that became impossible and I just wrote the truth: "She doesn't want to go to school today." I was ready to pay the price but I could not lie.

A historical dilemma concerns vegetarianism, and currently veganism as well. Many ask: "Was the Buddha a vegetarian? What did he say about vegetarianism? Were the Buddha alive today, what would he recommend? And what about eggs and dairy products?"

In his lifetime, the Buddha forbade monks to eat meat if someone killed an animal for them. The monks only received leftovers from the families in the villages, whatever they were, but if someone invited them to a meal and wanted to slaughter a chicken for them, they were not allowed to respond. It was more important to let go of need and greed, preference and self-interests, than to be choosy about what leftovers they ate, meat or not. But nowadays the situation is different. We are not monks. Meat, eggs and dairy are the products of a huge food industry which causes enormous physical and psychological suffering to animals and people working in it, as well as severe environmental damage. If the Buddha were alive today my guess is that he would advise us all to have nothing to do with such products. At the same time, if we choose vegan food, we have to be careful not to fall into other traps of the ego – of being self-righteous, fundamentalist, orthodox and judgemental of those that don't keep our own ethical principles. This is harmful and hurtful and morally insensitive at another level and forgets the life teaching of non-preference and bringing harmony and goodness into the world. Is the Dalai Lama an unethical person because he eats meat?

These are not simple questions, and sometimes the aspiration for a moral life leads us along a bumpy road. For example, we often need great courage and energy to speak out or act with moral sensitivity, where the consensus social view is brainwashed and xenophobic. We can easily get branded as traitors. Are we silent in situations that demand us to cry out? Are we afraid to intervene? Are we concerned only for the poor that we know, and indifferent to the oppressed who are far from us? A painful recent example is the treatment of the Rohingya in Myanmar. Their villages burnt, attacked by the army, they fled into Bangladesh in the hundreds of thousands in what the UN described as a major act of ethnic cleansing. By Buddhists. Clearly being born a Buddhist gives you no automatic access to goodness. The five precepts, like the Ten Commandments, have to be practised deeply otherwise ethics can fly out of the window at any time.

To understand how to act we need wisdom and attention. We must carefully examine what we do and say and the results of our actions. Do we contribute to an increase or reduction of suffering in the world? In the Biblical myth of Noah, he is picked out as a unique example of ethical behaviour at a time when the rest of humanity was corrupted. He was asked by God to save the animals from the coming flood by building an ark for them. The Talmud asks what was special about him. The answer was that he knew what every animal needed and could take care of each of them. His ethics was based on a great awareness and big heart. Let us be like Noah, lift the curtain and create an empathic connection between us and all other creatures. When people ask me if I eat the chickens that I keep, I answer; "Would you eat your friends?" We need to see all life as a community and then we will take care of other beings. If we see how all other beings suffer like us, we will not cause more pain. The joy of others makes us joyful too.

The accepted way of life in the West revolves around the desire for comfort and pampering and for endless consumption. We are generally not interested in the harm it brings to others and the planet. We don't think about the working conditions of children in Vietnam or Bangladesh who are sewing our clothes. To put my benefit over the well-being of others creates an ethical minefield.

The Buddha was asked a fundamental question: "How does it help me to keep the five principles of morality?" The Buddha replied that a person who commits to stop harming gives all beings in the world more freedom from fear, freedom from danger, freedom from anger and freedom from oppression. Because he too is one of the creatures in the world, he gets back the gift of freedom from fear, misery, anger and oppression. This is a circle of transmission and reception – those who transmit ease also receive it, freedom returns to them like a boomerang. This boomerang supports us during our spiritual life because it helps us to climb the mountain without the weight of regret, fear or oppression.

This view is based on an understanding of karma. This is the knowledge that every action we take, every word we say, every thought we think, sows a seed. The seeds do not disappear – they produce fruit. All beings in the world are connected in a network of interactions. Everything we do creates a message of a certain kind, and it resonates within and without. We broadcast and receive constantly. There are four types of karma, divided by the actions that create them:

- **An act full of light** brings light to the world. An action full of light is one that is consistent with the five precepts.
- **A murky act** that is harmful results in a muddied outcome.
- **A mixed action** is what characterizes us in most cases, and is created, for example, when we lead a fairly pure life, but are occasionally a bit aggressive, or drink alcohol or watch a stupid television programme.
- **The ideal action** is peaceful and creates no karma at all. It is an action that seems to happen by itself, and takes place when life flows through us. It happens when essentially there is no "I" separate from and ceaselessly trying to control the world. This is liberation.

But until we get to this high place, we should appreciate that our actions are heavily influenced by our patterns, tendencies and habits, called *sankharas* in Pali. And they create further *sankharas*. What kind of person creates this action, that word, that thought? And what kind of person do we build from them? We recreate ourselves every moment. If we look at it this way it is easy to see how pure action fosters joy, calmness and harmony in our psyche, while a murky act has the opposite effect.

We die and are reborn constantly, recreating ourselves every moment, with every thought and action. This is the early Buddhist teaching on rebirth, which is something that happens in the present. The moment called "death" is only one death among many, the death of the body. From this point of view, the power of action becomes clear: we are not born again, but our actions are. Or in the words of Chögyam Trungpa: "The only things that are born again are our bad habits." Therefore, we must be careful and pay attention to every action, word or thought. As it says in the *Dhammapada*: "Even small negative actions can cause great suffering in the world, similar to a poison that even a small dose can harm, yet positive actions, even the smallest ones, bring joy to our next and subsequent lives, just like a small seed can give rise to an abundance of crops."[1]

How can we balance both right action in the world along with spiritual practice? Each stage in the development of consciousness requires a step up in our sensitivity to our actions. This is especially true for great teachers, who have to be very careful. There are many examples of teachers with a high-powered consciousness who do not understand this, and allow themselves to get contaminated by desire for money or sex, for example. They maintain ethics 90% of the time and not 100%; their students can get badly wounded, karma takes it further, and then everything collapses.

CHAPTER 3
SIMPLY RIGHT

During 40 years of work as a consultant and writer in the area of herbal and complementary medicine, one of my frequent assignments was to go to health product trade fairs, and give talks there. They are bizarre and enormous, with thousands of manufacturers pushing health products for all their worth. I used to go regularly to Expo West, in Anaheim, California, a mammoth jamboree of around 10,000 stands, all pushing, explaining or giving tastes of their products. I used to spend days wandering around, grazing like a cow; tasting organic delicacies from all over the world, sipping juices from exotic fruit, snacking on "forbidden" foods that are actually all made up of soya beans, and, when quite exhausted, getting doses of herbal pick-me-ups. The inventiveness is extraordinary. There are lots of dedicated people who really believe in what they are doing. And lots of others who are only interested in the bottom line. There are good products, and useless ones. But it does raise a question: is our own health and well-being, and that of the planet, dependent on what we buy? Or rather on what we do not buy? There is surely no problem in choosing more wisely what we decide to eat, and what we bring into our home. It is indeed helpful to our health and the environment to choose less processed, organic and healthy food, to be vegetarian, and to have a preference for safe natural medicines rather than toxic drugs where possible. But there needs to be a more careful examination of what and how much we consume, and more generally, what really matters, what is important.

Our instinct to fill our lives with more and more, feels like an escape from our basic existential dissatisfaction. It leads to shopping as an automatic response, encouraged by the whole of the social discourse. We are usually quite unable to see it as a problem. We are convinced that if we had this new car/flat/

holiday/computer/dress/shoes etc we would be happy. And it can make us happy, but only briefly, because happiness is to be found in being, not in having. We are *human beings* not *human havings*. And too often, when the having loses its magic, we are left with depression. There was, apparently, a study carried out in the US that surveyed how long lasting was the happiness resulting from the purchase of a new car. It was on average four days.

It is helpful (though not essential) on the road to real happiness, to be more simple. Not to be overwhelmed, drowned, in things that we accumulate. These can be physical possessions that pile up and we find ourselves constantly busy with them, or they can be mental possessions – ideas, attachments, views and a great deal of mental clutter. It drowns us. We need to let go a bit, not to hold onto things in order to feel fully alive. As one Zen master said: "Why should I let go? Because it all piles up!" It is basically letting go of expectations that the world is our provider, letting go of the need to control everything, and to keep having more. A traditional Christian sect, the Shakers, created a song called "Simple Gifts" that expresses this:

'Tis the gift to be simple, 'tis the gift to be free
'Tis the gift to come down to where we ought to be
And when we find ourselves in the place just right
'Twill be in the valley of love and delight.

As Western culture is so deeply bound into a culture of buying, we may need to go against the stream. There is a phrase going round – "only dead fish go with the flow". Are we going to turn round and swim against the current? How?

One of the most well-thought-out alternative ways to live was that of Mahatma Gandhi. He taught a community life that was fundamentally ecological, joyful and dignified. Symbolized by the hand-operated spinning wheel which he took everywhere, he taught that joy comes when you restore your connection with the most basic things in your life, by doing them or making them yourself. That does not necessarily mean that you need to spin your own cotton thread as in village India. But at least you can consistently cook your own food from simple raw materials of grains and vegetables. You can bake your own bread. You can grow your own food given the smallest plot of land, or window boxes, and you can learn how to treat yourself with medicinal plants and grow them in your own garden or in pots in your house. We find that as we do these things we establish a real contact with those crucial and forgotten life essentials. We bring more joy and ease into our life, and we notice that stress just vanishes in the renewed intimacy with our lives. For around 15 years, I grew wheat in a small plot of land, enough for the family for the year, and I used to bake bread in the early mornings for many years, and it was one of the most joyful experiences of the day – the movement of the body, the aromas of the wheat, the concert of birds outside against the background quietness of the morning. I also used to grow some of the herbal medicines we all needed: again the simplicity of growing and preparing your own medicine chest as people have been doing for thousands of years. What a joy.

But there is also a deeper letting go that is a major help in our spiritual journey. Too often, our spiritual quest can translate into a restless mindset of shopping, having and gaining – another weekend, another course, another teacher, another book, another practice ... none providing the deeper peace and joy of simply being and being simple. We need to let go of the need to experience certain things we have heard about, of expectations that the path or teacher should provide us with certain results, of the need to control outcomes, of the habits of judgement and criticism. As we let go on this deeper level, we may experience a great relief – that much of the accumulated spiritual "possessions" were not needed in the first place. Though there is no doubt that realizations, inner freedoms and wisdom are precious, but there may be a place where the gifts turn into baggage. Sometimes our longings are the neediness of a demanding "adolescent" self. As we let go those voices in us demanding control and outcomes, we may find that a much deeper joy creeps up on us when we are not looking. A real contentment that previously escaped us. Ramana Maharshi once said that a passenger on a train does not need to keep carrying his baggage. He can put it down and allow the train to take him and his baggage. Let life take us and our baggage. The journey will lead us naturally through the "valley of love and delight", as the Shaker song put it. Wisdom travels light.

CHAPTER 4

LIVING TO WORK OR LOVING TO WORK?

Rabbi Harold Kushner once remarked: "No-one ever said on their deathbed 'I wish I'd spent more time at the office'." Some of us really seem to enjoy our work and find it meaningful and fulfilling. Others find their work draining and meaningless and they only work because they need to survive. Nonetheless there is a fundamental challenge about working life – and that is its control over most of our life. How are we to make sense of this primary difficulty that we all face – the fact that our work occupies most of our lives, yet often seems the opposite of a liberating experience.

How can we shift from living for work, to working for life, from living to work, to loving to work?

The great wisdom of the dharma teachings offer some illuminating insights into the problem. First, to clear the ground, we should do a basic screening of the moral implications of our work. This is a kind of fundamental housekeeping, in that if there are questionable moral issues around our work, it may be hard to find it fulfilling, since the impure karma, or seeds sown every day by our actions and intentions, may bear uncomfortable fruit. There are boomerangs, which seem quite invisible but can steal our fulfilment. A pure mind and heart is the best guarantee of a joyful day's work.

The moral issues, as defined in the traditional teachings, are centred on not harming others. We should not be involved in the making and selling of weapons or intoxicants, the harming or selling of animals or people. We should not be involved in deceit or tricks or violence, or in gaining wealth through untrue promises, including spiritual promises.

All of this seems at first straightforward – your initial reaction may be that you don't do any of these things, but it's important to look closely at the ramifications of what we do, and be brave enough to ask some questions.

What promises am I, or those for whom I work, making? What values are we encouraging? Could the substances or materials or services we are supporting or selling create any harm or addiction? Is there discrimination, oppression or harassment in the culture of my workplace? Are we condoning suffering, abuse or exploitation that is not so visible, maybe in the chain of production and resourcing that source a certain product that we may be selling or using?

We may not always be able to change our work situation, and the way things are done. We may not have the courage to speak up, or there may be no-one there to listen. But the inquiry is itself a practice, bringing to our work moral energy and sensitivity, making us feel more in touch with values.

I knew an American meditation teacher who earned his living mending computers. What he really liked about this work was coming into houses, often of lonely, needy people, and bringing friendliness, warmth and light into those homes.

Can we crawl out from under the bottom-line mentality, from what is in it for me, what is in my pay packet, to what can I bring, what can I contribute? Helping others can bring meaning and joy to our work. As the Dalai Lama once said: "It is so much more joyful to give to others than to give to oneself, because there are more of them."

When considering what kind of work to choose, many people on the spiritual journey are choosing the caring professions because it brings meaning and arouses compassion. There may be less money in it, but the open heart is a sweetness that is with us night and day, and is worth much more than gold.

We need to appreciate that as we spend so much time and thought and energy on our work, it deeply conditions us. For this reason "right livelihood" is one of the basic practices of the eightfold path, (the way of life according to the Buddhist dharma), and on the same level of importance as meditation. So we need to ask what is it doing to us, what have we accumulated at the end of a day, a month, a lifetime of work? We may find ourselves committed and enthusiastic for our work, but it exhausts and drains us. We may find that we want to work in a certain career, but that the atmosphere in the workplace is full of criticism, cynicism and judgement. Or we may experience disconnection, alienation or a hierarchical structure that generates fear. Or, again, we may find ourselves strung out by moral dilemmas. Do such psychological and emotional conditions take up residence in our mind and heart? Do we find ourselves talking in the same language, or holding the same views, consciously or unconsciously? Do we take the same atmosphere and bring it home to our family and our bed?

In such cases, as time goes by, we will feel contracted or even depressed; work becomes a kind of jail which we suffer for the sake of the money. It will need sensitivity and mindfulness to catch the problems as early as possible. And then what?

Well, we may indeed have to give up or change our work to save our inner life.

This is sometimes inevitable. However, there is also another way. To change the atmosphere – to make a difference, to find rewards in bringing something human into a place starved of the heart. Here is where meditative inner work is invaluable.

A commitment to and practice of *deep listening* can dramatically heal an environment of alienation and distance. Insightful awareness can perhaps show us that if we are exhausting ourselves it may be because of some kind of resistance or friction or restlessness constructed from patterns, wounds and anxieties.

The Buddhist practice of *metta,* the broadcasting of loving kindness, can bring warm sun to a frosty climate of criticism. We may be able to initiate a new dialogue that includes honest sharing of feelings and experiences, or group yoga in the mornings. Intention to change conditions can integrate outer work and inner work. For some years I used to go one day a week to a large and quite polluting fertilizer factory, and work there as a consultant to an herbal extract company that was located on the site. I got to know the CEO quite well, and would constantly and subtly try and move him toward more environmental sensitivity and awareness. And every time I was there I would barge into another office or shed and strike up a conversation with the workers there, listening to them, bringing friendliness and interest, breaking barriers.

Many times I have been asked by people in the armed forces if it is against the Buddhist teachings to serve. At first sight, one would think that it would be completely unspiritual to be a soldier. This is not so – if to be a soldier meant, for example, to stop other soldiers from harming or abusing people, or to bring more respect, communication and humanness into a soldier's life.

One would think that it would be unbearable to work in the slums of Calcutta. It was not so for Mother Teresa. When things are difficult, we do need to ask ourselves – are we able to make a difference? Do we have the inner strength, steadiness and inner peace to make change? Are we radiating kindness in a hard world? As Mother Teresa said: "We can do little things with a great heart!"

If we look at things this way, at higher resolution, with care, and awareness of what is really happening moment by moment, it seems that it matters less what we do, but rather *how* we act, how we work – what are the qualities that we are manifesting? In the moment by moment experience, with mind and heart engaged, there is no such thing any more as work, only actions. The concept of work dissolves into life. To quote Psalm 90: "Let the grace of God be in our work and let the outcome of our work be right."

CHAPTER 5
MONEY:
THE SHINE OF GOLD?

Just imagine for a moment, an observer from outer space, examining living beings on this planet including the human species. She may assume that human beings are rushing about all their life after food and essentials, in a similar fashion to mice. She might ask:

"So they are running about after food and shelter?"

"Not exactly. It is after a substance that they call money."

"That's really surprising. Where do they get it from?"

"From others who have it."

"What do they do with it?"

"They pass it on to others to obtain necessary things."

"So when they have those necessary things, do they stop rushing about?"

"No, They can't stop so they continue rushing to get more."

"What do they do with it then?"

"They store it."

"So those that have stored a lot of it, do they stop running about after it?"

"No. They are often even busier running after it than those who have less."

"And do those who have it stored feel happier than those who don't?"

"No, generally they are not so happy."

"And those who have a lot stored, what do they do with it in the end?"

"They die and leave it all behind."

Money is a medium of exchange and passes between people freely, just like water. In the process it is used to do things, like water is used to drive a water wheel. Since it is associated deeply with getting what we want, it has taken on a hugely important status. Since it seems to make available necessary goods and pleasures, it symbolizes all goods and pleasures. But then, as a symbol, it loses its connection with necessary things and becomes the necessary thing itself. As a result we become poorer not richer, because we lose the direct appreciation of those sensory things and just measure them against their monetary value. I remember collecting stamps when I was a boy, and I loved every stamp – the pictures, the series, the fantasies about what each country must be like, based on their stamps. I would sit for hours sticking them in albums and found great delight in swapping them with my friends. Until I discovered that any stamp in the world could just be bought with money. A rich boy could just have it all in an instant. The magic left. From that moment I never collected another stamp.

People have one single precious life, yet they devote almost all of it to money, despite the fact that life passes by. There is an Indian story about a king who was wandering in the desert. He ran out of water and prayed to the gods: "Gods, I will give you half of my kingdom if you provide me with water." "Fine," said the gods, and he found a pool in front of him. Next day he found he could not urinate and was in great distress. "Gods," he said, "I will give you the other half of my kingdom if you will just unblock my channel and let me urinate." "Fine," said the gods. "We will do it, but you should know that you have given your entire kingdom away for something that just passes in and out." So it is with money.

It is an icon. It is worshipped, thought about, dreamed about, and the main topic of conversation of all people around the world. The reason is its intimate relationship with human insecurity. The more insecure we are, the more we need to feel constant access to those goods and pleasures. We are nervous, not at ease, under stress, and as most of society behaves that way it is legitimized by the community and becomes a kind of suffering norm. So how can we be free? Can we really be free and poor? Can we really be free and rich?

The main shift that is needed is to take the special status away from money. Make it less and less interesting, less of an issue. We need to see it as a necessary medium of exchange and no more than that. This will work if it is accompanied by a deep inner journey, a look in the mirror, to uncover and take care of the insecurities themselves which are projected onto money. Or to uncover and take care of the greed that is similarly projected. In that journey to freedom, as our obsessions, fears and worries dissolve away, it will automatically make us more balanced in relation to money.

We also need to begin to ignore the social pressure to regard everything as purchasable. It is the dominant view that if we had more money we could do more, enjoy more, live more. Actually the opposite is true. Our real joy of life, our real contact with life, is in the vast territory of *being*, not in the small space of *having*. As our contact with life deepens, we begin to realize that money is less and less relevant to the important aspects of life: our values, our spiritual journey, the meaning invested in our moment-by-moment experiences. Yes, we will need to buy things now and then, spend money now and then, give money now and then. But the essential things are beyond the consumer marketplace. They cannot be bought and sold. This is well expressed by the story in the Gospels concerning Jesus who answered followers who were concerned about the taxes that they needed to give to the Romans. Jesus pointed out that on the coin was the head of Caesar, and wisely said: "Give to Caesar what is Caesar's." The implication is that the coin is his, but the rest of life is yours.

All of us have the potential for expansive, spiritual and non-materialistic lives, and in principle it doesn't matter whether you are rich or poor. Though it must be said that it is often a little harder for the rich to be free as they have more encouragement to be busy with money than others. But whether we are blessed with more money or less, what matters is the holding on and attachment. If we are blessed with money, one of the best ways to abandon holding is to give it away. It is joyful to give, it brings ease to oneself and happiness to others. It is also a primary value or ethic, part of a process of inner purification. If we have no money, we can free ourselves by not constantly wishing for it.

But on a deeper level money is just another form of exchange, of giving and taking, in which all beings participate. In the teachings of the Buddha, this exchange and giving (*dana*) is clearly experienced as an operating principle of the universe itself. The sun gives to the tree, the tree gives its leaves to the earth, the earth gives its nutrients to the tree. The whole of existence is one great ecology in which all things give to all other things, and take from all other things, in which everything, all life, is a web of interrelationships. Nothing is held back. We cannot imagine the tree saying to itself, I want to hold on to my leaves and not let them drop to the earth, I want to store them. We consume and in the end are consumed. Money is an example of this. Its nature is circulation, exchange, flow. It passes from one to another making things happen on the way. But in the end no-one can take it with them and it must be given away whether you like it or not. The *dana* principle is a life perspective rather than a self-perspective. The insecure human self often does not see this flow of giving and is under the painful illusion that he can hold on, grasp at things, and accumulate possessions. This is a stopping of the flow of life, a kind of death. The Greek myth of King Midas illustrates this. King Midas was obsessed by gold. He prayed to the gods that all things that he touched should turn to gold. The gods granted his wish, but of course everything he touched became dead gold, including his own daughter.

CHAPTER 6
"I JUST CAN'T DECIDE"

Sometimes it's agonizing. Usually it's stressful. We just cannot decide about something. It may be as trivial as which restaurant to go to tonight. Or as important as whether or not to get married. It seems particularly acute when we are younger; choices such as which subject to study at university can create sleepless nights and obsess us for weeks or months on end. I remember the gut-wrenching nights when I was just 15 and the school required that I choose the humanities or science.

Faced with the endless possibilities of what may happen in the future, the mind spins scenario after scenario, trying to predict the best outcome. This is what causes the stress. The reason that the mind does this is that it is driven by a "me", a "self" which has as its job description the search for the safest and most comfortable outcomes for itself in an unpredictable world. Essentially, it cannot be done. The future is unknown. The best we can do is to write possible future scripts based on our experience of the past, or of who we know ourselves to be. For example, "I will buy this white shirt not the blue one as in the past people told me I look good in white." Both reference to the past and current taste are unreliable as guides to the future. The past is gone along with the situations we found ourselves in. And we ourselves are changing constantly and may not be sure exactly who we are and what fits us at any point in time.

What we forget is that much of what happens to us is not our choice. Can we choose to be happy or miserable, in love or angry? We find ourselves at a fork in the road struggling to choose left or right, and meanwhile we forget all the non-chosen events that brought us there. We try to decide whether to take an umbrella, but we did not choose the experience of cloud-covered sky which created that question in the first place. Much of what occurs to us happens anyway. We just imagine we are choosing everything, with a rather inflated view of our own power. Or, to be more precise, the "self" that sits in consciousness like a big boss or overseer has an inflated view of its own powers.

Let's do a small exercise. Try and remember the last time you "chose" to go to a coffee house, and "chose" something from the menu. Notice how you paid attention to just those many tasty offerings on the menu, not to the sequence of hundreds of small or big influences that resulted in you finding yourself there – you were already in the area, you were attracted by the décor, you were hungry or deprived of caffeine, you had a positive memory of that place. Even the item you "chose" on the menu – did you really choose it or is it simply likes and dislikes that were conditioned by past experiences, such as the kind of food your parents used to give to you when you were small, or the great coffee you once had somewhere. We swim through a sea of influences and so we have less freedom than we think. This helps us to reduce the pressure that we have to decide all the time, we can just relax and go along with what arises because it is happening anyway.

But the opposite is also true. Paradoxically we also actually have more freedom than we think. Our life is often lived on automatic pilot. We are run by our own habits, and the biggest habit of all is forgetting. If we notice how we keep following the same tracks of thinking and acting, if we remember to be there fully with every moment of our lives, we see how playful and open it all is and how much more power we have to change things and make new choices, to do the unexpected, and to be original and independent. A classical example of this is the conditioning we absorb daily from the media, advertising and our peers. As soon as we realize how all this stuff shapes the mind and reduces our power of independent thinking, a whole new world of choices opens up.

Choices in life are therefore made radically easier if we wake up a bit, and live according to three main insights:

1. **Events condition and create us from moment to moment. We do not choose events – they choose us.** This takes away a great deal of pressure from us to continually decide or to try and design our future. We can watch the present continually unfolding and offering us its surprises, without the need to decide. We can be much more child-like and fresh, appreciating what comes instead of manipulating outcomes. When we do have to decide, between the blue shirt and the white one, between this course and another one at university, we do so with much less stress, because we don't feel in charge of everything. We just go in the direction that seems most fitting.

2. **If we live mindfully, and not on automatic pilot, a world of greater freedom and spontaneity opens up.** We do not want to be entirely passive bystanders in our life, carried along by events as in the story of the man who went into the bedroom to change his shirt for an evening dinner, but then assumed it was bedtime, undressed, and went to sleep, much to the consternation of his guests. If we wake up to the original nature of each spontaneous moment, we live with much more potential and possibility. More choices open up.

3. **All choices are actually made spontaneously in the moment.** If we look carefully, most of the intensive calculation, speculation and hardship that goes along with choosing, is actually like treading water. It doesn't go anywhere. When the choice is eventually made, it is always in a moment, often when we have given up from exhaustion after a great amount of fruitless speculation. If we wake up to this, if we live with more awareness, we can shortcut our decisions drastically, learn to make spontaneous, intuitive and instant decisions, and cut through all the useless churning in the mind.

These awakenings are not complicated. They are part and parcel of a more spiritual and aware life. In this kind of life, pressure to choose is replaced by something else. This is intention or direction; a real sense of what is good for us, what helps us, and a wholesome and steady direction to our life. A long-term vegetarian when offered a ham sandwich does not need to choose whether or not to eat it. This is the big picture which makes all the choices less critical. After all, most choices are on the level of what I want or what I don't want. If our wants and needs are less holy, choices are no big deal. There is a background sense of rightness, harmony or what is fitting to us and the world and from that place we will know what to do.

CHAPTER 7
DANA: THE ECONOMY OF THE HEART

Dana, in the Pali language of ancient Buddhism, means generosity or giving. It is a crucial human quality that is of great significance and importance in Buddhist spiritual practice and the world view that goes with it. It has been a cornerstone of religious culture in Buddhist societies and countries for thousands of years. In Thai villages the giving of food, gifts and possessions is often the way Thais would define themselves as Buddhists. When young Thais or Burmese first enter monasteries to become monks, they are generally not started off with meditation instructions. Instead they usually spend much time in serving and giving to others. It is seen as an essential purification of the inner landscape, a reduction in self-importance, and so a powerful force for success in subsequent practice of devotion, meditation and so on.

Let's leave aside its Buddhist roots and context, for the moment, and consider *dana* both as a personal quality, a deep truth about the nature of things, and as a source of action and meaning in our life. We understand that it is much more than simple generosity. It is not just about money. It is the process of giving self to others. It is about opening the heart to listen to and feel what the other needs, and giving accordingly. It may be money, but it may be food or teachings, it may be giving attention or respect, often gifts worth far more than money. It may be the gift of giving your time to another, whether a mother who devotes herself completely to her child, night and day, when it is convenient or when it is not, or a carer helping a patient. It can be quite subtle. For example, we have a tendency to put those close to us under pressure, criticize them or put them down. *Dana* may be the gift of space and freedom to others to be themselves, the gift of our friendliness and sympathy instead of our negativity.

A good example of *dana* is breastfeeding. The mother does not give milk only if she gets some credit or reward. She does not try to hang onto as much of it as possible and not let go of her milk. That would be painful. She does not measure the milk according to how many smiles she gets back. She and the baby are one, united in a flow of giving and receiving.

Some of us find it difficult to let go and give things away, others find it easier to give to others but not so easy to receive from others. In the end, *dana* is about both. The giving is not in one direction – it is in all directions, including to oneself. That means it includes receiving as well. "The gift" is a basic form of communication in which the giver and receiver are joined and connected by a primal and universal action.

There is a lot more to giving and receiving than being nice, or a moral imperative. *Dana* is a movement in the soul, in the atmosphere and in the community that is felt as ease, sweetness and lack of pressure. It is emphasized again and again that *dana* is an aid to seeing the world in terms of *being* rather than *having*. And as this movement is the basis of spiritual realization, *dana* is a direct aid to awakening. It creates joy and release while the constant tendency to want more, to be unsatisfied with what we have, creates suffering.

For these reasons, *dana* has now become the operating principle in most vipassana retreats. As a teacher, for 20 years I have not asked for a fixed sum from anybody, but just have a box there for those I teach to express their support and appreciation in a real and practical way. It pays the bills. Sometimes I teach for organizations that do have a fixed payment schedule, and I just go along with whatever they usually do. Just as a meditation course gave *dana* in terms of teachings, accommodation, care and support, so the participants give *dana* back. Giving and receiving. In Israel, where I mostly teach, the organization I founded (the Israel Insight Society – Tovana) also works on a *dana* basis. That means that no-one is asked beforehand to pay for their residential course, the food or accommodation, the overheads to run the organization. They give *dana* at the end of the retreats. The trust and ease this generates in the retreats is deep and palpable. It is described as an alternative economy, the economy of the heart, in which everyone gives according to their means and their heart, rather than according to a fixed price. It has had the surprising result that many young people, students, or those in the army, now join the retreats, and the average age of participants is going down, whereas in other places where there is a fixed charge for residential accommodation, the average age goes up, as only those established financially can afford it. Does it work? It just about works. The courses more or less cover themselves. The problem is often one of educating people to this different economy. Coming from a life in which everyone is busy trying to get the most out of each other, some people are confused: it is strange, almost too good to be true: "There must be a catch!" There is no catch. It is *dana*.

This is also a traditional way of doing things. You can go to a monastery or meditation centre in Burma, stay for a year, and no-one will ask you for money. The local people maintain the monks with *dana* of food, one of the main practices in traditional Buddhist communities. The monks give in turn the *dana* of teachings, healing and pastoral care. Behind this is the principle that spiritual teachings are the birthright of all of us. They cannot be bought and sold. Their value is beyond money. No-one should make a profit out of your spiritual thirst. This is unfortunately not always the case in the world of spiritual teachings, which are not always so clean around the issue of money. Spiritual teachers that drain their students of money should learn the principle of *dana*.

But *dana* goes deeper. The *dana* principle is a life perspective rather than a self-perspective. Our actions can be guided by the insight that all of life is a dynamic flow and exchange. Everything, including our own bodies, is received and given away. The insecure human self often does not see the flow of giving and is under the painful illusion that he can hold on, grasp at things, and accumulate things. This is a stopping of the flow of life, a kind of death. Practising *dana*, therefore, is not just the practice of giving. It is the uncovering and realizing with total clarity and conviction an essential truth of life. As we know it in our being we live it. And living in the flow of *dana* is a joyful awakening.

CHAPTER 8

SICKNESS: CRISIS OR OPPORTUNITY?

We all dread the moment when we are diagnosed with some serious disease. It can strike any of us at any time. It feels as if we are skipping along living our life and we get stopped dead in our tracks. A life-threatening health problem, such as cancer, is one of the most severe challenges we can face. The mind is besieged by fears, worries about what will happen, concerns for our children or family, plans and strategies for fighting the disease, and intense questions about causes. We also build lots of narratives and scenarios, for example we may blame ourselves for the problem, or we may be angry at life or at others around us (such as the medical system) and jealous of those who are healthy. All of this creates emotional turmoil, confusion and despair, and makes the struggle for health seem sometimes impossible.

And then, if someone (or a book) comes along and tells us that a disease can be an opportunity, a turning point in our lives, and it is not all as bad as it seems, it may sound absurd, unreal and even infuriating: "How on earth can you say that, you don't know what it is like to be where I am." Yet there is a profound truth in it, which often cannot get through to us because it is presented as words, and not experiences, and because we are so overwhelmed by our suffering that we put up a stiff resistance – there is no room to listen.

So first we need to give ourselves a little space, some room to look directly at our situation and not at all the projections around it. Then, with a little wise reflection, an open heart and some persistence, we can open new channels in us to messages that actually we long to hear, and that will transform the situation.

To illustrate this I would like to discuss an intensive weekend, which I taught with two other teachers for those with major health problems. There were 50 participants, most of whom suffered from cancer, fibromyalgia, and other diseases, some severe.

At the beginning, the despair and confusion was palpable. The room was heavy with the personal stories that each person carried, and shared, the tears flowed and it seemed impossible to lighten the load. Yet something miraculous happened during our time together and at the end of the short weekend there was laughter, and lightness, there was hope and hugs, there was deep gratitude, and most of all, the participants felt truly alive, in some cases for the first time in a long time. I would like to describe here the methods we used and how they worked.

There were some underlying values that helped to clear the emotional ground. First, there were no professional agendas. There were no promises that "professional others" would fix, cure, treat or lessen the disease. Second, as teachers we did not come over with a system, a belief, or even a special status. In some way we tried to show that we are all the same, the situation of human suffering is universal, that there were not sick and healthy people there, but just people, all with different issues. Third, we made sure the weekend was inexpensive and not-for-profit, to create an atmosphere of trust, and of giving rather than getting or exploiting.

A basic tool was mindfulness meditation, using breath and body as the main focus. We taught this in several sessions throughout the three days with plenty of real-time guidance and imagery. One of the main images that went along with the meditation was that of coming home, of finding a genuine refuge within us rather than expecting it to come from the changing and often distressing conditions of our lives. Steadily, moment by moment, all of us worked together to develop the sense that there is a deep home inside us that nothing can steal from us.

Mindfulness meditation not only expands our awareness but also brings it back to the immediate lived experience, creating a sense of wholeness and intimacy with our life, which is quite beyond the disease. Being in touch with the feelings, sensations and activities of our mind-body helps us to see that all our projections, fears for the future, scenarios, memories and worries are in the end just chains of repeating thoughts, however loaded they seem. Experienced for even short moments, this kind of mindfulness takes some of the weight off.

Resting in the experience of the natural flow of breath and sensations in the body is not only a safe place but also a place in which we discover that there are messages within us of healthy lived experience. The disease is shouting so loud we cannot usually hear other quieter voices within us. For example, we usually don't know we have a head unless we have a headache. We don't know that our hands are perfectly fine and enjoying their life, and telling us so, with messages of "okness", if we are only focused on the pain in our back.

Taking the disease down off centre stage and replacing it with our lived experience creates a profound shift in attitude. Our situation lightens, we can become a participator in our fate and not its victim. There is a profound and yet subtle power of intimacy with present-moment experience to take us to a place beyond disease. This is beautifully and poignantly illustrated by this quote from Treya Wilbur, from the book about her life and death by her husband Ken Wilbur, *Grace and Grit.*[1] She was dying from cancer at the time:

> If I do become well for long periods of time, will I lose this deliciously keen knife-edge of awareness I now have? … new creativity pours forth under pressure of this illness, I would hate to lose that … there are moments when I feel practically ecstatic just sitting on the veranda and looking at the view at the back of the house, and watching the puppies play. I feel so blessed in this moment. Each breath is so incredible, so joyful, so dear. What am I missing? What could be wrong?

Learning to reconnect with the present moment of breath and body is a great help in coping with stressful and painful situations such as hospitals and treatments. One or two conscious-aware breaths and the anxiety fades and we are in a different place. In addition, as is well known, meditation is a tool that can be used to help support our healing and the life force in us.

Another important element of that weekend was sharing and discussion in groups. Here there was a chance to air fears and experiences, including issues of death and dying. It was a chance to listen to others and feel the support. The groups on the first morning were indeed full of tears and the most difficult stories, but as the retreat progressed, the dialogue shifted – toward inquiry into the meaning of being ill, toward illness as a personal journey. Several times participants raised the issue of control. Do we have control? Is it better to fight even though that may bring expectations and anxiety, or is it more helpful to surrender? The groups helped to cut the "demons" down to size, reducing the denial and avoidance which generally increase the suffering. On the second day the groups were actually like alchemical vessels in which change happened because of the intensity. New insights emerged into how life could be lived, new directions were realized, joys were shared, and there was laughter at the absurdities of hospitals and the discomfort of acquaintances. I insisted that one of the group sessions be devoted to our relationship to death and dying, even though some felt it was too risky and even explosive. But it turned out that the groups dealing with death and dying were those in which the laughter rang out – it was as if the valve of the pressure cooker opened and let off steam. The holding, denying and suppressing was much more painful than bringing fears and concerns out into the light.

A further exercise that we used was to open the heart to ourselves and to others, by means of several guided visualizations. We cannot easily "befriend our cancer", especially if we are told to do so by well-meaning but annoying givers of unwanted advice. But we can be friends to ourselves.

We can bathe in soft appreciation. We can feel gratitude for those ordinary moments, which are in fact quite miraculous. We can experience softness in our belly, softness that can hold all the pain. We can feel compassion to ourselves and to all others who suffer. We can feel the preciousness of ourselves and of each other.

Behind the veil of ordinary life were the realizations that were always ready to emerge and surprise us. They often centred on the truth that the experience of the disease is not the disease. The consciousness is freer than we think. We can be bigger than the problem. We need not be drowned in an ocean of despair when we truly discover our vulnerability. Our vulnerability itself can help us to live fully, live on the edge, live with uncertainty, and surrender to the unpredictable nature of life. This can be liberating and freeing. It is the place in which sometimes the sick have an advantage over the healthy.

I have had the privilege of working with several cancer patients over long periods. To illustrate this I would like to describe an extraordinary three-year journey with Liora, who had had cancer for nine years by the time I met her in 2005.[2] We started our monthly meetings in a coffee house with the existential and practical question: What is my real experience and how is it different from the world of fears, projections, struggle and despair? The long struggle with her illness and the constant sense that death was not far away over the horizon created a sense of urgency, a thirst for meaning, a deep curiosity about existence and a commitment to unfold spiritually. Mindfulness meditation practices became a refuge and also a fascinating new territory. Gradually this territory took shape. Instead of being a victim, she became a courageous and wise explorer into awareness of the moment, the inner landscape, full of its thorns but also its meadow wildflowers. And it was not death that was being explored, of course, but life: moments of grace in the early mornings; the joy involved in writing her thesis; the fun and games with her young daughter; deep peace when finding meditative concentration; the flow of living messages and intimacy with her body (the healthy parts with their healthy messages and the sick parts with theirs); the compassion and sympathy arising spontaneously when meeting other patients or the doctors.

Cancer, for her, became a label, a definition, a concept, that in the flow of experience no longer held power. In the same way, pain, confusion, physical and mental limitations, when unpacked or deconstructed by an inquiring and meditative mind, lost their solidity, their terror. When she needed to take morphine for a long period, she asked me how to find clarity even with morphine. I remember advising her not to be attached to a model of how she wants the mind to be. Instead of clarity, we worked together to convert the dream-like qualities produced by morphine into inner work with changes of consciousness.

In our dialogues we explored the fundamental issue of our human fragility and the transience of our life and all experience. A deep sense of her vulnerability became the cracks in the prison wall that let in the light. There are few that have this blessing. Liora herself more than once thanked her illness for bringing her beyond ordinary life into a place of depth and meaning. Liora holds an enduring memory for me – and what shines out is her example in converting the struggle for life into a deep and rich awareness of truth.

We do not need education, degrees, money or medicines for this. We only need to have a genuine interest in our experience, and the courage to be authentic rather than go with the herd instincts, which are mostly around anxiety. It is a shift in attitude and when it happens, even slightly, something irreversible occurs. We can never be quite so drowned again. There is always a little voice to remind us that a serious health problem need not be pure crisis. It can be our opportunity.

CHAPTER 9

THE SECRET THAT GLOWS IN THE DARK

I want to share a secret,
About the gentle radiance
Of those last years
So clear, so soft, so good,
That even the doctors
And the visitors who come and go,
Stop to take a breath
And will never forget you.
You are not ill
Illness is our label
Inscribed by our fears.
You know no illness nor wellness
Just there-ness.
No fear of death
No anxieties of what the future may bring,
Or may not bring.
No pain, no blame,
No loss, no regret
No anger at those who abandoned you
No time, no purpose
But the gentle kiss of life itself
The grace that comes when all else goes.
To what do you listen, so intently?
Is it the music of your heartbeat,
Tapping celestial rhythms
On the gates of your soul?
Or is it the humming of bees
On that summer's day?
Or the barking of your dogs,

That only you can quiet,
Or your fingers in their thick fur?
Or dreams of play and play of dreams
The kaleidoscope of past in present
Uninterrupted by our harsh reality.
As I lie next to you,
And feel this life flow through
And watch your face,
No frown, no wrinkles,
Just open presence,
Then, like the moon that shines between passing clouds,
Beams a joyous smile,
That vanishes so fast,
That I do not know if I really saw it
And now, again, you teach me,
About a life without fear, without walls, without end,
Just as you did when I was born
And, like then, share your happiest years.

Poem I wrote about my mother when she was
totally incapacitated by Alzheimer's disease

CHAPTER 10
AGEING WISELY

Ageing is a hard time for us all. I use the word "us" intentionally, as sooner or later, it is all of us. It is hard to watch as one by one our powers weaken and abilities deteriorate, quickly or slowly. We may feel abandoned and side-lined by others who are always busy and whose attention is focused on getting on and achieving in a predominantly youth culture. Frequent health issues keep us endlessly concerned and occupied with medical matters. On top of that, there may be expectations from others, be it family, friends or society, that somehow we are there to look after them – whether babysitting for the grandchildren or giving away presents, money and possessions. And there is a struggle in relation to our role. Too often it is as pensioners who are ignored, dependent and rather useless, and at best do not cause young people too much trouble. Which tends, unfortunately, to be the standard Western model.

But there is another possibility entirely: to arrive in old age skipping not crawling. To be feisty, energetic and full of the spice of life. To enjoy this time as a time of freedom from cares, freedom from ambitions, expectations and concerns. To be delighted that we are not still a slave of the endless race for success and achievement. To live lightly without too much thought of tomorrow. To appreciate all the life wisdom that we have accumulated, donate it freely to others, and usually receive in return the honour and appreciation due to us. This can be a time to enjoy and share the memories and stories that we live by, and at the same time to be the holders of culture, and preservers of skills, values and ethics. We could radiate steadiness and bring confidence and meaning to younger folk who have lost their way. Why not be the "wise woman" or the "tribal elder"?

If that is our aspiration, we have to start early. Ageing begins at birth. It's just that we don't notice it as such. To age well we have to live well. It takes practice. If we spend our whole lives busy, ambitious, demanding, and full of expectations and needs, it is not easy to switch channels in such a drastic way, so as to let go so completely in older age. We have to practise letting go before that. In a way, since ageing is loss of powers, loss of capacities, and loss of many other things, there is dying in it – dying to what was and to our imagined needs, and to what we think we have and don't want to lose. Practice then means practising to die a bit during our life, to genuinely live with less grasping onto things and to life itself. One meditation teacher described this well after he contracted Alzheimer's disease. He said: "You have got to get your dying done early!"

On the level of the body, preparing for ageing well is about living with simplicity and harmony in relation to the world. If you look at the lifestyles of communities or individuals who tend to live a long time and are healthy and energetic into old age, they generally engage in physical work, are not overweight, eat little and regularly, don't use industrial or processed food, and are not under stress or subject to a great many contagious diseases. Science backs this up, and confirms that one of the main ways that we can increase our lifespan and general health into old age is to consume less – to reduce the amount of calories and chemicals that our body consumes and then has to get rid of. At the same time if we are active in our life we will be more likely to continue that into old age. It is interesting that science has failed to find any one herb, remedy, pill, vitamin, food supplement or drug that can substantially prolong life, but has confirmed repeatedly in many studies that restricting food intake is the one change that really can prolong life safely.

It happens that my doctorate is on the way cells age, and I have written many scientific papers and a book on the ageing process. What stands out is that there is no one mechanism or a programme that controls the ageing process – it is more the lack of a programme. As we age, more or less everything gets more chaotic, uncontrolled, unregulated. It is as if evolution has designed us to reach maturity and have children, and then after that loses interest – like a car that is designed to go for 300,000 km, but after that everything seems to go wrong. If that is the case, then wise ageing is to get more mileage out of this body by using it carefully, without stress, burnout, over-consumption, toxins and extremes.

However, much of this preparation is of the mind, not the body. And the mind that ages well is a mind that is cheerful, positive, curious, kind and attentive. These are the qualities of mind that we need to sustain in our life, so as to keep them when we are older. This is not the mind of a couch potato. This is not the mind that spends most of its waking hours either working in front of a computer or sinking in front of the TV. It may be a good idea to reduce the amount of non-nutritious stuff that the mind is consuming as well. Inner peace does not go well with endless worries and concerns about what was and what might be. What we do with our mind really matters – what we direct our attention to, and what habits of mind we develop. For example, I am a great believer in different forms of meditation, to give focus, balance and steadiness of mind, to reduce fear and runaway concerns. Meditation not only brings concentration and inner peace – it also embodies those qualities of mind we mentioned. If we see our inner landscape clearly with our inner eye, we are no longer controlled by it. We can be more intimate with ourselves, and free, and see the truth of things, even if they are not so pleasant, and this brings us much ease and joy. I remember during a course on meditation I was teaching to elderly people, during one particular session there was a wonderful sense of peace and deep quiet that kind of took us over. After the session I asked how it was. One woman said: "Do you realize what a relief it is just to rest in the awareness of my quiet breathing? I was no longer a 70-year-old lady, I did not have arthritis, and I did not have a crowd of noisy grandchildren and demanding family. I was just breathing. I was at peace."

This can help us to cope with the really big challenges of changes to ourselves, our circumstances and our body, such as loss of capacities. With an ability to be a "fair witness" of the changes that happen to us, we do not identify with them so much ("my problems") and we will tend to take our changes more easily, to take things as they come. Embracing our changes also includes embracing health and sickness. Nature is being expressed when we are born, when we age, and when we die. We don't need to take it personally. Here is part of a poem I wrote on my sister's 60th birthday:

> This is a great age
> If we don't hold on too tight,
> Turning to our life,
> Filling it with warm colours,
> Love inside boundaries
> That no longer quite protect us
> But are breached in unexpected places
> Which seem like aches and pains
> But is the sweet vulnerability
> Of the world getting in.
> This dialogue between health and sickness,
> Is like two neighbours arguing,
> Across a fence full of holes,
> That divides the same garden

Once, so the story goes, the Buddha as an old man was being given a massage by his attendant, Ananda, and another monk. They too were old at this time. As they gave him a massage, the Buddha exclaimed: "Look! How the skin is falling in folds! How amazing!" They all laughed. "Look", he said, "how the flesh is so dry and withered! Isn't that something!" "Yes," they replied, "amazing", and they all laughed. They were like little children looking at their changed selves with surprise and delight, not old depressed people complaining and worrying about their bodies.

Part of this freedom to flow with change is to live in the present moment. In a deep sense, in the present, there is only moment-by-moment experience, which is spontaneous and immediate, beyond time. In the moment, truly experienced, there is no ageing, no measuring, no comparing with what was and no concern about what will be. There are no labels or commenting about my problems, my issues and my age. We can meet the moment by letting go into it, just as we let go into the touch of the wind on our cheeks, or the beautiful early morning song of the blackbird in our garden. We can actively surrender to whatever the moment gives us. We need to give ourselves permission to stop struggling, to get out of the battle. This is what allows the moments of grace that, after a long life behind us, we deserve. This is the wisdom of age – a life rich with experience culminating in peace, reflection and full presence. It is this wisdom that makes us role models to younger people.

Isn't this period of our lives the one when we can leave behind our duties and concerns and devote ourselves to our inner life, the life of the spirit? In India there are traditional life stages – the first quarter (20–25 years) is growing. The second is establishing a family and working. The third is gaining wisdom and preparing for departure, and the fourth is to leave home and wander the land in search of spiritual realizations. Maybe we don't want to physically wander the streets of London, New York or Tel Aviv. But we can fly free, like a great bird soaring over the great landscape of our life, celebrating the view!

CHAPTER 11
WHAT ARE WE SAYING?

You are reading words, perhaps on paper or on a website. Our mind largely packages its thoughts into the form of words, which dominate our inner and outer lives. We should ask ourselves: How do we speak? What can we say? What is worth saying? How do we purify our words so that they bring blessings to ourselves and others and not pain?

It is worth first of all understanding both the power and the emptiness of words. The power is obvious. Think of the power of the words of a politician that can whip up emotion in millions of people, create insecurity and fear of an enemy, imagined or real, and incite terrible violence. Think of an insult that we suffer that stays with us and revolves around our mind for years. Think of the climate of criticism and putting down that is so prevalent in daily life, often stealing the joy from everyone within earshot. What a huge personal result will ensue from the words of a doctor who tells someone that they have cancer. Words can also be the power and beauty of a blessing, the relief of a confession, the sweetness of appreciation, the dramatic echo in the heart when someone says the words: "I love you." Words can radically change our life. Nisargadatta Maharaj received a few words from his guru, Siddharameshwar Maharaj, that entered his consciousness like a virus. He worked with this blessed infection for some years and it brought him to awakening. The words were: "You are the Absolute. Now go and realize it."

But at the same time words are empty, made of nothing. Words are empty vessels carrying agreements. No matter who speaks them. The barking of dogs are their words. Words are nothing more than agreements in the mind. They arise as conceiving, which may be shaped into a word, which is converted to sound waves in the air, or written shapes on a page, which travel, land in someone else's mind, where they are unpacked and can trigger similar meanings. Or they can trigger great misunderstandings and disconnections, as the agreements need to be learned and are never secure. They signify things but are not themselves things. They are the map but not the territory. In that sense they are never completely satisfying. And if we want to express anything more subtle or deep we are mostly lost for words. T S Eliot, one of the greatest poets in the English language, had to admit in his poem *East Coker* to 20 years largely wasted in attempting to use words, that every attempt was a different kind of failure, that it was "a raid on the inarticulate".[1] No wonder many spiritual teachers teach in silence and communicate their teaching as a stream of non-verbal contact. You either get it or you don't. Chuang Tzu, the ancient Taoist sage, said that "Words never communicate reality. So show me the man who has given up words. I want a word with him."[2] In other words, we have no choice but to use these imperfect tools of language. But at least we can do so with the awareness of their emptiness and yet their power.

So what is "right speech"? The Buddha defined right speech as one of the eight primary paths leading to awakening. So we do have to take it seriously, and cannot put it aside and assume that spiritual practice or religious life is all about meditation or worship, after which we can scream at our partner, or lie to the income tax, or cause people to hate each other, or make untrue promises to customers in order to sell them things. The Buddha defined right speech as follows:

> If it is not true and not helpful, don't say it.
> If it is true but not helpful, don't say it,
> If it is not true but helpful, don't say it,
> If it is both true and helpful, find the right time.

Wow! This is a demanding definition. It may seem that only angels can speak like that. Do we have to be monks in order to keep such high standards for our speech? I don't think so. And here is why. The first and primary intention is to bring our speech into awareness. To be more mindful of what we are saying. This turns speaking into spiritual practice. What does this mean in practice? It means being more awake as to the source of the words within us, and to the effect of the words we are saying both on ourselves and on others. Words are the result of thought, which is heavily influenced by emotion and feeling. Thoughts themselves arise out of consciousness or mind, much as waves arise out of the ocean but are also made of water. Consciousness is pure, it is our Buddha-nature, our pure being. But as it is expressed in forms such as thoughts and then words, it takes on the shape of our memory, our conditioning, our personality, our habits and patterns. In order to purify speech, our awareness needs to extend in both directions – to the source of words and to the results.

In relation to the source, we can dive into the feelings and kind of awareness that gave birth to these words. When we speak harshly, does it grate inside us like sandpaper, creating friction somewhere in our inner life? If we are used to talking too much, can we feel the sense that we are covering over something with our words, that silence is painful? If we speak very little, is it an inner quietness, in which we don't speak because we are contented without words, or is it an escape from disturbance, from the noise of the world, or is it some personal shame that we are grappling with deep inside that blocks us. Many years ago, I joined co-counselling for a couple of years, as I felt in need of some help in opening the channels to my own emotional life. One woman who I counselled with announced one day that what I needed was to go into the forest and scream. I absolutely resisted, considering it unspiritual to scream and shout. But I soon realized that it was even more unspiritual to be attached to some kind of inner cave. So I went out to the forest every week and shouted my head off. It was an amazing way to open the channels of the heart and of speech.

In relation to the results, we need to be aware of the quality of our words and whether they are helpful, kind and reduce suffering in the world, or do the opposite. How do they land within someone else's inner life? Do they cause confusion, disturbance, defensiveness, anger? Or do they help trigger calmness, confidence, clarity and kindness? For example we may have a pattern of needing to control, which makes us give unasked-for advice to everyone. But we can bring the pattern in ourselves to the surface when others get irritated and even disempowered rather than empowered. The dialogue becomes a useful mirror. It boomerangs back on us and helps us to see ourselves.

Here are some examples to illustrate this. These examples come from people I met within the space of a few hours. In one case a young man began to talk to me very fast and very intelligently. I felt that I could not get a word in edgeways, as the expression goes. As he rapidly talked and talked, I felt almost physically that he was pushing me away with his torrent of words. I felt compassion for him, sensing how he had created a wall around himself, protecting a wounded self, not letting others touch him, and how lonely and unloved it felt inside the wall. I suggested that he could practise just watching, without judgement, and sympathetically, and see how his speech distanced others from him, and at the same time he could meet and know the vulnerability behind the wall of words.

I met a woman who was talking about her work, and her language was peppered with criticism and blame of others, of almost everyone, from the prime minister to the office cleaner. It felt like a cloud of negativity. Her practice would be to notice how her criticisms backfired and caused relationships to be painful and disappointing, and to know the pain inside her that projected out onto others. Mindfulness of speech would also show her how her softer words created positive conditions around her, allowing others to get closer to her, and how that felt.

There is some wise traditional advice in Buddhist monasteries on how to admonish a monk who has slipped up and broken the rules. First, get permission from the monk for you to offer admonishment. Second, do it with kindness and compassion, not anger. Third, speak with right speech.

Fourth, find the right time. Fifth, don't admonish someone about something they are doing if you yourself are doing the same thing!

The practice of awareness of speech is able to bring us into a present moment which is wonderful, always surprising and even sacred. A word of the Bible can be sacred to Jews as the word created by a spontaneous brush stroke can be sacred to a Zen monk. It is the deep attention that makes it so. If we are genuinely aware, a lie can feel really crude, rough and painful. A word spoken right, that encourages the best in others and creates healing, can be felt directly as a moment of joy and ease. It creates an atmosphere that spreads in all directions. It spreads out to help others. It spreads back to lighten our own inner life, and it spreads into the future to sow seeds that benefit all.

Words do not need to interrupt silence. They can arise from silence, they can carry silence and they can create silence. And silence does not need to interrupt words. We need not be afraid of silence; sometimes it can help us listen to our precious inner messages.

CHAPTER 12

WAR: DO WE REALLY HAVE NO CHOICE?

I am writing this in July 2024, after six months of unimaginable violence and suffering in the Middle East. A significant number of Israelis were killed, wounded or captured on October 7th, and Israeli soldiers were still being killed after that. While in Gaza there has been catastrophic death and injury of a huge number of civilians, and massive destruction making most of the population homeless. In actual fact I wrote much of this article in August 2006, during the war between Israel and the Hezbollah in Lebanon and revised it 10 years ago, in July 2014, when large numbers of people were killed and injured and made homeless in Gaza, and Hamas rockets were raining down on Israel. And the tragedy is that the text of the article is mostly the same because nothing has changed, though it is much more devastating now. War follows war, with temporary respite in between. Each frenzy of violence prepares the way for the next. During the Lebanon war I was in the firing line. The days had been constantly punctuated by loud blasts of katyusha rockets which had been landing intermittently, randomly, suddenly, and anywhere and I had given up repeatedly seeking cover. At the same time Israeli artillery had been thudding continuously day and night. Today, July 2024, I hear again the booms and bangs mostly from Israeli guns bombarding Lebanon. Then as now, I feel the blasts in my being, sensing their violence and the suffering which they bring. I feel a huge sadness and compassion which knows no boundaries and does not take sides.

Then as now all the participants draw motivation from a consensus that 'we are justified', 'we have no choice' and 'we must defend ourselves'. This view stands behind most wars and conflicts, and the encouragement of this view by groups or leaders prepares the ground for war by providing the necessary justification. It is certainly the case with the current onslaught on the Palestinian population, which is based on the view that Hamas has to be destroyed so as to protect Israel. The defence of 'Freedom' provided justification for the Vietnam war, and 'Weapons of Mass Destruction' for the Iraq war. 'We have to get them before they get us' is a common refrain that initiates slaughter, such as that of the First World War. And the conviction that there is no other way, that 'we have no choice', somehow makes it possible to inflict so much harm and suffering on so many men, women and children. So it is crucial to ask if it makes any sense.

Ethical decisions are never easy, and our actions, though often spontaneous, do depend on all the wisdom and heart that we have built over our lives. For that reason it is our responsibility to develop our awareness, empathy, big vision and wise heart during our life so that if we are confronted with challenging violence we will choose a path that causes minimum harm to self and other. People often ask me, what would you do if someone came to your house with a gun to kill you. Would you kill them first if you could? The answer is that I have no idea. I would try and protect life, both mine and the other. One view would hold that genuine self-defence is possible, but only as a last resort when all other options have been used up. It also requires that we use just the minimum of force necessary to disable or restrain the attacker and no more. The Buddhist tradition, for example, does not forbid self-defence, and has developed techniques of martial arts such as kung-fu and aikido that protect the attacked without hurting the attacker. Clearly this is not the case in the huge death and destruction in Gaza today, and in other current conflicts such as between Russia and Ukraine, in which maximum force seems to be the rules of the game rather than minimum force.

In actual fact, cases of genuine self-defence are extremely rare, and in virtually all cases of conflict there are wise and heartfelt solutions that are not seen and not taken. "We have no choice" generally means "We don't have the wisdom to act differently". Most wars, including this one in Gaza as I write this are fought because of fear, insecurity, anger or revenge. But these are individual and national emotions, often stoked up by media and political leaders. The emotions create narratives, which is usually a national blindness, in which neighbours become demonised and labelled as 'the enemy'. Then it becomes impossible to really communicate with 'the other' and sort out any problems together. Fear and insecurity are not problems in themselves, but are dangerous when they become fixed as uncontrollable narratives such as being the victim, which then justifies the violence. If we clearly see these emotions that sweep through the social atmosphere, then we can take responsibility for them, take care of them, and not allow them to be converted into bombs and rockets. We can deal with the fears and their ensuing narratives internally, rather than attempting to destroy the source of them externally. If we reduce identification with these emotions and the belief in the views that arise from them, everything looks different. All of a sudden, the so-called terrorist becomes a Palestinian youth who has suffered dearly and needs to be heard, the so called 'Zionist aggressor' becomes an Israeli family man whose parents died in the Holocaust, the Israeli soldier and the Hamas militant can both be seen as young men, patriotic and resentful but also wounded in their souls, and suffering while giving and receiving violence. If we are unable to do this, we have severely limited our vision and our freedom to act sanely. If we will not put ourselves in the other's shoes, listen to him or her, understand the fears, angers and pain that drives them to fight, just as our own fears, anger and pain, and know what we ourselves can do to help each other to get out of conflict, how can we say there is no other choice?

There is a choice to see things entirely differently. To see 'us and them' as a habit of mind and not a reality, to see how much we are connected, not separate, even as we fight together and certainly as we live together on this same earth. Pain and joy, love of life and fear of death know no boundaries. We and them can both wake up and realise that our happiness depends on the happiness of our neighbours, and vice versa, and our real safety is in togetherness not in intractable conflict.

The current Gaza war, according to Israelis and many others, started when Hamas invaded and killed Israeli citizens on October 7th. But to Hamas, this was a response to a very long period of occupation and failure to allow Palestinians their independence and a sense of hope, as well as the years of siege by Israel of Gaza which happened after the previous Gaza wars. And so the chain goes back and back for generations. Violence goes in chains. Each act of violence breeds another act of violence. Each act of violence creates the conditions, especially the emotional climate, for the next. Each act of violence makes it harder to initiate acts of peace. Each act of violence conditions the collective consciousness to feel that peace is impossible and only violence is left. But it doesn't take much wisdom to see this process happening, and unroll it in another direction. It is possible to create chains of peacemaking, to turn acts of aggression into acts of healing, to look for windows of opportunity for communication, dialogue and understanding of 'the other'. Where this is not done, it can hardly be said that "there is no choice". There is. To stop the chain. To take another road. In nearly all cases, 'the other' will be relieved and run to sit down with you over a cup of coffee. Non-violence does not mean doing nothing. It means an energetic attempt to create another climate. This requires strength and steadiness, qualities which are shown by genuine peacemakers. Mahatma Gandhi said: "Non-violence is the weapon of the strong". We can always make this choice.

For many years I brought groups of Israelis for weekends with Palestinians in the Palestinian town of Nablus in a program supported by the People to People program, part of the Oslo peace deal. The program was called 'The Transformation of Suffering'. It was based on a simple and profound insight derived from Buddhist teachings, that acknowledging, expressing and sharing our suffering together, is the fastest way to create empathy and put ourselves in the other's shoes. It worked powerfully and dramatically. The labels 'terrorist' and 'brutal occupier' vanished, and a human being just like ourselves emerged in their place. One young Palestinian with tears in his eyes, said "I grew up as a terrified child with loud Israeli soldiers controlling the streets at night. Now meeting you I know that after all there is goodness in the human heart."

What is needed is the intention to be serious about peace-making. Which raises another question. What are our real intentions, what is our real vision for the future? The habit reactions and the basic assumptions – are they about peacefulness or about conflict? Do we really and deeply yearn for peace or do we just say so? Each side must ask: are we really trying to make peace? What seeds am I planting for our common future? If we longed for peace, our speech, our motivations and our actions would be peaceful, and war would not arise. We all would begin a process of dialogue, healing and support with the same resources and determination with which we wage war. It would be simply impossible for an Israel intent on peace to take land and water from Palestinians, and settle all over their territory. Palestinians with a hunger for peace and a willingness to let go of past hurts, would utterly discourage the madness of suicide bombers and rockets, and would spread friendliness and appreciation for Israelis in the media and schools. In such a climate, neither side would have any incentive to bomb anyone. If we yearn for peace, we would have it, and the region would be a light to the world.

CHAPTER 13

IS SPIRITUALITY NATURAL?

Is the transcendent world a natural part of ourselves that just needs to be uncovered or something beyond us that needs to be sought? It sometimes seems hard work to seek for heaven. Yogis through the ages inflict on themselves austerities, the Buddha went off for seven years of intense practice and asceticism, monks sit in the desert alone, and we today busily consume piles of books, go on endless courses, chase after teachers and still find that we haven't "got there". Is all this hard work because "there", the spiritual or enlightened dimension, is apart from us and has to be hunted down by superhuman effort? If not, and it is a natural part of ourselves, why does it seem so inaccessible?

Part of the confusion comes from the definition of spirituality. We are somehow used to describing it as a state, or a thing which, like all other things, has an existence independent of us. However, we could define spirituality in the words of the Dalai Lama: "To be concerned with those qualities of the human spirit – such as love, compassion, patience, tolerance, forgiveness, contentment, a sense of responsibility, a sense of harmony – which brings happiness to both self and others." Then clearly we have nowhere else to look other than inside.

All the great spiritual traditions are clear on this. Christianity may preach salvation, and Judaism the Messiah, or Japanese Buddhism the Pure Land, all of which seem to be an ideal place or event coming from somewhere else, but spirituality always talks in terms of liberation existing inside. In each of the above the mystical or deeper understanding explains salvation, Messiah and Pure Land as an inner process. This process is one of uncovering layers of mud or dross to reveal the diamond within. As Rumi says: "I kept knocking on the door of heaven. Eventually it opened. I found I was knocking from the inside!"

The language of Jewish mysticism describes the spirit as veiled or covered by peels, which need to be peeled off. Traditional Chinese Taoist teaching describes *shen*, the great power of the heart, as flowing only when yin and yang, our primal energetic and constitutional opposites, are in balance. Buddhist teachings state that our awareness is limited by *kilesas* or thieves that have stolen our spiritual insight. It comes from the basic idea that we need to understand what the obstacles are to awakening, and work to gradually dissolve them, and then awakening will be revealed by itself. If we hunger for an imagined goal it is another attachment that restricts and channels us. The Buddha did say that attachment to the goal of a liberated life is the best attachment that one can have and better than all the others, but nonetheless that too needs to be abandoned eventually.

In any case, in the fundamental Buddhist teaching of the Four Noble Truths the third truth – the cessation of suffering in nirvana – is not given as an unreachable goal that is unrealistic and exceptional, but rather the truth as it stands already. Just like the fundamental axiom of the first truth, that dissatisfaction and suffering cannot be avoided in the experience of all living beings, so the third truth expresses the axiom that liberation is also an integral part of life, though, as the second truth states, it is hidden under attachments.

Even the neurosciences have something similar to say about this. The spiritual experience itself is (thankfully) not amenable to research using the crude scientific instruments that we have now. However, there is research showing that 80% of those whose temporal-lobe region of the brain is stimulated electromagnetically in the laboratory will have a mystical experience.[1] This must indicate some kind of hard-wiring that facilitates such experiences. Another finding is that meditation increases access to the right brain and balances

the activities of the right and left hemispheres. The left brain
tends to filter experiences and select those that fit our view of
self and the world. Right-hemisphere cognition tends to be
a more expansive, truthful and insightful, and is usually less
developed. Higher states of consciousness may arise through a
more balanced left and right brain functioning.[2]

Think of the Garden of Eden, paradise. At its centre is
the tree of life, the lived experience. Man was tempted away
from it by the other tree – the tree of knowledge of good and
bad, or perhaps more accurately good and bad *for me*. This
deeply archetypal myth tells us that paradise is not in some
other place, unobtainable and forbidden, but is tied to the
tree of life, the lived experience itself. It is accessible if we stop
favouring the fruit of the tree of me.

Take another example. All of us are drawn to nature. We feel
an affinity and a sense of harmony when we are within nature
that is quite difficult to pin down in words. Something in
nature talks to the nature within us and we feel more peaceful.
If we look more deeply we may also sense that in nature we are
less pressured to be somebody, we are less identified with our
careers, desires, interests, and roles. It is not in nature itself that
we find transcendent feelings but in the natural spirituality
within us that is triggered when we are in nature, such as
sitting watching the waves by the sea.

So why does it seem so hard? One clue also comes from
neurology. Our brain makes maps of the world and of
memory, and these consist of neural networks. In other words
the normal, automatic and functional mode of awareness is
built into our minds by a strong conditioning process from
an early age that is more or less engraved in our minds. We do
need quite an effort to restore flexibility and wise innocence,
so as to be able to see things differently, and in a more open,
expansive and liberated way.

The peels, the shells, the thieves, the stains, the veils …
these are all images of conditioning and habit. We are creatures
of survival and creatures of habit, and in the daily obsession
with our interests, we have forgotten so much. Philosophers

have joked that man's main activity is forgetting. We have so consistently forgotten the big picture, the child-like innocence, the inner freedom and power that we do not know where to find it again. It is in there, but we need an archaeological dig to get to it. Interestingly, the word for Buddhist mindfulness meditation in the original Pali language is *sati,* which is loosely translated as "remembering to be aware".

But this does have important practical consequences. If our spiritual search is for something that is already within us, though buried, then our practice or inner work should emphasize uncovering, or a kind of dropping into our innate awareness, rather than an intensive search for something outside of ourselves. We may, on the way, derive benefit from the outside, such as a book, a guru or a deity. But this has to be a stepping-stone into a pre-existing and forgotten reality. Good teachers know this and may intially encourage devotion, practice and surrender to something or someone external, including themselves as guru, but then encourage the same surrender to what was there all the time and within all experience. Spiritual practice, whether meditation or any other, needs to reduce the control of our conditioning, creating the inner space and emptiness that allows the truth to bubble up like the laughing waters of a spring.

And actually our realization that spirituality is natural, a birthright, and already part of our make-up, does make it all much easier. If it is outside of us we have to go through a long period of preparation, waiting and purification until it happens to us. We need to practise heroically to make us ready, which often seems an endless process. An example of this is the Christian desert fathers who fasted and prayed for grace, which came from long periods of *expectatus,* waiting with deep longing for it to arrive from "above". However, if we know it as part of ourselves and the nature of things, then our training becomes much more like learning to listen. It is a bit like learning to play the piano – we have a musical capacity, and it needs some practice to open it. The great thing about the spiritual journey within is that, like learning to play the piano, we can enjoy the music we make right from the beginning, as well as in the middle and at the end. And there is some more good news. Neuroscience has recently come to understand that there is more plasticity, flexibility, in the neuronal networks than was previously thought. We can make a real difference to our inner landscape without heroic effort, and it can often feel like listening to the music of our soul.

Let's go a few steps further, in fact let's go all the way, and ask what is this natural spirituality, our basic but ignored Buddha-nature? The answer is that spirituality is not only natural, it is itself our fundamental true nature because there cannot be any ultimate reality in the thoughts, subjectivity, concepts, ideas, perceptions and interpretations that we think of as our nature, since they are the result of a fabricated construction process that we learned. Moreover they constantly arise and pass away. These are like the movies projected onto the screen of our real nature, which is at one with the universe and the totality of things. In other words, even if we think our thoughts are very close to us and they are our nature, this is an act of ownership not an uncovering of our natural spirituality. Natural spirituality, our real nature, is even closer – it is being itself. Pure, aware, perfect, primal and unconditioned. From which place all our passing experiences, and the story of our life, emerges.

CHAPTER 14

DIAMONDS SPARKLE IN THE AIR

Diamonds sparkle in the air
And are quenched under water
Salt once was money in the desert
But worthless by the sea
Value is noticed when it is missing
The pure shines out of darkness
But is invisible among the angels
Insights illuminate space
But are lost among themselves
We hold precious what is not ordinary
Until we know that the ordinary is precious
And water that hides diamonds
Sparkles like them.

PART TWO
HOW TO PRACTISE

(SAMADHI)

CHAPTER 15
TRUTH AND AUTHENTICITY

According to Buddhist tradition, spiritual practice is not only for the sake of spiritual experiences and insights, but leads to the gradual development of refined qualities or perfections (*parami*) such as generosity, determination, serenity and patience. Lifelong practice enables these qualities to take root within our personality. We live them, and how we live in each moment becomes more important than what happens to us, or even who we are. The quality of our actions takes the place of our sense of self importance. Seeing the way these *paramis*, such as generosity or equanimity, grow within us reveals the manner in which practice affects our daily lives.

One of the perfections is *sacca,* which is usually translated as honesty. However, the original concept in Pali is much broader, and it may be understood as authenticity or truth. How does this perfection manifest in our lives?

Upon close examination we find that living an authentic life is not at all a simple matter. Since we are all vulnerable and sensitive creatures that cannot exist in isolation, we tend to believe things that we are told; we hold onto others' beliefs and positions as though they were our own, and live, think and speak them long after we have forgotten their origin. We hang onto perceptions and tales that we read in newspapers or pick up from the television, and adopt the social conventions of our childhood homes. These voices and views trickle and seep in and take hold of us unawares, and so our thoughts and inner voices actually originate from external sources. We can find a typical example of this in the unconscious similarity between ourselves and our parents in manners of speech, inclinations and habits. Even after having left our parents' home, thinking that we were totally free and on our own, a bystander would easily recognize behaviours and thought patterns that we inherited from them. We give voice to others' views and ideas so often that we have trouble identifying our own true voice. If we were to decide to be totally honest with ourselves, what does that actually mean? What is that self that I would like to be honest with? This question has no simple answer. Authenticity is no simple matter.

Dilemmas about the authenticity of experiences can come up in the context of practising meditation. To what extent are experiences authentic if they are directed by external guidance and instructions? For example, if I practise meditation on compassion and loving kindness, how authentic are the feelings that arise as a result of my intention to nurture the perfection (*parami*) of love? When I practise mindfulness as the direct and immediate knowing of what I perceive moment· by moment – what is my genuine experience at this moment? These questions are not simple to answer.

Nonetheless, it is much more difficult and painful to exist inauthentically, so, in a way, we are given no choice. It is worth noticing the suffering brought on by the experience created when we are captivated by inauthentic positions. Such a position, for example, is "us versus them", when the other is identified as the enemy, and conflicts turn into irrefutable facts of life. Such is the conflict in the Middle East, which is perceived as a perpetual fact of life. We are born and grow up to a state of conflict, we internalize it and perceive it as an indisputable truth. It becomes an underlying assumption that guides us – circumventing our awareness. An automatic thought process ensues, "us against them", "them against us". We mindlessly adopt the consensus thinking, feeling great vulnerability, bobbing up and down in a sea of beliefs, assumptions and prejudices – a state of enslavement, ignorance and suffering. This is where Buddhism offers inquiry as a central element of practice. It is a beautiful dimension unique to the Buddhist way. Fundamental to the practice is a search for truth, stemming from the understanding that truth leads to liberation, while the quest for comfort leads to subjugation.

Rahula, son of the Buddha, received his first lesson when at the age of seven he joined the community of monks. The lesson was dedicated to the importance of telling the truth. The Buddha demonstrated this unequivocally, in a disconcerting way: he overturned a water dipper, spilling all the water, saying to his son: "If you tell a deliberate lie, your spiritual life will be as empty as this water dipper. When you lie you toss away your spiritual life. In the same way, Rahula, when anyone feels no shame in telling a deliberate lie, there is no evil he will not do."[1] This may sound overstated, but the Buddha was adamant that honest truthfulness was the foundation of spiritual life. Following this principle to this day, Buddhist monks are obligated to present truthful accounts of their experiences in their interviews with their teachers, neither embellishing nor diminishing them, and without pretending to have experienced events that have not occurred. A breach of this principle could even lead to an expulsion from the community. Speaking the truth is considered the first stage in the practice of truth, whereas inauthenticity in speech can lead to inauthentic consciousness. Truth is such a basic necessity for the spiritual way, that one who does not strive for the truth loses his way.

Dedication to the truth is evident also in the way the Buddha approached questions on the existence of God or a creator. He left those questions unanswered and advised his followers to refrain from such questions or beliefs. Such speculation not only offers no benefit, but can actually undermine the spiritual quest, which is founded on direct realization. It can cause the mind to wander off to a world of opinions, arguments and discussions of ideas that cannot be proved. The Buddha likened preoccupation with questions that are not part of authentic inquiry to a row of blind men leading each other. So honesty begins with an awareness of our utterances. This is a practice of inquiry that begins with honesty and leads to the depths of authenticity.

The sutta[2] that deals with this says that when a person expresses an opinion it is of great importance that he state that "this is only an opinion". When he is aware that an expression is only an opinion, he is actually stating that "this is something I heard that makes sense to me" and avoids the statement "that's the way it is, it's a fact". He takes responsibility for adopting a particular opinion. This is a defence of the truth, but not yet an awakening to the truth. Such an awakening happens on a different level, in which honesty and authenticity are used as a basis for a deep investigation into the nature of experience.

The second part of the sutta approaches the deep level of truth and deals with our illusions and vain thoughts about ourselves. When a person says, "I know" – who is the one who knows? What is the source of his knowledge? When the knowing stems from a presence that is awake, pure, has no illusions, is clear and wise, and devoid of self-interest, repulsions, desires or attachments – then we are dealing with an awakening to truth. The way of dharma begins with respect to truth, continues with sustained awareness of truth and leads to an awakening to the truth. Thus states the sutta: "The Dhamma [dharma] … is profound, hard to see and hard to understand, peaceful and sublime, unattainable by mere reasoning, subtle …we realize with the body the supreme truth and see it by penetrating it with wisdom."

This short and powerful description of the dharma is repeated time and again throughout this and other suttas. It offers two key teachings that are paths through the wilderness. First, it maintains that truth is realized, or perceived, with the body. This challenges the almost universal assumption that it is the mind that distinguishes true from false and that truth in is the territory of ideas. Instead of relying on those external voices of questionable validity, the awakening to truth is attained by a direct knowing of bodily life. There is something deeply authentic in listening to the voices of our cells, tissues, feelings, emotions, and even thoughts as thoughts. It is a direct, immediate knowing, without the need for interpretation, or commentary, and invites us to be present and connected with our life. The second key teaching is contained in the word *penetrating,* which expresses diving under the surface – uncovering what is hidden. The iceberg has only 10% of its mass above the surface of the ocean, and 90% below. What really matters is invisible, to quote *The Little Prince.* We will not be limited to the 10% that is obviously visible, particularly the superficial concepts, ideas and thoughts about ourselves, our needs, our issues and activities, but instead dive into the ocean of our being and be astounded by what we can discover there. The dharma, the nature of things, the unconditioned, is profound and not easy to see with just a brief glance. It needs a penetrating gaze.

Under the surface, we are in an existential realm. "What do I really know? What is really happening here? What is my genuine experience?" These are no longer philosophical questions. They are the source of an enthusiastic energy of inquiry to uncover things. There are no correct or specific answers to these questions, but if we persist in asking them they begin to undermine the fixed mental structures that we have accumulated and that imprison us. It shines a light on our beliefs, opinions and concepts about ourselves and the world. We move out of a sense of living on automatic pilot. Though at first it may be discomforting or even scary to see that what we assumed to be our safe house was actually a castle built of sand, soon we relish new-found freedoms and possibilities we hadn't dreamt of before.

In general, it is better not to regard these "what is" questions as mantras to be recited, rather they are in the background to help us to develop a continuous quality of inquiry and fresh awareness of the present moment. However, there are some Buddhist schools that do recite these questions verbally, and then they penetrate the subconscious and there shake the foundations of the apparent known. Korean Zen, for example, has a practice where as soon a disciple enters the monastery he repeats the question, "What is this? What is this?" incessantly, for a lengthy period. There is an entertaining story that has been circulating for some time. A Zen teacher and a Tibetan Buddhist teacher were on stage at a university seminar in the United States. The Zen teacher gave a dramatic example of Zen practice. He raised an orange in his hand and asked: "What is this? What is this?" There was silence. Again he asked: "What is this?" The Tibetan teacher maintained his silence. The Zen teacher kept asking: "What is this? What is this?" Finally the Tibetan Rinpoche said a few words to his interpreter, who turned to the Zen teacher and said that the Rinpoche had asked: "Have you really never seen an orange before?"

Perhaps the most important field for inquiry is the sense that I am the king and owner of my castle, that I sit on my throne within its walls and from there rule my kingdom. The firm habitual belief in a solid and enduring *me* inevitably causes us pain and suffering. For example, we hold onto a variety of rigid beliefs about ourselves, such as: "I can't do that"; "I'm not good at this"; "I'm depressed"; "I'm critical and judgemental"; "I'm great"; "I'm a failure"; "I'm young"; "I'm old"; "I'm sick"; "I'm a victim". We harbour endless masks, labels and descriptions that we attribute to ourselves, with which we construct an identity. We hide behind and protect this identity and keep out others, finding loneliness under the armour. These beliefs are buried in the deepest layers of the way we perceive the world and ourselves in relation to it: "This is me and that's the world out there." However, in the light of awareness, we can begin to see the sense of self as an experience and a belief, rather than a thing. I am not really a solid *someone*, I am merely a belief that I am someone. None of us are what we think we are although we all act as though we are someone specific. I act under the belief that I am Stephen. Clear observation cuts through the solid feeling that I am someone specific, whom I grasp as "I". This belief cannot stand up in the face of honest inquiry.

We may think it easier to seek comfort – turn on the television or have a beer, just like everyone else. "Leave the quest for truth to the Buddha, I am more interested in the football results!" Continuous authentic inquiry of the immediate experience does, indeed, demand courage and energy. It is not a simple thing to pause and ask: "What is really happening here?" However, as we persist we will gradually get more comfortable with the mood of inquiry and will discover that it introduces an additional level of interest into our lives. Besides, it doesn't need to stop our interest in the football results. It does not shut us down – just the opposite – it opens us up. When we emerge from restricting beliefs and automatic thought patterns, we begin to feel like a snake shedding its old skin. We become freer and more playful. We develop the capacity to view life as it is, devoid of barriers or illusions, and we are no longer saddled with a bundle of beliefs, assumptions, automatic reactions and external voices that weaken us. Thus the inquiry itself empowers us and nourishes the continued process with energy and interest. It kindles a fire within us.

We meet paradox on the way. In loosening our hold on the secure world of assumptions, in holding the known and the unknown more tenderly, we may meet contradiction and uncertainty. A Zen saying asserts "little doubt – little enlightenment; medium doubt – medium enlightenment; total doubt – total enlightenment". This does not mean a paralytic doubt that stops us from continuing, but rather a doubt that leads to a fruitful confusion about boundaries, facts and beliefs. A cup used to be just a cup. Now a cup is understood to be known as such by agreement and a perception built on memory. My dog doesn't see it that way. So what is a cup? This doubt allows us to linger in the unknown, even dance with it. Nothing is self-evident. We allow differing points of view to coexist, making no effort to adopt one and regard that as the truth and all others as false. For example, take views of spiritual practice – one view stresses gradual progress via formal training, while another claims that things are perfect as they are and there is ultimately nothing that needs to be changed. On the one hand, if reality is already perfect, why practise? On the other hand, how would we know that if we did not practise? Therefore, we must practise! How is it that

I need to sit here with eyes closed and follow my breath? It's boring. Wouldn't it be better to go outside, take it easy and spend time with the birds and the trees, and just enjoy myself? Both are necessary. Both views together paint a picture that is broader than each one separately. We climb the path up the hill, aiming for the summit. Why shouldn't we admire the scenery and enjoy the flowers on the way? We shouldn't tarry and fall asleep for 100 years but neither should we take the path itself too seriously and make the journey a burden. We aim for a dynamic middle way that lies between diverging paths and embraces coexisting paradoxes. If we do not take opposing viewpoints too seriously we will find that they create interest rather than trouble.

From within the realm of doubt and uncertainty we reach a new understanding, and a freer level of knowing. We need to stay close and intimate with the unknown so that it gradually reveals its secrets. It is impossible to go beyond the known while relying on ideas about it. Instead, we keep sitting at the doorway to the unknown until it opens, and we pass through.

This authentic inquiry can be part of our daily life and also formal practice that offers quiet and comfortable conditions for observation. Meditation creates a space where we may meet ourselves and take a deep gaze in the mirror. There will be pleasant experiences and unpleasant ones; we will identify our anger and limitations, and also our joy and freedom. Whatever arises becomes the raw material for observation. We are constantly awake and aware, steadily and honestly observing what emerges moment by moment. What we see in the mirror may seem like small personal trivialities. We may feel that our personal story is petty or silly, a sort of a soap opera unfolding in front of our eyes. Of course, that's not a problem: that's our life! With trust and courage we identify things as they are, realizing the truths that they represent. If we persevere and look directly at the view unfolding before our inner eyes, we will find that it dissolves and transforms. Things are not what they seemed to be at first. For example, the distinction between *myself* and the *world* begins to dissolve.

We discover our interrelations. When we look at ourselves we are actually observing the world. When we look at a tree it is joined with us, seeing it thus, in a moment of togetherness. The importance of the inquiry process is in that it teaches us about ourselves and the world and the way the two merge. This is an intimate connection with unity at its centre. We realize that there is an ongoing flow between us and the world which co-create each other incessantly. The inner voices we attribute to ourselves, that we think we own, actually belong to the world, to what has arrived through the senses, to our parents, our influences, our culture. At the same time who we are, what we think and say and do, influence the world. Knowing that intimacy and "inter-being" between us and the world allows a deep relaxation, an end to the struggle. We can let go. The search is no longer a burden that we have to carry on our small shoulders. We realize that there is no need to hunt for the truth; it is truth that seeks us.

CHAPTER 16
THE BODY IN MIND

We are born into a body. No-one asked our permission first, at least I don't remember any such request. We simply find ourselves in a body. And there begins a long complex love-hate relationship. First and foremost, we will spend more or less our entire life looking after this body, satisfying its every whim and caprice, and making sure it is as comfortable as possible. We have to feed it three times a day, and add to it constant snacks and cups of coffee to keep it quiet. We spend around two-thirds of our life working to keep the body active, in good shape, engaged and busy and the other third unconscious so as to give it enough rest. We also spend an extraordinary amount of care and resources making it look nice and dressing it up. Anyone reading this who has teenage daughters may well be able to read most of this book while waiting for them to get out of the bathroom! Our minds are constantly occupied in defending the body against insults, enemies and hurts, and its self-image against failure, blame and so on. After all that, the ungrateful body often hurts us with pains and illnesses. It is enough for anyone to want to leave this burden behind and get out. Except that leaving the body is the last thing anybody wants to do. We are entirely attached to this big needy baby.

Since being in a body is not easy, our usual response is to keep shutting out these nagging voices of need, of pain or discomfort. We shut them out by instant gratifications, such as sugar, stimulants, social drugs or alcohol, or by instant relief such as painkillers. But this only quietens the shrill cries for a short while. Instead we need to re-examine our relationship to this body. We need to ask some hard questions. If the body is telling us things, do we know how to listen? For example, pain is the way the body cries and calls for our attention. Do we block the crying with painkillers or do we listen to what the pain is telling us? And if we do respond, do we think only in terms of a solution, a treatment, a way again of silencing the uncomfortable voices, or do we pay deeper attention? Perhaps we are misusing or abusing or stressing some or all of our body and we do not know it because it is under the radar of our attention? One example that comes to mind is our heart. The core of our being. A large proportion of those who suffer a heart attack report that a heart attack was the first sign that there was something wrong with their heart. How is it that we don't know our own heart? Or to take another example, we use our eyes intensively. And often suffer from eyestrain, headaches and short or long sight. Yet we cannot imagine giving our eyes the rest, attention, support and love that they crave instead of sticking glasses in front of them. In our relationship to our body, or its parts, are we like a mother who shoves a dummy into the mouth of a crying child to shut it up? Or are we like the mother that responds to the cry with love and careful attention, and can read the subtle signs to know what the baby really needs?

Much of our relationship to our body is placed in the category: "It's ok. It doesn't need me, so I can forget it." We don't notice our teeth unless we have a toothache. We don't notice our head unless we have a headache, and we don't fully experience one breath in a million … unless we suffer from asthma! We guide our body in its life by automatic pilot. However, meditation, body-centred psychotherapy and especially mindfulness bring the automatic into awareness. We can begin to feel the living body, and what it expresses to us. We can open the experience of the body and discover a fascinating territory. What usually goes unnoticed comes within range of our attention. We don't just notice one breath, we notice one thousand breaths, each different, each telling us something about the sources of our life. We begin to see how the experiences of our daily life leave their tracks and traces in our bodies too.

It is common knowledge that we need to relax, and many of us do, perhaps combined with yoga, tai ch'i and other forms of movement. However, there are many dimensions of deep restful body awareness way beyond relaxation. Deep listening to the language of the body takes us much further. We know the stresses and strains in real time, as they happen, and so can prevent health problems at the earliest stages, we can guide ourselves to relax and care for whatever part needs us, in the right way, at the right time. And we know how to talk back to the body in its language; we can send our attention as a kind of healing internal massage, warming, softening and soothing. For example, we can feel straight away any strain around the eyes, and so we can close and relax them at the right time, at the same time as bathing them with sensitive loving attention. One Cambodian Buddhist monk I knew, who was at least 100 years old when I met him, said that his daily morning practice was to move his awareness over the body, part by part, and, conversing with each part, he would ask, "Right ear, how are you? Fine! Good. Left ear, how are you? Fine! Good. Upper lip, how are you …"

Steadily, my body and me become more intimate partners in the journey through life. As we move from avoidance, and open a new channel of dialogue with our body, we have a constantly available source of joy in the experience of the living body. But at the same time it can be of major benefit if we are in pain or difficulty. We can completely shift our attitude to pain. Instead of a nagging hurt, it becomes a changing kaleidoscope of shifting unpleasant sensations, always changing according to moment-by-moment circumstances. Instead of being a victim, we become a partner, instead of pain plus suffering, there is pain without suffering. That is the reason that deep mindful attention to the pain, diving into the waves rather than running away from them, is a key technique used in many chronic-pain clinics around the world, used when other therapies have failed, with a large amount of backing evidence.[1]

It goes much further still. The body can become a window to the universe. If we have the skill to pay deep attention to our body, it becomes a kind of weather vane, to direct us toward what is wholesome and healthy and harmonious in our daily lives. Our bodies can warn us of frictions, conflicts and anger, almost before our minds know it. Our feet take us in the right direction, our belly tells us its intuitions, our muscles show our defences, and our whole being dances to the impressions of the world around us. This is our body directing our minds, just as our minds are directing our bodies. This is spiritual work. It can be deeply enriching and liberating, because it is the discovery of the truth that mind and body are one continuum. There is no basic division between mind and body. Witnessing the life of the body, the greatest show on earth, will tell us that the mind and body are constantly creating and intermingling with each other. Bringing mind to our body is bringing our body to mind.

CHAPTER 17
THE MIRACLE OF MINDFULNESS

In this book I have chosen to focus on mindfulness in the wide sense of waking up to our lived experience moment by moment. However, mindfulness in a more specific sense is a relatively new term that is being talked about everywhere. It seems to be taking us by storm. It has changed the face of modern psychology with CBT (Cognitive Behavioural Therapy) and ACT (Acceptance and Commitment Therapy). The new mindfulness-inspired methods are taking over from traditional psychodynamic psychology throughout the modern world.[1] MBCT (Mindfulness-Based Cognitive Therapy) has become a key psychological and psychiatric self-help training as an alternative to medication, particularly for depression.[2] In the British Parliament, a cross-party committee has recommended strongly the take-up of mindfulness in the prison system, in schools, in the workplace and in primary health care, especially in dealing with mild and recurring depression and anxiety.[3] More than a hundred members of Parliament have taken courses in it. We hear about "Mindfulness-Based Stress Reduction" (MBSR), a structured mindfulness training that is now available in most hospitals and medical centres[4] that is used in specialized ways such as in chronic-pain clinics in the US when all else has failed.[5] Of course mindfulness meditation is also a spiritual technique that is being learned and applied by millions across the world who go to classes and retreats. There are now thousands of research papers on mindfulness in a number of areas: improving well-being and happiness;[6] treating anxiety and depression;[7] improving the life and health of cancer patients;[8] dealing with insomnia;[9] helping to improve the atmosphere and reduce stress in the workplace.[10] But it is not clear to many people what exactly it is, how it is done, and how it can help us. So let us explore that here.

Mindfulness is a translation of the word *sati* in the ancient Pali language of the early Buddhist texts. *Sati* means to remember to be aware or pay attention to what is actually happening right now: it has an element of being present, and an element of returning or remembering. Before the translation to the English word mindfulness, the old-fashioned English word "recollection" was used, which also suggests a movement of coming back to ourselves. Mindfulness has come to the Western world along with the introduction of Buddhist spiritual and meditative practices over the last 50 years. It is a central practice of most Buddhist traditions, and indeed, in one form or another, the practice of being aware is part of all spiritual traditions. It is one of the techniques of spiritual training that has emerged from the monasteries of Burma and Thailand, which has become packaged for the modern world as mindfulness, much as yoga has arrived from its Hindu spiritual source.

In the early texts it is very clearly described – when you breathe in a long breath you know it is a long breath, when a short breath you know it is a short breath ... when stretching out the arm you know it, when turning, walking, sitting and eating you know it ... and so on. You know sounds and tastes, touch and smells. That is on the level of the body. It gets subtler of course. When a thought arises you know that you are thinking and you know what kind of thought it is. You know when you are attracted or pulled toward something you like or pushed away from something you don't like. You know the arising of intentions and will, of moods and states of mind. You know the inner emotional climate, subtle or gross forms of anger, joy, love and every other feeling. You know what it is like to be you at every moment. In other words, you are fully present and aware at each moment. It is like waking up to the true experience of each moment, or shining a light on phenomena that are actually occurring as they arise. This knowing is directly meeting a phenomenon, such as a pain in the back, without the intermediate agency of concepts, interpretations, commentaries, wishes or projections based on it. We are like a king sitting in the palace of our body-mind. But we don't know what is there, most of the rooms are dark and closed. But we can open the doors and illuminate what is there even if it has been dark and abandoned for a long time.

What is the opposite of mindfulness, what is it to be non-mindful? It is being distracted and unavailable to ourselves. Instead of being awake it is sleepwalking through life, living on automatic pilot. We breathe thousands of times a day and don't know one of these breaths. We walk about throughout the day but don't know one step and don't know what our feet are doing or what they are experiencing. So waking up to what is already happening is a good description of mindfulness. As in the quote of John Lennon: "Real life is happening while we are busy making other plans." Shakespeare said it beautifully: "For where thou art, there is the world itself [...] And where thou art not, desolation" (*Henry IV* Part 2 – Act 3, Scene 2).

This is no easy task, and it is usual to take it step by step, training the attention by regular practice or in intensive retreats. The training involves staying steady for longer and longer periods, with some slice of our sensory impressions in the present moment. For example, if the breath is used as the point of focus, the training is to stay with the breath, observing it fully, for as long as possible. After a period, the mind is distracted and goes off on its usual tracks. One lets the mind go, and returns to the breath. The contact of the foot with the ground while walking, of the body on the floor while lying, or the taste of the food while chewing, are all possible places to train our mindfulness. Gradually, mindfulness becomes established for longer and longer periods, and one becomes more sensitive, more able to notice things, and present with whatever comes up. Continued practice can bring us to a deep spiritual transformation as life opens itself up to our penetrating attention.

But fortunately mindfulness is highly effective even in small doses. Preliminary exercises and training may start just with taking time to really experience the eating of an orange, or to fully catch the experience of just a few breaths. At this level it can help us come back to ourselves, feel at home with ourselves, engage more effectively with the ups and downs of daily life, and feel that we are living more fully. It works because it opens a window to the basic truth that we live our life only in the present moment. And in this present moment we experience a flow of ever-changing impressions and experiences. Getting closer to this truth we begin to feel fully and wonderfully alive. Much as we were when we were children, with every moment full of wonder and interest. And with that same innocence, if something is painful we can cry, but immediately afterwards we have moved on and the sun shines again.

Mindfulness works because it runs counter to inner tendencies and habits with which we usually perceive the world, such as the assumption that daily life is a Sisyphean task of coping and endless struggle, which causes stress, depression and suffering. There is a tendency for our minds and ourselves to be completely and endlessly caught up by things we like or do not like. If we have a task, we are totally occupied with what we need to do, with its success or failure. If we have a pain, we are completely absorbed in dealing with it and trying to stop it and in being the victim of it. If we have emotional or relationship issues, they keep going round and round our minds and we may feel submerged or depressed. It is as if we are under an enchantment, and we forget the changing, dynamic and free nature of our real experience in the present moment. For example, we forget that we breathe unless we have asthma, forget that we are standing on this earth when we are waiting impatiently in line at the bank, forget that there are birds singing outside when we are working at a computer under pressure to reach a deadline, and so on. If we become intimate with our true experience, remarkable things can happen. If we begin to turn toward physical pain instead of away from it, and bring mindfulness to bear on it, we may find that it is not a solid and unpleasant block of pain, but rather a changing experience like any other, now strong, now weak, now urgent, now uninteresting, now evident and now vanished. In this way mindfulness training can help chronic-pain patients to completely shift their attitude from sufferer to participator, and they find that the pain is far less of a problem. Mindfulness softens the scars of living, and brings them back into circulation.

This is even more crucial when dealing with mental and emotional pain – patterns, habits and tendencies, our repeated negative thoughts, our angers and frustrations or the lack of meaning; in other words the struggle and reactivity that often seems to run our life. Mindfulness allows us to meet these burdens at eye level simply as phenomena that arise and pass. We call them by name and they gradually cease to run the show. They can be fully seen and known as just the flotsam and jetsam floating past on the ocean.

In a deeper sense, there is no real problem in the present moment, even though we may have unpleasant as well as pleasant experiences, if we are aware enough not to build up unpleasant experiences into a state of suffering. In this present moment things feel new, simple, meaningful and direct. Each living moment opens itself to us anew in the full gaze of our attention. This is what makes life sacred. Mindfulness takes us, in the end, to a place of non-dual knowing, in which the separation of me, the observer, and whatever is observed, dissolves. We merge with the object, and what is happening is just liberated awareness. We become the water that we hear and see. And we lose ourselves in the process – what is left is awareness.

The Vietnamese monk, Thich Nhat Hanh, who was one of the pioneers of mindfulness in the West, said: "I must confess it takes me a little longer to do the dishes in mindfulness, but I live fully in every moment and I am happy. Each second of life is a miracle; the dishes themselves and the fact that I am washing them are miracles! Every conscious step we make a flower blooms under our feet."[11] One of his further observations: "People usually consider walking on water or in thin air a miracle. But I think the real miracle is not to walk either on water or in thin air, but to walk on earth. Every day we are engaged in a miracle which we don't even recognize: a blue sky, white clouds, green leaves, the black, curious eyes of a child – our own two eyes. All is a miracle."[12]

CHAPTER 18
STOPPING

Most of us feel at times that we are like one of those hamsters that keep running inside a small wheel in a cage. Life can feel so relentless, fast, busy, stressful, anxious and uncertain. The Greek myth of Sisyphus is especially relevant in the fast-paced life that we lead today. Sisyphus was condemned by Zeus to roll a large boulder to the top of a hill only to have it roll back down again, over and over again for all time. We often feel that our working life is Sisyphean, endless and pointless. We keep dreaming of holidays, of lazing by the sea, of walking in the Alps, of getting off the wheel. If you ask people under what conditions they feel most well-being and peace, you would probably get responses like: "When I sit watching the sea"; "When I am walking in the forest"; "When I am sitting on my veranda with a cup of tea"; "When gardening"; "When breastfeeding my small child". If at the end of your life someone were to ask you what do you regret most, who would answer: "That I didn't spend more time in front of the computer."

But stopping is not so easy. We feel peace during short moments of a break, relative to the busyness that was. But if the break continued for long we would soon begin to lose that peace and want to do something, go somewhere, anything rather than just doing nothing. Even if we really go to that cave or desert island that we dream about, how long would it take before we begin to feel bored and restless, miss people we are close to, or feel that life is passing us by? Even if we have that holiday we have been saving up for, it may not feel that much different from regular life, as we run about busily sightseeing, or arguing about what everyone wants to do.

It is not easy to stop because we have strong built-in habits of restless activity. So the first understanding is that stopping has to happen gradually. In one of my mindfulness classes for the staff at a college, the dean who was really speedy kept rushing about trying to make sure everyone came on time, and then of course couldn't settle. I joked with him about rushing to stop. We have to get used to slowing down and stopping, then we will get to love it. It is like stopping the great ocean liner the *Titanic*. It takes some time to slowly stop, and if it is stopped by force it can sink. Our body tells us the pace. We can try the experiment of sitting quietly and watching how long before we need to move – probably not more than a few minutes initially (unless we are sitting in front of an exciting movie, but then our body is stopped but our mind is racing with the story). But if we sit quietly every day, soon the body can sit for longer and longer, as meditators well know. Nonetheless, it will take us a long time to be able to beat the sitting quietly marathons that my cat seems to be able to do without any problem whatsoever.

In fact we don't really want or need to stop. It is only a reaction to being controlled by busyness, such that we long for its opposite. But the opposite of a lot of activity is a lot of anaesthesia, passivity or inertia. What we actually want is to be active and energetic in life, but with peace not agitation. And if we want to know real peace, we will need to deal with the habits internally not just the conditions externally. And this needs some effort and skill. Paradoxically, to stop and know real peace is quite an active process. It is an art. One of the main tasks is to really know and clearly sense what the experience of agitation actually is like, with its nuances, layers and underground sources. This will engender intuitions as to what exactly makes us restless. We need to recognize and let go of the stress and the habits of unease. This is a psychological and meditative investigation. For example, we can sit or lie in deep relaxation and check in the body where the regions of stress and contraction are. By meeting each and letting it go, we introduce a deeper state of inner peace. But it goes deeper than that, because those habits are connected to basic human survival drives, which have a tendency to take us over. The basic need for sustenance becomes a relentless drive for more, in which we are constantly unsatisfied, and needy whatever the setting. It moves people to restless shopping. On my visits to New York I was amazed to see how much time and energy was spent on choosing which kind of restaurant to go to. Our views, opinions, conflicts, thoughts, fantasies, memories, disappointments, frustrations and so on, all written into our biography, will be a constant source of agitation.

It is not so easy to meet and work with the sources of our restlessness, our dissatisfaction. When we try to reach and meet those sources we don't quite know where to look and how to work with the material. Meditative reflection, contemplation and mindfulness will help us catch the restlessness as an actual present-moment experience. Then we can use the acronym RAIN:

- **R is Recognize**. First we need to clearly recognize and acknowledge what it is that is arising that is stealing our peace. For example, if it is a habit of self-criticism or judgement, we need to see it clearly, and name it.
- **A is Accept**. It is helpful to accept what is arising as just that – what is arising. And accept ourselves as we are. This is instead of setting up an internal battleground in the name of inner peace – which of course won't work.
- **I is Investigate**. Look into it, see its dimensions, its projections onto the body, the way it runs through our mind-feeling-body system.
- **N is Non-Identify**. It is taking a step back and becoming a witness of the uncomfortable phenomena that are arising. It is about reducing ownership of them. That will allow us to remain in peace even in the presence of these disturbing guests that, as Rumi said, invade our house and overturn our furniture.

Clearly, stopping cannot be forced, it is not achievable by aggressively trying to control ourselves, which just generates resistance, more noise in the system of mind-body, more waves. Nonetheless we do need a bit of persistence because sometimes the habits seem so ingrained that we give up. "This is too much for me, I will just go and get a cup of coffee instead." However, there are aids that help to quieten our minds. Use of a mantra, of the breath, or of a candle, or listening to guided meditations are obvious examples. This is easy to learn, but not so easy to sustain. It does not need a great deal of mystique or religious mumbo-jumbo, nor expense. It simply needs some kind of regularity of practice to deepen the concentration or steadiness of the mind. In one course that I gave to the staff of a mental hospital, there were some participants who enjoyed taking a break from work to go out and smoke a cigarette. I used the image of a "cigarette break without the cigarette" to drive home the simple message of how to stop in the midst of the busyness.

In fact we don't need to hunt for inner peace, it is already inside us, though often much covered over. We enjoy that quiet of the forest, the sea, the cup of tea on the veranda, because it brings us back home to a place that we already know, going right back to the experience of the deep peace of feeding at our mother's breast. The Sanskrit word *samadhi* is used for deep quiet, serenity and concentration, and it actually means to gather ourselves together, to bring ourselves back home.

There is an ancient Buddhist story about a forest brigand called Angulimala, who was commanded by an angry guru to kill 1,000 people. He killed 999 people and was looking for his 1,000th victim. The Buddha heard about him and against the advice of his concerned disciples insisted on entering the forest alone. Soon Angulimala found him and began to chase him. The Buddha walked, steadily, smiling, but for some reason Angulimala simply couldn't catch him, no matter how fast he ran. So he shouted to the Buddha: "Stop, Stop!" The Buddha turned and looking at him straight in the eyes said: "I stopped a long time ago. You stop!" This was such a surprise to Angulimala that all his aggressive intention evaporated and he asked him what he meant. Of course it gave the Buddha the opportunity to explain to him the teachings and soon Angulimala joined the forest monks.

What the Buddha meant when he said that he stopped a long time ago was not that he became a couch potato! He meant that he stopped making waves, creating damage and disturbance, harming himself or others, creating friction and suffering and stopped generating more karma (see chapter 38 on karma). He got off the wheel and stopped in nirvana, which is another word for cooling the fire of restless activity. Stopping is living freely without resistance, with the stream of life – not struggling against it and not sinking under it.

CHAPTER 19
SURFING THE WAVES OF EMOTION

Emotional life can sometimes hit us like a tsunami, in particular in those uncontrollable and unwanted surges of rage, reactivity, despair or depression. But even positive emotions like falling in love can take us over and turn us and our lives upside down. Emotions can be more subtle but equally disturbing, such as chronic anxiety and worry, criticism of self or others, irritation, or gloom, which can contaminate the bright flowing waters of life and steal joy and ease.

Emotions always start with the first immediate seeds of responsiveness to what's coming in through the senses. Sensory stimulation always does something as it arrives in the system: it is pleasant, unpleasant, or neutral, as if a little "Like" or "Dislike" thumb instantly appears at the gate of our perception. It is fast and mostly unconscious. We usually only notice it when thoughts and perceptions are constructed out of the sense impressions, a moment later, coloured by those likes and dislikes. We turn so as not to tread on a pile of dogshit, or turn to meet our pet dog bounding along the road toward us and we don't know why we are doing it until the action is in full swing. Or something pulls us away from the computer and only then we know it as the aroma of freshly brewed coffee.

The first animal-level responses on which emotions are built are called in Pali *vedana*, which comes from *veda* in Sanskrit, which means "to know". It is a kind of knowing, knowing based on feelings or knowing based on the heart. Indeed science has shown that every moment of brain activity, every thought and perception, is coloured by what is called "affect", fundamental emotional responsiveness, which is part of consciousness itself. We are not a computer. We are oriented toward survival, and just like the amoeba will move toward what is sweet and away from what is salty, so a person will express preferences and a push-pull responsiveness to what is arriving through the senses and brain at every moment. We may not notice it – we may think that we go through our day without much feeling, but consider what makes us attend to one particular sensory stimulation and not another. What is important to look at when we cross the road? The mind is always saying, "this is relevant, pay attention". Our life depends on it. Consider the tragic disease of leprosy, in which the nerves don't work properly to deliver messages of pain. Though pain is unpleasant, it is vital to know if the body is damaged.

Emotional responses are constructed rapidly with *vedana* as the foundation. They collect around them perceptions, reactions, physiological responses, memory, habits, stories and the self as centre and owner of the emotion. As the wave collects all these components it becomes much stronger, even overwhelming, and we recognize it as, for example, anger or anxiety. Only then we know our buttons are being pressed. In the Tibetan tradition all emotions are basically divided into two categories that they call hope and fear, an inherent attraction/repulsion as part of the experience of all beings, human or otherwise.

Clearly, *vedana* as a rapid physiological response is not a problem. It does not make a mark in the inner or outer world. As soon as we build constructions out of it, conditions are created for all kinds of consequences. Feelings, thoughts, words, actions, intentions and habits are created or maintained. This creates karma. For example, someone close to you blames you for something you did not do. The harshness in the sound of their voice is the first rapid subliminal trigger of *vedana* and it is followed immediately by a still unconscious rise in defensive reactivity that becomes conscious as a thought: "How can they say that to me, don't they see that it wasn't me?" The familiar chain of responses follows, such as contractions in the stomach, and rapid breathing, rising heart rate, rising heat, discomfort, distant memories of hurt, familiar narratives of the self that goes down old tracks such as "they always do that to me", and more. We know the whole thing as anger and from anger arises our defensive/aggressive shout: "You are always blaming me for things I didn't do."

There are also feelings or emotions that are not reactive, that don't have much of "me" in them, a territory of deep feelings that are rather blessed. These are emotions that expand our inner world rather than contract it, and are less problematic from the point of view of the karma or consequences. Sadness when looking at the condition of the world or of others is one – it's not misery, it's not depression, it's not anger, and it's not fear. It connects us to a bigger picture and though there is pain in it, the heart is not just broken but broken open. Compassion is another. It is helpful if we can move the smaller self-emotions to the big ones. For example, we respond to someone with anger, but then we look at what is behind their eyes, we make the switch in our mind, and realize that the person we're arguing with is suffering, and both of us are joined through mutual pain. In that moment the anger can collapse and in its place compassion can arise. Obviously love, deep joy, contentment and even longing – these are liberating feelings that are important in opening the heart and connecting us to the world. The Buddhist teachings encourage these emotional states, stating that you don't have to have an emotion, but if you are going to have one, let it be one of those.

How can we detoxify emotional life and at the same time not suppress emotions or be enslaved by them? How can we experience emotions as a music of the heart and not distressing blasts of a horn? The way to work with emotions first and foremost is with awareness. The *Satipattana Sutta*, the key ancient Buddhist canonical text on mindfulness, guides us to a direct and immediate awareness of emotions. It says to be aware of feelings in the feelings, the "feelingness" of feelings, the quality of the feeling. Instead of looking at feelings from a distance, or thinking about them, it's knowing them from the inside.

It is important in mindfulness as a whole, and here espec-ially, to have a completely non-critical and non-judgemental attitude. If feeling is difficult or hard to deal with, we give it our kind attention, we recognize what the emotion is, we recognize that it is difficult or painful, and we allow it to be what it is, without adding to it any resistance or thought that it should be something else. The key to freeing us from the control of emotions is to see them phenomenologically, as passing expressions that arise, flower and die away. The ability to welcome them as either rowdy guests that are the negative emotions, or angelic visitors that are the positive emotions, and welcome them again and again as they arrive and depart, gradually frees us from their control. And when not fed by the automatic habits of reactivity, they simply get quieter.

An emotion like anger, or a specific ingrained fear, can be powerful, automatic and hard to get a handle on, let alone to be fully seen as it is. It is so powerful because it is grounded in self-protection and survival, our animal power, and the fight-or-flight response. It carries us away, and we may often feel that it is simply too immediate and overwhelming to hold with awareness. Here is where all the practice of mindfulness we've ever done in our whole life is needed. It will give us the power to stop and find the eye of the storm, to come to our senses and watch the storm as it arises and as it passes. We can also be helped by the fact that an emotional reaction is built up from many parts, including and especially bodily responses. These are usually easier to identify and get a handle on, and to see directly. We break down the whole construction of our overwhelming anger into a much more limited domain of: "How is my stomach right now?" I used to suffer terribly from fear of public speaking. I was a lecturer at the time at the University of London, and every time I had to talk in front of students I just wanted the ground to open and swallow me up. I wanted to die. It was awful. Mindfulness saved me. I would stand there as the students took their seats, breathe a couple of conscious breaths to bring myself into the present, and then focus on one of the physical symptoms of the fear – usually the stomach contracting or the heart racing. Others, such as dry mouth, short breath and sweating, were additional places to focus attention on now and then. I also worked on it while sitting in vipassana retreats. Simply remembering the last time I had to give a lecture was enough to elicit the same fear reactions but in a minimal homeopathic dose. Again, I watched it arise and pass through the system, disintegrate and vanish, like watching a wave surging onto a beach and dissolving into the sand. By practising again and again, the fear was reduced to peripheral and unimportant bodily phenomena, like pressing the minimize button on the computer. It no longer took centre stage, and eventually the fear disappeared and that was the end of it.

This kind of collected, focused and interested awareness is not just a passing glance. It is important to stay with the awareness of the emotion as deeply as possible. As in the English expression: "When the pot boils over – don't leave the kitchen." This needs some degree of courage, acceptance and also kindness to ourselves and to our inherent vulnerability, out of which the protective emotions such as anger arise. There is a tendency to try to get rid of difficult emotions, to suppress them or deny them. Sometimes there is the opposite tendency; to justify the emotions by encouraging their release and expression. But between suppression and expression there is an extensive territory that often goes unexplored. By acknowledging but not identifying with emotions we allow them to arise and pass as they will – they leave us in charge, wise and sensitive. More than that, because they are so powerful, if we really get a handle on them they can transform us. Ten minutes of the full practice of mindfulness of anger may be as useful as a longer time of quiet peaceful meditation. If the emotion is strong, the karma is also strong, so when we break it something significant can happen to us.

Emotions are extremely dynamic, free and flowing, like water. Even though we tend to make persistent emotions such as our anxieties solid and real, and we support and prove them with our stories and narratives, actually they change rapidly. Can we allow the emotions to pass through the system without making any tracks, like a bird flying through the sky, or like a line drawn in water? There is a Zen story of a student that came to his teacher and said: "I have a problem with anger, can you help me deal with it?" The teacher said: "Yes I can … bring me the anger and we'll deal with it together." The student answered: "Well at this minute I don't have anger, so how can we deal with it?" The teacher said: "So go to your room and the next time the anger arises bring it!" The student answered: "But master, in the ten minutes it takes me to get from my room to yours, the anger will surely disappear." The master said: "You see, even if you want to have anger you cannot. It is not yours, it comes and goes when it wants. It belongs to the universe. Be with that coming and going – that's all you have to do."

As we do this we do not become a kind of passionless zombie that somehow shuts down emotional life or censors it in the name of spirituality. Quite the opposite. Emotional life talks to us constantly, it plays the songs of the heart. We experience our feeling life like the changing weather: ok now it's raining, ok now it's cloudy, ok so it's sunny, ok so it's hot. By freeing up our feeling life, by engaging it with awareness and letting it come and go as it will, we feel the rising sun and the quiet moon, the love in the eyes of those near us, the heartful joy of the cool breeze and the tears of loss. It is like sitting next to a river, listening to the sound of the water. Emotions especially are like water. An emotional intelligence takes the place of being captured by emotions or shutting them down.

The domination that emotions have over our life can also be reduced by not feeding the automatic behaviours that arise from them. Behaviours that avoid emotions, compensate for them, amplify them or act them out, will often sustain them and their control over us. In Cognitive Behavioural Therapy (CBT) these are called "safety behaviours". For example, at a recent workshop on anxiety that I gave with my daughter who is a CBT therapist, television or screen watching came up as a widespread way not to engage fears of face-to-face communication with others, and instead seek a comforting substitute. The Buddha described how he dealt with a great deal of his primal fears, by living a pure and ethical life, by awareness, by kindness and renunciation. But he still had some left-over fears, such as when he found himself in the forest at night. He advised that if fear catches us when walking, keep on walking. Whatever position we are in when fear arises, don't change it. This reduces the authority fear has over us. I remember once I was sitting alone on a rock deep in a wooded valley in Galilee. All of a sudden there was a loud crashing sound in the bushes near me but I couldn't see what it was. Fear immediately arose, but then I remembered this text and decided that I would just remain where I was and do nothing. At that moment a huge wild boar, the size of a small donkey, burst through the bushes right next to me. Though my heart was racing, I kept my body still. The boar gave me an uninterested glance and moved on with a grunt.

Generally we don't really need antidotes to difficult emotions. Dancing with them in the way I described above will be enough. But sometimes antidotes are genuinely needed. We can change an unwholesome emotion (in the Pali language, *akusala*) to a wholesome one (*kusala*). It is possible to remember, in the middle of anger or fear, feelings of calm or compassion. In the middle of reactivity you may remember kindness. It's like rewriting the script, which is especially helpful if you see how much damage is being done to yourself or others. Through practice, we may be able to add the colour of compassion every time we find ourselves in worry, irritation or stress. We do this by zooming out of the self-centredness of the emotion, like a bird soaring up and looking down from above; we have a bigger view of ourselves and others, a sense that the emotion is not entirely personal, that we are all caught up in samsaric reactivity and conditioning.

Actually, if you remember a time when you were afraid or angry about something, or regretful, or guilty or jealous, and somehow you let the feeling dissolve and pass rather than taking you over, you may be able to notice a residue of compassion. When feelings are no longer trapped within us and fuelling our needs, our stories, or our issues, they open naturally to a bigger heart space, an aliveness that is experienced as compassion. If we are not entirely invested or closed in emotions, and let them flow and pass naturally, a bigger space opens up. This is where feeling life can lead us to inner freedom. The emotion or feeling beckons us into the garden, and then releases us there. There is a short poem titled "Eternity" by William Blake that says this beautifully:

> He who binds to himself a joy
> Does the winged life destroy
> But he who kisses the joy as it flies
> Lives in eternity's sun rise.

Emotions, such as anger, are a power because they collect or recruit great energy within our being, and this can be directed toward our inner freedom. Instead of being stuck by the road-side, we jump on a galloping horse into great open spaces. If we know how to do it, it takes us far. Otherwise we can fall off.

There a Zen story about a student that knocked on the master's door for his usual morning check-in – and this time the master didn't answer. The student found it strange and wondered why the master didn't answer. So he knocked again, and the teacher didn't answer. He got a bit irritated so he knocked again more loudly, and the teacher quickly opened the door and then slammed it in his face. An uncontrollable burst of rage and resentment rose up and overwhelmed the student. At that moment the door opened suddenly and the teacher commanded: "Now watch your anger!" The student had an immediate awakening experience.

We relate to the world through our constant, immediate and mostly invisible feeling responses. If they can be freed up from the control of self, we can find ourselves connecting to the world deeply as participators in the universe. We and the world are singing from the same hymn sheet. A natural sense of partnership with everything arises. For example, we go out into the street and we see a little kid riding a bicycle and all of a sudden our heart goes out to this kid, and at the same time to all kids riding bicycles and all kids in the world and from there to appreciation and joyful empathy with the enthusiastic life energy of all young beings, from puppies to chicks. We experience a deep connection with everything. It is not a thought about oneness but actually feeling it on the vibrational level.

There is an extraordinary Tibetan Dzogchen (non-dual) practice manual called *The Flight of the Garuda*. One of the instructions there is to remember an emotional experience, such as when one had been wrongly accused and humiliated, and then work with it:

> Brood on these things letting hatred arise and as it arises, look directly at its essence, at hatred itself. Then discover first where the hatred comes from, second, where it is now, and finally where it goes. Look carefully for its colour, shape or any other characteristics. Surely the vision of your anger is ultimately empty and ungraspable. Do not reject anger. It is mirror-like awareness itself.[1]

The author concludes this piece by saying that by continuing the practice emotions will recruit emptiness and liberating awareness as soon as they arise: "They will be triggers for freedom, and indeed, the greater the passion the greater the space of liberation."

All emotions resonate with the world. As resonance they are like the songs our body-mind sings in tune with the song of life. Though each emotion and feeling is experienced slightly differently, in the end they all resolve into the space of love, they are love expressed within situations, habits and conditions. Every emotion is a response, and the response to events and connections through the doors of our senses expresses our fundamental interconnectivity, or even identity with the world. This is love. Without a sense of me as controller or subject, it is the world responding to itself. This is liberation.

CHAPTER 20

A JOYFUL LIFE DESPITE PAINFUL MEMORIES

To what extent are we controlled by our memories, and what price do we pay for that? Obviously we need memory in order to function and stay a healthy person. We wouldn't last long without an effective working memory – not just to remember where we put our glasses or to turn off the gas, but even to remember to get out of the way of a bus on the road. However, we often find ourselves wounded and scarred from our difficult biographical experiences. As a living being mostly engaged with survival, discontent becomes much more important and interesting than contentment. So we tend to build our personality more from our painful memories than the joyful ones, circling around them like a moth around a flame, allowing them to take up permanent residence in our consciousness. We are not quite sure where they are, how they are and what they're doing to us but we live and feel and act from them. Persistent anxiety is a good example. It sticks because of lingering traumatic events, creating an unhappy anxious adulthood that is passed on to the next generation who have to deal with it as well.

Trauma is insidious, and can lodge deep inside. For example, soldiers coming back from fighting in wars, as we have seen recently from Afghanistan and Iraq, sometimes suffer from PTSD (Post-Traumatic-Stress Disorder), which sits in the subconscious. It is like the image of the elephant in the room. The trauma sufferer tries to close off the memory and the pain, to prevent it from being felt and acknowledged, and pretend it is not there, and so he or she is constantly dancing around the elephant in avoidance behaviours such as addictions, depression, violence, emotional deadness and disconnection with themselves and with others. Emotions, whether pain or joy, become truncated and suppressed and this contaminates relationships, especially within families, with a culture of denial and areas that cannot be touched. Sometimes the society puts the trauma on a pedestal and it becomes an icon, such as the Holocaust in Jewish society, which is another way of dancing around the elephant.

I remember growing up in the post-Holocaust immigrant Jewish middle-class society of north London. There was a sense of a suffocating denial within the families, expressed as compensation behaviours such as the need to be wealthy, fears of the unknown, emotional neutrality, distaste and aversion to the expression of pain, and a consensus of insecurity. One of my friends at that time told me that every time she was sick with a childhood illness her mother was furious with her – because she expressed, and so reminded her mother, of pain and trauma. I grew up determined to get out of such a toxic social and emotional structure and in the process shake it to its foundations. The 1960s psychedelic movement was for myself and many others a perfect antidote to the post-trauma of World War II. Though in hindsight I have to say that we went a bit too far in our indulgence, narcissism and idealization of love and peace, which also may have been coloured by avoidance of the elephant. It needed the 1960s to mature into the 1970s with the development of alternative lifestyles, new psychologies and spirituality, for the existential pain to be allowed in as well as the fun.

A story that illustrates the way such a strong cultural icon creates chains of consequences was told to me by my wife, Rachel, who was working teaching elderly Arabs/Palestinians in Western Galilee. On one occasion she took them to a local Holocaust memorial museum. Fifty elderly Arabs went on the tour, which included models of concentration camps. One elderly Arab summarized their impressions with a concise and poignant comment: "We never before realized just how much you Jews suffered in Europe. But why on earth did you need to build your Holocaust museum on our olive trees?"

In Buddhist psychology, memory is one type of mental form or construction, called in Pali a *sankhara*. A classical metaphor of a *sankhara* is a potter making a ceramic bowl. Memories are cast or engraved onto consciousness. Western neurosciences would agree with this model and assumes that the brain patterns that allow us to recognize a tree, a person, an idea, or time and space are actual specific networks of neurons in our brain. And there is nothing wrong with that, except that we forgot that we built the world from external conditions and learning, and believe that the constructions in the mind must be true representations of the world. How can the world out there be a fact if it is made up of a construction in the brain? Where is the truth of it? The belief in our fabrication of the world is a self-validating loop and not reality!

The penny dropped for me when I was young, and read an old edition of *The Jungle Book* by Rudyard Kipling, again and again. I was fascinated that Mowgli, who was brought up by wolves, thought he was one as well. For him the networks in the brain say I am a wolf and this is a fact. For me my networks said: "I am a human child and this is a fact." So being Stephen was not a fact, it just happened to be like that, based on conditioning – it was a result of what I was told, and therefore there cannot be any real facts out there – the whole world was just a conviction, a happenstance. As a child I thought this was an explosive secret that only I knew, and as in the story of *The Emperor's New Clothes* I was alone as a boy struggling with the realization that the clothes were illusion but all adults seemed to believe that they were facts. We build a fictional self and a fictional subjective world, which we then think is the truth. This is described in the Buddhist world as ignorance (Sanskrit: *avidya*). We suffer from the attachments to narratives that give us pain because we think they are the way it really is. The sense of being inferior, for example, is a *sankhara* that leads us to look at the world through that filter, and we look for and of course find proofs of it every day. But it is only a view, a story, it is not a reality. Even if it's inscribed as a network of neurons. The philosopher Heidegger once said that we forget at least 99.9% of what we experience, and we are left with a memory of only 0.1% and that is what we call reality.

Surprisingly, Buddhist psychology holds that there are five external sense organs, and what arises in the mind as thought or memory is the sixth. When a memory comes up in the mind, consciousness receives it just like it receives a sound of a passing car which appears and vanishes. The Buddha said that in the present moment memory, just as with all other sense impressions, is like a line drawn on water that has no trace or track; as with the sound of a bird, it comes and goes. This is good news because it means that *sankharas* are much more dynamic than we first realized. The neurons, as we now know, can be reconnected – there is neuronal plasticity. We don't need to totally believe in the reality of these constructions, because when we really look at the experience of them we see how they come and go like a smell or a taste of food. They have a very short shelf life. The same is true for the memory of a painful experience, which may arise in the present moment naturally, making us cry if we need to, but then passes on like all the rest. We can let our stories come and go freely, however painful they may be, if we don't hold onto them, deny them, bury them, be obsessed with them, be controlled by them or identify with them. If we are aware of the fluidity of memory the stories become less personal and pervasive, and in this way our scars are healed. And as we open more inner space, we gradually discover a great freedom that was buried under the stories, which we forgot. We discover that the room that was blocked by the elephant, is actually vast and glorious.

An example of what this feels like is described in the book *An Interrupted Life*, by Etty Hillesum, a young Dutch Jewish woman who lived under the Nazi occupation in Holland. It is an extraordinary tale of freedom in the midst of incredibly difficult experiences because of an ability just to see the changing flow of life as it is:

[…] at unguarded moments, when left to myself, I suddenly lie against the naked breast of life and her arms round me are so gentle and so protective and my own heartbeat is difficult to describe: so slow and so regular and so soft, almost muffled, but so constant, as if it would never stop … I believe that I know and share the many sorrows and sad circumstances that a human being can experience, but I do not cling to them, I do not prolong such moments of agony. They pass through me, like life itself, as a broad eternal stream, they become part of that stream and life continues …[1]

What do we need to do to experience life like Etty Hillesum? Fundamentally it's about waking up to see clearly how experiences come and go in the present without suppressing them, or looking for them, denying them or projecting them. They become, as Etty said, just the stories that flow and enrich our life.

We might ask how it is possible not to identify with memory if it forms who we are and our individuality. Indeed, memory is a form of shaping. I live alongside lots of olive trees, which have an amazingly expressive character that clearly shows everything that has happened to them. If a branch has been cut or if the tree reaches out in a certain direction, or lumps are formed on the trunk or dry weather makes the leaves fall, you can see it. The shaping of the tree is its memory, its *sankhara*, a response to conditions. The tree doesn't have a problem with that, and there is no reason why we should have a problem either; we are also just shaped, constructed, by life. We are given a body and it develops and changes dynamically according to conditions – and we arrive in each moment as we are, and the world arises and meets us as it is, and all we need to do is to appreciate it and let it be. Stories are just stories, narratives are just narratives, and embodiment is just embodiment. If we let go into this flow of life, the wounds will dissolve, the scars will be softened and brought back to life, and we will find ourselves in the garden of the now instead of the prison of yesterdays. A difficult experience can come up just like an unpleasant visitor arriving in our house, we can cry and the next minute we can laugh and then he's gone.

This may seem like an encouragement to forget the past, but actually it is the opposite – it is a living engagement with the past. In the community in which I grew up, the fear of forgetting the Holocaust was, and maybe still is, so strong it verges on social panic. But such anxieties do the opposite of what was intended. It turns the Holocaust into something it is not, an icon, an obsession, a social identity, a symbol, an oppression, even a convenient means sometimes of getting what you want, instead of what it is – a hugely painful past experience leaving wounds in the present. Experiencing it as it is when it comes up, we may be deeply touched, and then we move on. We know the painfulness of it, we know the suffering that exists for us, we know it's also not entirely personal but part of the experience of all embodied beings human or otherwise, and we just allow it to be what it is.

Meditation is a very effective training of the mind to let go of its chains. The Buddhist mindfulness practice of vipassana is especially good at helping us see things as they really are instead of our usual projections and beliefs about them. Not only is it a place beyond the familiar circles and loops and cacophony of the thinking mind, but it helps us to see that we don't need to get rid of the stuff that haunts us, because we see directly that it comes and goes by itself. We do not need to struggle to be free of difficult memories, because if we look with mindfulness at mental content we see that it flies by and cannot control us. Of course the opposite is also the case, that we cannot control it. We can't design our stream of consciousness, much as we would like to. But there is much more to meditation than a window on memory. Meditation is also a way to discover natural quiet, inner peace and inner spaciousness. It is as much about the white page as about the narratives written on it, as much about the room as the elephant in it that we are trying hard to avoid. And it is not that easy. To touch deeper *sankharas* and fully meet inner life often does need time, practice and some direction, and sometimes supportive conditions, such as an intensive retreat.

We also need to be kind and balanced in meditation practice. We shouldn't force it, or push ourselves too hard. During a retreat I was teaching, one man said something interesting: "I can invite and become mindfully aware of any pain, which reduces it, but I will not touch the pain of my childhood in the Holocaust. This is outside the territory of my meditation practice." This shows a wisdom about how far he could go and how far he couldn't go, just as when we have pain in the body, our wisdom will tell us when we can explore it and meet it with mindfulness and when we have had enough.

A beautiful word often used in the Buddhist texts to describe the way we can let go of attachments once we see them for what they really are is *disenchantment*, in the original meaning of the word – to wake up out of enchantment. For example, we may hold a story of a humiliation that rankles, and all of a sudden we realize that the story we believed in as completely true is just a story. As if a kind of spell has suddenly been broken. Many times we say: "I don't know what I will be without my story; I need my stories, even the most painful ones, if I lose them, who will I be?" And yet when we become disenchanted afterwards we always feel a relief, and cannot understand how we could have carried such a heavy burden all that time.

Dharma practice moves us continually toward more freedom, and nirvana, awakening. These are big words but they mean being fully alive and yet unconstructed, unattached, unclosed, unboxed. This is a continuing work of liberation, which starts by dealing with the scars and the wounds, touching and bringing life to the difficult places and just keeping on going toward a fundamental existential freedom. Like Etty Hillesum says, "life is just life", it brings the biggest tragedies and the biggest joys, and it is uncontrollable. Our aspiration is to become a free open vessel for this eternal life. As we do so our heart embraces a wider world than our own suffering, and becomes able to respond and resonate with all other beings.

CHAPTER 21

NO NEED FOR NEED: BREAKING THE SPELL OF ATTACHMENT

We may think that pursuing happiness by fulfilling our desires and avoiding harm and difficulty is what life is about, and it cannot be wrong as all life does it from the smallest amoeba upwards. But actually if we stop for a moment and reflect, we may see that as humans we have a far greater potential, and that simply following our interests from birth to death is a form of slavery. It is shutting down life, not embracing it. The Second Noble Truth of the Buddhist teachings is clear – the pain of life is not because of unpredictable and uncomfortable events. It is because of our endless attachment to what we want or don't want from life and our need for things to be other than they are.

Of course pleasant and unpleasant sensory experiences are natural and inevitable for all living beings whether man or amoeba. A burnt finger will hurt the Buddha or you and me. These immediate sensations are termed *vedana* in the Pali language. But the difference between Buddha and non-Buddha, or awareness and non-awareness, is what we do next. Do these experiences blossom into thoughts, actions, needs, automatic behaviours and self-definition, which control all our waking moments? Or are they just pleasant and unpleasant experiences that do not call for automatic reactivity, passing like water under the bridge, leaving our conscious awareness unchained and free "like a deer grazing in the forest", to use a Buddhist image. The difference is in attachment. It is attachment to our needs, to comfort and control, which keeps us chained and makes us feel we are living our entire lives helplessly running after what is pleasant and away from what is unpleasant. Attachment is *upadana* in Pali, which actually means feeding – what is it that we feed with our thoughts, words and actions? What kind of life, what kind of person, and what kind of mind are we serving? There is a saying that expresses this well:

> Sow a thought, reap an act,
> Sow an act, reap a habit,
> Sow a habit, reap a personality,
> Sow a personality, reap a destiny.

According to traditional Buddhist teachings there are four kinds of attachment and identification. The first is attachment to the senses – that means feeding pleasure and desire, what I want, or need or like, and avoiding what is difficult, unsatisfying, or what I don't like. A classic image of this is the monkey trap. A coconut shell with a small hole in it is fastened to a tree. A banana is put inside. A monkey comes and grasps the banana through the hole, but he cannot withdraw his hand while grasping the banana, and he will not let go of the banana, so the hunters come and catch him. Some other examples might be:

- "When I feel down or bored, the only thing that helps is shopping in the mall."
- "I watch several hours of TV every day, it helps me switch off, though I feel quite drained afterwards."
- "I know it's bad for me but I can't stop it."
- "My neighbours are so disturbing, I can't stand living here any more."
- "I feel so anxious all the time about what might happen."

The second kind of attachment is to views and opinions – views of myself, views of the other, opinions about the past and the future, prejudices, obsessions and beliefs, world-views and what I think. Here are some examples:

- "They just want to kill us. They are all terrorists."
- "I am always failing at what I do. I will never ever make it."
- "Only technology can solve all the problems of today's world."
- "My life will be much better if I could earn a lot of money."
- "It is all the fault of …"

The third kind of attachment is dependence on rituals, religions and systems, attachment to principles, rules, forms, gurus, teachings, teachers, worship and all of that. I remember the first year I spent in Varanasi, I had a room that opened out onto the bank of the Ganges. Nearby was the station of a yogi who was all dressed up in the full paraphernalia of a Shiva sadhu. He also had the disease elephantiasis, which meant that his testicles were the size of grapefruit. There was a whole queue of village women who would come one by one, bow, reverently touch his testicles, and ask for a blessing, for example that a sick child would recover. Here are some common examples:

- "I know I will be more successful if I pay the priest/rabbi/ Brahmin to pray for me."
- "If I don't make an offering to the Buddha, something bad may happen to me."
- "I need to wash my hands every time I touch a door handle otherwise I might catch a disease."

Fourth, the big one, is attachment to self, to the fundamental idea of me and mine and identity, the sense of being the subject, controller, experiencer or victim, of all that happens.

- "Since I had the diagnosis of cancer my life is finished."
- "I deserve to have better than this."
- "This is my land and no-one can take it away from me."
- "I am working night and day to become well-off."
- "No, I don't like this one – I want the other one."

All of these attachments at the very least restrict our freedom, but they can also lead to the most terrible consequences. Wars are fought on the basis of a mass conviction and labelling of the other, fuelled by group fears, or on attachment to views such as democracy, empire, superiority, or religious ideas. We forget that we made those assumptions and they may have nothing to do with the truth of things. A tragic example is the war raging in Syria, in which hate, revenge, and views of "them and us" appear to be an unquestioned truth. Meanwhile, the country is being destroyed, the people are starving, the children are traumatized, there are millions of refugees and hundreds of thousands of people have been killed. At what point will they wake up from the disastrous sleep of illusion and ask: "Is this helping anybody?"

On a fundamental level we build constructions (*sankharas*) of me and the world: patterns, habits, identity, objects, things, definitions, time, boundaries – all the content of our stream of consciousness, which we are busily maintaining or feeding every time we think or act, every moment of our lives. We forget our role and responsibility in making and maintaining these constructions, they seem to be real, and we feel like we're inside a kind of matrix, an enchanted dream universe which we take to be absolutely real. I once saw a wonderful take on *The Matrix* called *The Meatrix*. It was an animated film in support of vegetarianism, about a whole farm of penned-in but docile and contented pigs. But there were two pigs that woke up, and they tried desperately to tell the rest: "You're going to be eaten, you're being bred by a farmer, you don't realize, wake up guys, wake up guys!" All they got for their pains were grunts.

What helps us to break the spell of attachment, to become "dis-enchanted" and wake up? One crucial alarm call is the recognition of pain and suffering. Pain and suffering (Pali: *dukkha*) are not just our enemies – paradoxically they can be our best friends. It is obvious that pain is the shout with which the body tells us to wake up and pay attention because there is something wrong. Emotional pain too is often a call to respond to something in our lives. Pain shows us where something is out of harmony; like a compass it points us to where we need our awareness to go, what messages we need to listen to. Life – unpredictable, wild and uncontrollable – doesn't fit our structures and expectations. For example, it sends viruses or bacteria that make us miserably sick, snatches away people or things that we love, confronts us with unpredictability in the future, and fires slings and arrows at us when we least expect it. Life doesn't listen to our beliefs about it, nor our needs, desires and aversions that we project onto it. Life is just life – it isn't busy trying to provide us with what we want. *Dukkha*, in the form of feelings of discomfort and dissatisfaction in the mind and body, arises from the mismatch between life that's free and uncontrollable, and our attachments and constructions driven by the need to be comfortable in the matrix. For example, much of the suffering from a serious disease comes through thoughts, identifications, struggle, emotional responses, relationship issues and views that arise along with the diagnosis. I have taught many retreats for people with cancer or other chronic conditions. One of the key shifts that can happen is the full realization of how much unnecessary suffering arises through this self-labelling, and how possible it is to let go of all that baggage and live a full and joyful life despite the diagnosis.

Dukkha tells us where to look, and the wisdom eye is the eye that knows how to look. We need to stop and look long and carefully at what it is actually going on, starting with simple things, the breath, the body, the touch of the ground on which I walk, and continuing with intimate awareness of all the aspects that constitute our experience – our perceptions, feelings, narratives, responses, and the way we constantly and automatically orient ourselves toward what we want and away from what we don't. We see our stories as stories and not reality, we see our views as just that and not facts, we see how we build ourselves from our narratives and memories and no longer need to believe them as truth. In the example just mentioned, when all the constructions, fears, creation of a victim identity, and other narratives are seen for what they are they have much less power to control, and freedom to live fully takes their place.

Habits, views, addictions, obsessions, psychological loops and patterns imprison us when not seen and not known because we simply are them. We are inside the prison cell but don't see the walls let alone the doorway, which is actually open. Once seen clearly, once we become completely familiar with the pattern or attachment as an unwelcome partner and not a hidden enemy, we can take responsibility for it. We can examine the walls and find the door. Mindfulness works subtly – it is not about banging your head against the wall or shouting to get out, but about noticing where the door is and that it is already open. There is a Sufi story of a man in prison who wrote a letter to his friend outside asking him to send him a hammer so he could break the lock and get out. A parcel arrived, he eagerly opened it and was greatly disappointed to find only a prayer carpet, which he threw angrily into the corner of the cell. But after some time, since he had nothing better to do he started to pray regularly to Allah using the prayer carpet. Some weeks passed and one day, while praying with his face close to the carpet, he noticed for the first time the pattern woven into the carpet. He realized it was the blueprint to the lock on the door, and using it he walked free.

Mindfulness is a way of dealing with attachments subtly, powerfully and irreversibly. When you see things as they are, you see that they arise and pass by themselves. In other words, you don't have to get rid of attachments because they go by themselves. They didn't really belong to us in the first place but got stuck to us through life experience and memory. In the present moment every pattern, no matter how stuck it may feel, is just an experience that arises and passes and therefore we are not made of it. We can watch as even what seems to be a monster of a pattern, such as self-judgement and low self-esteem, arrives, flowers and dies away. It will come again, but when seen as passing, the next time will be slightly less solid. There is an irreversible realization that all things arise and disappear. *Dukkha*, when it comes, it comes; when it passes, it passes. It is extra to us. We just need to make sure that the door is open and the unwanted guest will leave by himself. He may come again, but each time the goodbye gets easier. Letting go, although much misused as a slogan, is actually a good word for this as it implies that it does go anyway, we just need to stop hanging on to it.

The walls built by our attachments crumble when they are looked at with a penetrating gaze. Seen as they really are, we realize that they never were more than an assumption in the first place. When the walls that separate us from the world begin to dissolve, and the world is let in, life rejoices through us.

As we read this we may be forgiven for thinking that it is all very well to let go of painful attachments, but there are many that seem healthy and fruitful – the attachment I feel to my family or my work, the drive and will that makes sure I get up in the morning and achieve what I want to do in life. Surely if I give them up I will end up in some state of passivity, a spiritual zombie. Attachment is in fact a good word in psychology, indicating ties and a sense of belonging. It is indeed helpful to develop a natural and beneficial connection to others, but beyond that, attachment can tie us up too much and this is one of the places where psychology and spirituality part company.

T S Eliot in *Little Gidding* used the image of detachment and indifference growing in the same hedgerow but being as different as life and death. Letting go of attachments is not an invitation to indifference, which is shutting ourselves down, death-like. It is an invitation to live more freely in a bigger space, to relate to our life and the world, not through the narrow filter of our obsessions and addictions but as dance, as love, as play, as open exploration. This is close to the positive sense of *upadana,* namely feeding. If we feed non-attachment rather than attachment, we feed aliveness. Take the example of ambitions. If we depend on attachments, the drive to succeed, to get us up in the morning, we may find ourselves unhappily driven like a hamster turning a wheel in a cage. But if we get up in the morning motivated, not by that drive to succeed, but instead by a readiness for a new and fresh meeting with life, we will do so with at least as much energy and positivity, and a lot more joy. Take the example of close relationships with a partner or in the family. We may think attachment is absolutely vital otherwise the connection would not survive. But in many ways the opposite is true. Attachment brings control ("You must do as I say. Why do you do those things that you know I hate?"); it brings jealousy and possessiveness ("I get mad when you talk to other men"); it brings pride and ego ("You bring shame on the family by betraying our beliefs"). And real lasting successful relationships are based on a non-attached deep love, deep respect and listening to the other, seeing what goes on behind the eyes, and wide open free communication and connection.

Similarly, we may be concerned that our desires are what makes us tick, and we don't want them reduced. Indeed, desires themselves may be entirely natural. Hunger draws us toward the kitchen. But then what happens? Does natural hunger become attached hunger when we open the fridge every time we are bored? Does it, as desire tends to, just increase itself so we think of food much of the time even though our body does not need it? Does it captivate us, so that we end up like the millionaires that just want more and more? Besides, desires can be helpful or harmful. For example, what about desire for liberation? Indeed, longing for freedom is still a desire but the best one we can have, and it is well worth replacing unhelpful desires with that one. But in any event, when liberation begins to happen we don't need the desire any more so we can let it go. It's temporary, like all desires, and they all need to be left alone to arise and fade away.

Memory too seems like something absolutely natural and is functionally vital to life. Without it we could not cross the road. Yet, confusingly, it also holds us in its grip. Like the monkey trap, the tighter we hold on to it the more we are trapped by it, and if we open our hands we are free to be with all the memories that we have. In particular, the memories of psychological scars and wounds from a difficult childhood are largely held unconsciously. However, like other attachments, if they are hidden they just project into life, colouring it with difficulty and suffering. It is like the elephant in the room that is carefully avoided and so takes away the space. As soon as it is exposed and clearly seen, identified but not identified with, the elephant is revealed for what it is, even loved, and as he comes and goes freely, the space of the room opens for us to dance in. Memory, in Buddhist psychology, is a dynamic changing source of information that appears freely in the present moment, a doorway just like the senses of hearing or touching. Seen as it really is, without our attachments, it is a rich source of engagement and interconnection with the world. As T S Eliot expressed in *Little Gidding*, history can be servitude, but history can also be freedom.

What is precious is that space that opens up when we do let go of our needs and attachments. We cannot see it beforehand, while we are wrapped in them; they seem to be the only way things are and the way they ought to be. We cannot imagine ourselves without them. Our identification with our attachments is the source of our resistance to dropping them. We are like a passenger on a train who is carrying his heavy bags instead of putting them down and letting the train carry them. But then suddenly it dawns on him, and in the same way we can put down our baggage and let the train of life take us and what we were carrying. What a relief! A space opens up, a lightness, a sense of freedom. It reminds me of my chickens. They live in quite a big caged area and they have never gone out. When I feed them I leave the door open because I know they don't see it as a door. It sometimes happens that one flies out by accident and finds itself outside, and usually it tries to get back inside in a panic. But rarely, one that escapes suddenly realizes that it is feeding in great new horizons, and it is not at all easy to return it to its cage.

This increased space is the ground and source of genuine spiritual development. Spiritual life depends on a seemingly endless amount of renunciation of our conditioning, of rooted patterns, habits of thinking, blocks and definitions. Liberating insights come from inner freedom, from letting go of the security of the known, from being outside the box of our beliefs and concepts. As the saying goes, the only reason we are not the Buddha is that we believe we are ourselves. Attachment keeps us stuck in the mundane world even if it is attachment to the apparently sacred. Even the spiritual practices that get us to the point of realization have to be abandoned in order to move on. As the Buddha said, all means to transformation are like rafts. When we get to the other shore we have to let them go. That space of awakening is like love, is living in the unknown, is endless mystery and wonder.

CHAPTER 22

EMPATHY: HOW TO PUT YOURSELF IN THE OTHER'S SHOES

Empathy is a quality that all of us know something about. It is our ability to feel with others, to feel what they feel, to know something about what they are going through. Empathy is about feelings, it is not about cognitive processes. We can be aligned with the views of someone else, belong to the same group, understand what they are talking about, and yet empathy is missing. We will not really feel that we belong or are fully accepted and our participation will be a bit awkward. Our daily life is full of such encounters in which we are as distant at the end as at the beginning, whether or not there is agreement. And the opposite is also true – with empathy we can get a sense of what is going on behind the screen of the other's eyes, and know where they are coming from, even if we disagree with their views.

Empathy is the kind of intuitive and emotional knowing that reaches inside the other, inside the well-manicured public face, inside the mask that we all wear to face the outside world. It is a knowing that is non-verbal, non-conceptual and non-cerebral. It is beyond time. Empathy is in the first impressions, the immediate sense we have about the inner world of another. If we have to think about it, we have already lost it.

Many of us feel that we don't have enough empathy, and indeed this is often the case. It is most clear to us in the field of family and couple relationships, which can be a garden if there is empathy and a prison if there is not. How often do we hear the refrain – "He doesn't understand me"; "She doesn't know what I am going through"; "We are living in separate worlds";

"I can't get through to them". In those situations we can feel completely helpless, frustrated with our inability to know what someone close to us is feeling, and we don't know how to develop that power.

A huge amount of parenting problems are in this territory. So many parents are trying to be better parents, trying to learn from experts, psychologists and books, what to do and what the child needs, and what is a better direction, when actually the child is saying – all I need is to be fully seen and fully understood.

But we all do have empathy to some degree, from childhood. Before learning speech, children communicate by body language, emotion, signs and so on. They know immediately what a mother is feeling toward them. It is an intuitive reading of subtle clues and subliminal messages that express outwardly the inner climate. We all start off with this power, although in some cases such as in Asperger's syndrome, it may be reduced. But then, while growing up, something happens and we usually lose it. Where did it go? The answer is that it didn't go, it got covered over by layers of logical thinking, concerns, busyness, planning, information and the emotional anaesthesia that we often need to cope with the demands and threats of the adult world.

Learning to be more empathic is as much about removing the blockages as learning emotional intelligence and intuition. One of the best ways both to develop empathy and remove the blocks, is mindfulness meditation. This is the practice of paying mindful attention to what is really happening in the present moment, rather than to our comments and thoughts about it. Mindfulness meditation can be practised by careful and persistent attention to the simple experiences of life that are usually missed. The touch of our feet on the ground as we walk, the weight of our body on the chair, the rising and falling of the stomach as we breathe, the sensation of the breeze on our cheeks, the sounds of the birds in the trees, the moment of stopping when we look up into space from our computers. From there we can move into the world of feelings, paying a similar close and caring attention to the peaks and valleys of the inner emotional landscape of our life. We embrace with our awareness all the range, from ecstasy to misery and everything in between. Intimacy with this territory in our inner world will help us become familiar with the inner world of others. We will know what is behind someone's eyes when they look at us pleading for understanding and contact, because we will have seen it behind our own eyes. Mindfulness practice is anyway as much about outside as inside – it is not a withdrawal but an engagement. The feelings, presence and expression of the being of another is as much a place for mindfulness as ourselves.

We can also train ourselves to be more empathic by just being interested and curious about others as we go through our daily life. It simply needs an intention. As we go into a shop, can we feel what it might be like to be in the shoes of the sales assistant? Or the clerk at the bank, the bus driver, or the woman walking her dog in the morning? It needs an energy, a bit of effort. Look people in the eyes, watch their body language, look what they are saying with the lines carved into their faces. How is their life treating them? Let our intuition speak, let first impressions and spontaneous insights arise, and give them space and significance. The effort needed is not just about watching, as if we are a good policeman. We need to get out of our comfort zone, to jump out of our perpetual self-concern and self-importance and let the others in. At first this will be difficult, but if we persist, it becomes easier and easier. So in your next work meeting, just take the time to look at each person as he or she speaks and ask yourself again and again what is really going on with him or her, what it is like to be in their shoes right now. Suddenly this meeting will become a spiritual experience for you – just watch how it changes the atmosphere.

Your heart responds to others if you can be totally there for them when they tell you their story. There is nothing that can bring you as close to someone as deeply listening to their honest expression of the suffering they are going through. Listen deeply, drop perpetual self-interest and self-obsession, and let your heart resonate with the experiences of others. See how your heart expands. Empathy drives compassion, and compassion drives empathy.

CHAPTER 23

OUR GREAT COMPASSIONATE HEART

It is obvious that almost everyone would help a blind man to cross the road if they could. Although it is painful to know that this is not always the case. Once I was on a bus in New York and I looked out of the window on a shocking scene. An elderly woman fell down in the road and her husband who was also elderly was desperately trying to pick her up but did not have the strength. Five young guys were standing in a circle around them and laughing. I remember thinking that this is the end of civilization.

For the most part we do have empathy, a natural goodness that is hard-wired in the brain. Neurologists have discovered that we all have mirror neurons, brain cells that automatically and unconsciously reflect and mirror others. For example, we instinctively know how someone near us feels from subtle signs in their eyes and body language. Animals too have goodness, and are able to decide not to hurt or harm or eat another if the circumstances require it. I am amazed sometimes how kind my own dog can be, looking after and caring for everyone around: the cats, the chickens, the young children, even if they climb all over her and take her food.

Empathy is intuitive, immediate and built-in, starting from the moments of togetherness of mother and baby sensing each other. But it is also based on a subconscious understanding that others are like us, and this makes us care. Since we know what hurting is like, we do not want others to hurt like that. We share their hurt so long as we are not anaesthetized to others' feelings. Just as we are happy and love life, so intuitively we know that others love life and we rejoice with them and do not hurt them. This affinity, at a deep level, expresses the fact that all of life is interacting, interconnected, and similar. The traditional Buddhist text the *Dhammapada* says: "Having empathy for others you see that all beings love life and all beings fear death. Knowing this one does not harm or cause harm."[1] This understanding can and should be developed in us to form the ground of both ethics and compassion.

However, unfortunately we often feel the opposite. We get constantly irritated by the difficult neighbour that annoys us day and night, we get frustrated by a close family member that doesn't listen or take us into account, we can't help feeling some anxiety about what those others over there may do to us, we find ourselves caught in reactivity and anger that lands on anything and anyone – the local authority, politicians, schools, doctors. The scars we accumulate can often make us build protective walls that we are endlessly busy maintaining: my needs, my religion, my survival, my possessions, my family, my comfort, my car, my money, my group. With this contraction into the self there is not much room left for empathy, compassion and natural goodness. It is not lost, it is simply closed off. In times of conflict, when a madness of anger and revenge takes over, even then, natural goodness surfaces in the midst of the darkness, as with the courageous life-saving work of the White Helmets in Syria. Eventually people wake from such a collective nightmare, and then natural goodness always finds its way back.

Embodiment, arriving in a body, is itself a source of suffering, since much of life is devoted to maintaining, feeding, protecting and sustaining this body and the inflated self that seems to run it. This is samsara, the cycle of suffering. Natural goodness becomes compassion when we see that we and all others share this busyness with survival, endlessly turning the wheel of samsara like hamsters, and so suffering together. Compassion arises when our hearts are touched by the struggles of all living beings. For example, one of my grandchildren, when she was not yet four, was running around next to my house and she saw a tiny black mark on a stone. One had to look carefully to realize it was a wing of a small black beetle. As she run past it she looked briefly at this little black wing and said: "It was definitely looking for its mother."

The Pali word for compassion is *karuna,* and it is defined as the quivering of the heart when faced with suffering. It is one of the four immeasurable and limitless powers of the heart, called *brahmaviharas,* which can be roughly translated as celestial mansions or "kingdoms of heaven". The other three are: *metta,* love or loving-kindness; *mudita,* mutual joy; *upekkha,* balance and equanimity (see Glossary). They are all based on unconditional love, an expanded and connected responsiveness, an enduring friendliness with everyone and everything, at all times. For example, a primary tone in meditation and spiritual practice is that of embracing whatever arises with kindness and attention. The sense of allowing things to be what they are, without selectivity, judgement, blame or criticism, is the quality of radical acceptance and enduring friendliness. But if the experience is painful this love takes on the colour of compassion. Every time we embrace with soft mindful attention a painful thought (such as guilt, anger or anxiety), or an unpleasant feeling or emotion in our mind-body (such as tension in the shoulders), we are acknowledging difficulty or pain or suffering with compassion. We invite the pain in for a cup of tea, and engage with it rather than trying to shut it up, stop it or fight it.

Compassion has the quality of holding or containing. Just as a mother would not reject or fight her crying baby, but would hold it with kindness and careful attention to what is wrong, compassion holds our cry or the cry of others. The Hebrew and Arabic word for compassion comes from a root word meaning "womb". The English word compassion comes from the Latin *compati,* meaning "to suffer with". It is a primary quality of Jesus and one of the names of both the Jewish and Muslim God: it is a divine quality. The womb not only denotes a protected space but it allows life to be born. Compassion is active, like all the *brahmaviharas.* It is as if we collect the energy of the heart and radiate it out to ourselves and others. Compassion is the active aspect of awareness, which is manifest in life as heartful engagement.

The "near enemy" of compassion, which sometimes looks a bit like it, is pity. When we pity somebody we feel higher than them. But compassion is a grace, which is like rain that falls on everyone, rich and the poor alike. We would have compassion for the tiger that eats the lovely deer, as well as for poor Bambi; both are caught in the same uncontrollable wheel of samsaric pain. Compassion is not selective, it is for the oppressor and the oppressed. They are both part of the same picture.

Compassion has become in a way the signature of the Mahayana/Tibetan vehicle. Mahayana split off from the early Indian Buddhism around the beginning of the common era, when the latter became increasingly intellectual, philosophical and analytic. Tibetan Buddhism started with some real wild northern Indian mystics (the 84 Siddhas) who realized that compassion is not an add-on to wisdom and liberation of the consciousness. Compassion itself was a liberation of the consciousness. Subsequently they defined themselves as Mahayana, the "great vehicle", and renamed the Theravada, which means the path of the elders, as the Hinayana, the "lesser vehicle" – not a compassionate determination. This is changing today in the face of a historic modern creation of a new Buddhist vehicle that we may call Western Buddhism, in which old religious distinctions and labels are breaking down.

How can we overcome the blocks to compassion, and learn to manifest it in daily life situations? One essential step is to discover and be familiar with the limits of our compassion – then we will be able to dissolve those limits. We walk forward because the ground has friction, and it is often the case that we can develop love only against resistance. If we are a doctor or social worker, what is it that dries up our heart, brings emotional distance and makes us treat our patients mechanically? If we meet the disturbing neighbour, what is it that pushes our buttons and makes us continually react with irritation? What is it that makes us respond with immediate caring when our own baby cries and immediate annoyance when it is the neighbour's baby? What is the source of the compassion burnout of so many in the social change field? What is it that drives us to help others if they are in our own group, but not those further away we do not know? And mostly, what makes us forget to have compassion for ourselves when we criticize ourselves or internalize criticisms coming from others?

Another limiting pattern that we may find if we look at our responses to others is what is sometimes described as "idiot compassion". For example, giving endless sweets to a child or complaint-stopping pills (tranquillizers, sedatives and painkillers) to adults in order to shut them up. Idiot compassion is also about stopping our own unpleasant inner voices by all kinds of escapes, comforts and addictions – drugs, food, sex, money, status. It is based on an unwise compulsion to stop, to fix or neutralize something, which actually may be adding to the problem or increasing it later on. A similar example of unwise or limited compassion would be the "helper syndrome", a compulsive need to keep helping/serving others, and an exhausting and frustrating pattern of trying to repair a broken world, often at the expense of caring for ourselves. There are many charitable organizations with this syndrome, which can make the people in them frustrated, angry and depressed when they reach their own limits or things don't work out as expected. I have worked quite a bit with staff in charitable organizations that work for peace but have board meetings that somehow end up in angry shouting matches between everyone's different views. It leads people with potentially great hearts to leave such work in despair because of stress, exhaustion or illness. Instead, it is helpful to realize and get to know this limit, add wisdom through reflection and meditation, learn the value of inner peace and deep listening as a source that keeps compassion flowing and balanced. By learning to say stop we can discover what it is like to give compassion as the best gift to ourselves not only to others. If there are a whole host of demanding beggars outside your guest house, as there was when I was in Varanasi, the depression caused by our inability to give to all of them is no better than the indifference of pretending that they don't exist. Both are not free.

The critical step is to pause, halt the chain of automatic responses, wake up and so notice the painful sense of reaching the limit of our compassion. Then just stay on that edge and allow what comes up. Understanding can flow in. We may realize how we are subject to conditions, pressures and stresses that contract us; we may notice how our own fears make us protective. If we see how it is to be in the other's shoes then our resistance usually melts away and is replaced by empathy and compassion. We may rediscover a sense of compassion for ourselves. In one of the many dialogues that I facilitated between Israelis and Palestinians, the Israelis were having a hard time coming to terms with what the Palestinians were telling them, until a 10-year-old Palestinian boy, with tears welling up in his eyes, said: "Why are the Israelis so distant? I don't want anything from them except one thing. And that is for the Israelis to listen to my story. I am sure that will bring peace when they hear about my life. Why is it that no Israelis want to listen to me?" Of course all hearts melted and compassion flowed and peace was indeed made, at that moment.

The fundamental way to expand our compassion boundaries is to be less full of me and mine, to be more connected to what is really happening, and not what I need and expect to happen or want not to happen. Through meditation and spiritual/psychological practice, we can dissolve the intensity of "selfing", of our habits of ownership of pleasant and unpleasant experiences. We may experience pain in the body, in thought or emotional life, but we don't do anything with it, we don't fight it or run away from it, we don't get busy with it, we don't try and analyse it, we don't automatically own it. We just allow it to be fully seen as a painful experience that comes and goes. It is a phenomenon that doesn't need to belong to me, nor turn me into a victim. We become less identified with it – more transparent – as the pain of ourselves and others touches us and passes on without making tracks.

We may be concerned, as our protective walls slowly crumble to allow in the full ecstasies and tragedies of human experience, that we may not be ready to cope with so much suffering. Surely the self is built from boundaries, from a defensive shield that I need, otherwise the pain of everyone will rush in and I will be overwhelmed, invaded, destroyed? This can be a concern for some sensitive souls, and it can happen that in the process of spiritual growth we can occasionally feel too sensitive and shaken up. But, in general, our sense of openness and awareness will be balanced by transparency. As we become skilled in listening to the painful voices but not giving them centre stage, we become open and free. We can allow natural vulnerability to be seen, we can be a life partner of vulnerability, looking truth in the eye rather than running away. We can surf the waves of difficulty rather than flee them, which just invites them to come crashing down on us. Pain does happen, but like life itself or like water, it passes through. And we soon realize that holding onto the character armour is itself painful, and the effort to maintain the comfort zone is actually a greater burden than the ease and joy of being completely available and present to whatever life may bring. As we become less and less self-concerned and more open, the emptiness allows us to be touched by more and more suffering in the world. The many Asian images of the Buddha with long ears express his power, based on emptiness and presence, to listen to all the suffering of the world and not be destroyed by it.

When things do get out of control, and our mindfulness is not strong enough to hold powerful painful experiences, compassion can be the default response instead of anxiety and confusion. When we go through strong emotional or physical pain that is too overwhelming to be held with mindfulness, when nothing else works, compassion is our best friend. It becomes the reason and motivation that drives our actions instead of the conventional motivation of seeking comfort. We become "baby bodhisattvas". As compassionate action becomes more and more a natural response to life, it becomes clear that it is not just about serving the world, but about awakening into the world. Our own inbuilt longing for transcendence, less suffering, and inner freedom, begins to be less personal and more global. We wake up with it in the morning and go to bed with it at night. It applies to ourselves and to others equally and so becomes the dominant movement of our consciousness. Compassion and awareness guide the mind instead of interests, and result in caring and attentive interactions with whatever arises in the present moment. It is as if every moment has the same immediacy and presence of mind that we use when preventing a child from getting burnt by a fire. There is a Tibetan image of the Shambhala warrior, who fights for peace. The warrior's weapons are compassion and wisdom and his actions are spontaneous – what is wise and appropriate and compassionate in the moment (see chapter 41 on the Shambhala warrior).

I asked my wife, who studies and practises the Zohar, Jewish mysticism, why compassion is on the male side of the tree of life, and she gave an interesting explanation. According to the Jewish mythological tradition, God first made the world according to laws and structure. But it just did not work. It couldn't exist for five minutes. So God had to make compassion equal to form and structure for the world to survive. And compassion in the tree of life is male because it is movement, active, whereas structure is female because it is ground or base. According to the Kabbalah, among other traditions, the world does not have to be there. It was made because of compassion. Since no-one can really know why the world exists, and it appears to be a dynamic creative self-sustaining movement, compassion may be good enough as a hypothesis. Compassion creates, compassion moves, compassion allows.

Buddhist practice holds that wisdom and compassion, mind and heart, have to be in balance like the two wings of the bird. Wisdom expresses the dynamic interconnectedness of everything, while compassion is the heart that moves through it all. The heart energy blossoms in the empty space of awareness that knows me and the world as one. If wisdom is lacking the heart can be sentimental, it can be extreme, it can be lost or lead to delusions and messianism. On the other hand, wisdom without compassion or softness becomes technical, theoretical, theological and analytic. Both in balance is the key to liberation. As Nisargadatta Maharaj said: "Wisdom teaches me I am nothing, love teaches me I am everything. Between the two my life flows."

CHAPTER 24

BRIGHT-EYED AND BUSHY-TAILED – OR EXHAUSTED?

Life is exhausting. We seem to be running from morning to night. We never have enough energy. Often we wake up tired and we go to bed even more tired and in between we never feel really on top of life. We feel as if our energy is stolen, our joy of life is undermined, and the place where our vitality has drained away is not at all clear.

Though we long to identify clear causes and correct them, our state of energy is a holistic issue, in which the sources of vitality or tiredness can come from any or all levels – the physical level such as the food we eat; the emotional level such as chronic anxiety, mild depression, despair or joy, enthusiasm and interest; the social level such as continuous tension and conflict within the family, or love, acceptance, being seen and appreciated; the psychological level such as stress, ego and inner conflict or clarity, ease and balance; the spiritual level such as meaninglessness, determination, inspiration and bliss. And they all may interact. For example, the state of our energy in meditation and yoga is influenced as much by emotional tension as by the level of determination. In all this web of possible causes, where do we begin?

It is a general rule in holistic self-care that we begin with the physical and the ground and work our way toward the subtle and the spiritual. Sometimes it is obvious that we are working too hard and we are drowned in an atmosphere of intense activity. We know we need a rest. But often it is not that simple. For example, we expect that a holiday will press our reset button, but it may not be enough, and anyway we bring our exhausting tendencies on holiday with us. So, starting from the physical, we should look at our diet. Is it in balance, am I eating wholesome food that provides the full range of nutrients? If we eat too much and too often, this can make us tired as the body uses up energy to deal with all this consumption. Excess carbohydrates, too much sugar especially in soft drinks, and too many coffees, are common sources of chronic tiredness. Regular exercise is crucial, and we cannot do without it. It can sometimes be as simple as that.

On the next level is stress, a blanket word that covers many kinds of pressures on our receptive selves. It is helpful to remember that our body-mind may experience stress even if we think we are fine. Research has shown that people who live near busy roads have much higher levels of stress hormones than others, even though they may not notice it and are quite adjusted to their daily life. Stress is not necessarily an issue of direct pressure. It can simply be the total amount of stimulation we experience day by day. If we work all day, and switch off in front of the TV at night, it may be that there is far too much input besieging our poor sensitive brains and hearts, and it would have been much better to properly shut the shop, relax totally, reduce the input, and allow the inner turmoil to gradually settle down. But there is a personal balance here, and everyone is a bit different. For some, too little stimulation, such as unemployment, creates stress, and for others too much. There are some tough nuts, such as Winston Churchill, who managed the Allied war effort with little sleep, vast overstimulation, plenty of brandy and cigars, and who died of natural causes well into his 90s. There are others who feel fragile and nervous. We need to carefully know ourselves and the nature of our vulnerability. Then we can work externally – reducing stress to the level we can cope with, even if it means moving house or changing jobs. At the same time we can work internally – building inner resilience and calm. Appropriate ways may include deep relaxation, or a daily walk by the sea. Methods of meditation that help here are those in which we reach a quiet concentration, in which we drop into a calm and empty place. The meditation needs to be without pressure to achieve anything, to have certain experiences, to fix a problem, or even to try to be calm. It needs to have a sense of ease and coming back home. Whether through following the breath, an object, sound or music, the return to our centre is a return to a place where neither we nor the world makes demands of us.

Yet often even these ways are not enough; they may seem to deal with the symptoms but not the deep causes. There is a sense that we are recharging the batteries in order to go out in the world and get exhausted again. We do not want to be like swans, which seem to be so serene above the water, but under the water their legs are paddling like mad. One of biggest sources of tiredness is the underlying pattern with which we paddle like mad to navigate through the circumstances that arise in our life. For example, patterns of worry or suppressed anger, of perfectionism, of compulsions (including the compulsion to be of benefit to others), of ambition, reactivity, guilt, confusion, even the pressure to change or the habitual need to escape from it all, and so on. All these undo inner peace. Here is the self in all its glory creating resistance at every opportunity – whether at work, home or in daily life – culminating in burnout. Here we need to work deeper to expose and liberate ourselves from the tyrannies of our patterns. This is partly a psychological work, but also wise use of the tools available to clean out the accumulated waste of unconscious tendencies, scars and destructive patterns. Methods of meditation need to be deeper, to work with content, not just with calmness. There needs to be a spiritual and psychological purification that gets to those deep places and frees us from the kinds of inner conflicts and stormy weather that drain us. This is a life journey. With heart, clarity, commitment and some good authentic teachings, we can go way beyond the proverbial recharging of the batteries, to find a natural freedom and original joy. The methods are given more fully in other chapters of this book.

But there are also energetic issues within the spiritual path itself. We usually approach spiritual life with exactly the same collection of patterns and issues that we bring to daily life. We can be striving and ambitious, trying to get somewhere fast (though often we are not quite sure where it is that we want to get to) or we may be passive, expecting others to do it for us, restless, negative. Are we a hero or a zero? An episode in the life of the Buddha touches on this dilemma. He was staying at a place called Uruvela, in a bamboo grove near the river Neranjara where he could bathe. He stayed there to continue his heroic asceticism and meditation practice even though he was dying from malnutrition. He described it: "My ribs stuck out like rafters of a ruined house. My eyes sank so far into my head that they looked like water at the bottom of a deep well."[1] In the nearby village a young woman, Sujata, who wanted to make an offering to the gods, assumed that the emaciated Gautama under the tree by the river was some kind of god and offered him sweet milk rice. He accepted and ate it, since he suddenly understood that in starving and tormenting his weak body he had also weakened and blunted his mind, and deprived it of the nourishment it needed for realization of the truth. He resolved to eat from then on, only a little but enough to maintain his vitality.

The now revived Gautama sat in deep and powerful meditation under the banyan tree. In due course he heard a party of female musicians passing nearby on their way to the village. They were singing about their stringed musical instrument, the veena. The words that came to Gautama made a deep impression on him. They sung that if the strings of the veena were tightened too much they would break, while if they were too loose they could not make music. They need to be stretched just right in order to make the best music, neither too tight, nor too loose. Gautama understood that neither a heroic inner struggle to suppress and beat down the body and mind did not bring results, nor the indulgence in the desires, needs, interests, likes and dislikes of the senses. It needed a middle way in which the right effort was balanced and healthy. It needed the soft touch of the feminine represented by Sujata and the gift of nourishment, like mother's milk, to balance the severity of the masculine striving for success. This was the trigger. With renewed strength and vigour in his body and mind, he abandoned both extremes, and was able to tune his mind to greater and greater subtlety, to give it transcendent power, which he described as a mind that was concentrated, purified, bright, unstained, pliant, malleable, steady, and equanimous.

This is the energy of the wildflower that can break concrete, not the sledgehammer. As in the traditional texts, we should perform any inner practice such as meditation like a chicken sitting on eggs, with a deep patience and quiet. No amount of wishing it to finish or imagining the chicks coming out more quickly will make any difference. They emerge when they are ready. We need a steady quiet persistence without pushing or giving up. When the Buddha was asked how he crossed the ocean of samsara he answered that he did so by not stopping and yet not struggling. He said that if he stopped he sank, and if he struggled he was swept away.[2]

As we continue on our inner journey, the quality of energy gets refined. We notice how struggle becomes more and more painful and unnecessary, as it implies a resistance to an imagined obstacle that is essentially just ourselves. We realize that there is nothing there to resist. Stopping or spiritual laziness is also not an option as it is experienced as an uncomfortable paralysis and helplessness. Letting go of problematic mind states that steal our energy, letting go of the dualities that create friction, we gradually find that the energy flows through us more and more freely, like an undammed river.

It is not only that the energy gets unblocked, there also seems to be more of it available as a natural fruit of the qualities that are developed along the spiritual path. If we live with purity (*sila*), something flows more freely as we come to live without regrets, guilts or aversions. If our heart is open, and our daily life is fuelled by compassion, a great spring of energy opens up as we respond naturally to the calls of the world. If we live with the power of giving rather than the contraction of taking, we find that that too energizes us. And if we constantly live with awareness and wakefulness, we find that we are dancing with change rather than resisting it, and as things get more subtle, we become like an eagle effortlessly riding on the currents and the winds, hardly needing to flap our wings.

In the deepest sense this is an aligning with the energy of life, the Tao. There is a Taoist story of a man sitting on a bridge watching a large waterfall. As he watched he spied an old man walking on the path to the waterfall. All of a sudden the old man jumped into the waterfall! The watcher was shocked and rushed down to the waterfall to try and save the old man. When he got there, he was amazed to see the old man emerge unharmed from the other side of the falls, and continue on his way. He ran to him and asked him how he survived. The old man said, waving his hand as he spoke: "The water went this way and that, and I went this way and that, and found myself on the other side."

I have witnessed the Dalai Lama's awesome energy – despite being in his mid-70s he taught from morning to night, with a playfulness, ease, and lightness of being. A few years ago I decided to go on a long retreat in my own home. In order to have some hours of quiet meditation before the household awoke, I started to get up before four in the morning. Amazingly, I found that my need for sleep dropped and to this day I am absolutely fine with four hours' sleep a night. These days, from four in the morning until around midnight, I am writing, teaching, communicating, walking, gardening, and I never feel tired. The energy comes flowing in from a place of ease that is indefinable and the day feels like a dance with arising circumstances. Let us have the patient steadiness and persistence of the swan sitting on her eggs, rather than furiously paddling up the river.

CHAPTER 25

LEVIATHAN: LIBERATING THE LIFE FORCE

Mindfulness practice, meditation and inner work raise awareness of mental patterns and tendencies, memories and fears, and not infrequently touch our limitations and difficulties. We learn to allow whatever arises to arise and to be what it is. We meet our host of friends and relations with varying degrees of readiness, insight and coping. However, we must also ask what happens to the material that does not reach awareness. This is material that we usually don't encounter, either because it is too painful for us, or because it is so ubiquitous that we don't even notice it. It is the buried stuff. Narratives, images, scars, voices and deep memories that are running in the background but don't emerge into the light of day. We all can think of personal examples. Some common ones would be: "I am not good enough"; "Life is against me"; "I am just a servant to my children/husband/society/boss"; "I am destined to be ... (fill in the blank)". We aren't even aware of the existence of such narratives until they suddenly pop up because of some circumstance or event. The narratives, hidden underground, are connected to our longings and hopes. They express deep and frustrated desire for purity, love and perfection. They are the life force imprisoned. And because this is a power chained, it is scary, something big under the surface. As in the saying – if you put a cat in a box, it turns into a tiger. It can be imagined as a monstrous leviathan (the old word for semi-mythological giant sea creatures) representing inflated issues lying beneath the threshold of our consciousness, issues that we are unable to direct or control.

Some of our greatest well-hidden narratives lying under the surface of our ocean are of course connected to death. The denial around death is endless. One example of this denial is the glorification of youth and health. Though it seems perfectly natural, it is in fact an expression of the leviathan concealed in the depths of our consciousness, in this case our fear of growing old, and of losses, endings and deterioration. In Jewish society, a potent example of the way a death-related hidden narrative lives powerfully within us and controls us from deep down is the Holocaust. It is running in the background all the time in the Jewish individual and social mind, and can produce a subtle restlessness, as if constantly alert as to where the next threat might be coming from. It is one of the psychological underpinnings of the intractable conflict in the Middle East. Behaviour can be deeply influenced by this narrative, even if we aren't aware of it. It can be lurking at the back of the German consciousness too, sometimes stealing the joy of life. We need to invite such undersea monsters to reveal themselves and then to meet and befriend them – "Come out of the depths, my friend, and dance with me in my life!" How can we do this?

I recently taught a retreat in Germany on the subject of the Holocaust with Israeli and German participants. Among other things we walked silently together to Sachsenhausen concentration camp near Berlin and meditated there for a day. The Holocaust felt to all of us like an elephant in the room; even though its presence was strongly felt, it was difficult to touch it or even to look at. But it can be seen by the pain it causes. This reveals it in the present. By means of dialogue, sharing and silent meditation we opened ourselves to see the elephant in the room, and at the same time to see the room, what is fine and healthy and nothing to do with the elephant. But something felt a bit stuck. In the small groups it was easier for the Israelis to talk, whose pattern tended to be the perpetual victim. It was harder for the Germans because of an inbuilt culture of silence. At a certain point I invited the

Israelis to look at things through German eyes and to try for a moment to leave behind their personal story. The Israelis saw that the Germans still carried with them painful leftovers of the war and the Holocaust in the forms of hidden guilt and unanswered questions about the actions of their parents and grandparents. They saw the pain of psychological dirt swept under the carpet and still there. At this stage the atmosphere in the retreat changed entirely and all felt relief and release. There was now the opportunity to share the depths of their pain with each other and to feel compassion for each other and for humanity as a whole. The elephant was invited to tea. There were hugs and communication, empathy and joy. The elephant turned into a puppy that wagged its tail.

The leviathan takes up a lot of space within us. We walk around it, are careful not to get too close, but don't understand the extent to which it drains our joy of life. Like a moth circling round a candle, we are busy with thoughts and behaviours intended to accomplish, to control, to compensate, to justify, to flee or to repress the hidden power, which can be our demon or our angel. Many in the Western world use antidepressants to avoid the leviathan. Such weighty unconscious narratives store large amounts of energy. If we succeed in identifying them and releasing them we liberate a powerful life force.

The leviathan is imagined in most cultures in similar ways. In the Bible it is a sea-serpent, and in the Vedic myths it is a lake-dwelling serpent, the naga. In Christian, Norse and Anglo-Saxon mythology it is a dragon. In alchemy it is a salamander. It populates dreams, mythology and esoteric teachings. It appears to us in our dreams if we ignore it while we're awake. I once had a recurring dream in which I was walking in an unknown land around a big pool or lake filled with black water. I didn't understand why the water wasn't clear until I noticed that the water was black because it was actually the dark grey back of a huge leviathan. At first I was afraid when I saw this huge beast, but then I was attracted to its uncontrollable and mysterious power.

These beasts are scary because they threaten our ordinary consciousness that is limited and committed to "business as usual". Ordinary consciousness regards these beasts as Satanic and wants to kill them, as in the image of St George who kills the dragon. But they are scary to the status quo just *because* they represent the extraordinary, the irrational, the mysterious, the hidden powers, the intuitive and non-conceptual, the sublime potency of life itself. The nagas in the Asian religions are frightening, but also worshipped as bringers of fertility, wisdom and life. Dragons are guardians of treasure. They often challenge spiritual heroes with riddles that can only be solved by intuitive wisdom. The serpent talks in primal language, the language of the animal mind, of the unconscious. In the Judeo-Christian world, based on Mesopotamian and Egyptian mythology, the serpent as a life power can tempt us into desire, as in the Bible story of the exile from the Garden of Eden, but also can heal and inspire. The snake on a stick is used to inspire faith and healing in the Bible, and became the symbol of the Greek god Hermes, who is the messenger between the divine and human worlds, and also the rod of Aesclepius, the symbol of healing and medicine, to this day. The snake and the stick are opposites and similar, the stick representing the straightness, the laws of nature, the rational, the left brain, and the snake representing the crooked, the subtle, the right brain.

So how do we become friends with these uncontrollable forces, with the unknowable life force? One interesting perspective comes from the Buddhist texts. Throughout the life of the Buddha, the demon Mara appears and tempts him with desire, tempts him to go back to dwell inside his comfort zone. Each time Mara appeared, in the many guises of ordinary daily-life temptation, the Buddha simply said: "I see you Mara." And Mara slunk away. Mara is with us all the time, but if we agree to meet him we connect to the source of his power. Only when we recognize our inner demons will we be able to overcome them. Recognize means firstly to be mindful of what is going on below the surface of our mind and heart, and secondly to be kind and welcoming to these forces. In many fairy tales a spell is cast on a handsome prince, turning him into a fearsome or disgusting creature. But if we succeed in overcoming the fear and the disgust, if we don't try to kill the monster but we kiss it instead, it will turn into the prince or princess we've been waiting for.

How do we actually do this? Let's take the familiar example of our primal shame and guilt – definitely a snake in the undergrowth. We may be ashamed to wear clothes that are too different from others (such as at work), we may feel shame at something that we have done in the past, we may feel under pressure concerning what people think of us, our role, status or personality, we may have a wounded self-image or we may just feel apologetic about our existence. How do we work with it?

- **Talk about it.** This is the classic way to surface the undercurrents and subconscious issues, and bring them into the light of day. This is the territory of psychologists, confessionals in the Catholic faith, and those great places of therapeutic encounter – the café and the pub.
- **Relabel it.** It is not a problem that we have to solve, but a visitor, a guest, a teacher or a partner in our life, however unwelcome it appears. Relabelling it from enemy to friend is a powerful step in accepting it and inviting it home with us to show its face and help us. Yes, I feel this shame sometimes but it is just appearing as it does and I befriend it with good humour and acceptance.
- **The kiss.** Regard our demons with kindness. They come from places of goodness, of trying to get things right, of protecting ourselves or others, of needing to be ok. Radiate kindness, and softness, like a mother to a baby with poo in the nappy. It doesn't actually smell that bad to the mother.
- **See its face.** Explore it, meet it in many different situations in life. Usually it is only visible by its uncomfortable projections and manifestations, such as the shame-based discomfort felt when someone looks at us strangely. See the discomfort directly, in our speech, in contractions or feelings in the body,

in reactivity in the mind. Be with these signs, with quiet mindfulness and inquiry. Track them back down into the unconscious voices within us. This may need meditation.

- **Seeing is not believing.** In Buddhist psychology, mental constructions, even those that seem entrenched and well dug in into the unconscious, are still only our own constructions, which have gained their strength by our investment in them through years of suppression. They are just accumulated moments of memory that have seeped into our self-definition and view of ourselves. In the same way as sense experiences, such as bodily sensations, seeing or hearing, they are only passing and labile raw materials entering our minds. We don't have to believe them, they need not ensnare us, for they are not the absolute truth.

- **All of the above together.** They add to each other, as in the example of the workshop with Germans and Israelis mentioned above – the elephant was seen, from trunk to tail, and invited to join the party, but it needed both the clarity and awareness of meditation and the openness of dialogue.

The Biblical story of Job deals with the same theme. Job was a good and successful man who played according to the rules. He believed, rather arrogantly, that his morality guaranteed that he would be "alright". But Satan, the uncontrollable life force, overturned his life to put him to the test. Because Job was a seeker and a man of inquiry he didn't agree to accept the explanations for his fate based on social conventions, and he set out to find absolute truth, the divine answer. Like the Buddha, he was endowed with a sense of urgency and with strong determination. At the end of the story Job receives an unexpected answer. It wasn't the explanation about human suffering that he was looking for, but even better – an encounter with the uncontrollable nature of the life force. God describes this force through the image of a leviathan in the ocean, a powerful creature that no man can capture or tame, and invites Job to see life in its irrational fullness, with wise and compassionate eyes.

CHAPTER 26
THE PATHLESS PATH

Most of us do need, or even long for, that sense that our life is going somewhere. We are not particularly happy when nothing moves, and are frustrated when we feel we are just marking time or idling in neutral gear. A well-known example of this is the suffering of unemployment. This sense of needing to go somewhere works subtly behind the scenes and can give us motivations and energy. We may be driven by manifestations of self, such as wanting success in our field, to make a name for ourselves or improve our status and popularity. Or it may be material drives, such as wanting to be financially secure. Or there may be deeper drives such as the quest for truth, for a spiritual realization and, of course, for happiness. And most of us, when asked, would describe this life as something of a journey; even if we spend most of our time sitting by the side of the road. But have we examined what this idea really means? Do we know where we are going? Are we indeed going anywhere? Do we know when we lose our way and when we find it again? Would we know it if we got to our destination? Are we given a path or do we make it with our own feet? And if it is easier to tread the path made by other people's feet, what is the price we pay by going down the common road? Indeed does a path exist in life? Jiddu Krishnamurti often described his teachings as "the pathless path".

The spiritual journey is not different from any other journey. At times we are busy with the path, with finding our way or losing our way, with the pressure to get there and impatience for the pleasures of arrival and rest. But at other times we forget the journey itself and find ourselves completely engaged in looking at those delicate flowers near our feet, the bird flying overhead, the empty feelings in a hungry stomach, or the pleasure of falling asleep under a great tree. All of these

are experienced in the present moment and are "pathless".
In other words, all journeys are a dialogue between time and
timeless, path and pathless, road and landscape: between
travelling and being.

When we come to spiritual travelling, especially at the
beginning, we may be inspired by a teacher or a teaching or
by the Buddha, or enchanted by the prospect of liberation in
this very life, or attracted by spiritual powers and fruits. This
often leads to a strong achievement orientation, a striving to
succeed. And one will find all the support for this attitude
from many teachers from all kinds of traditions. Teachers will
check you and offer you incentives to go to the next stage,
even a smile and private audience with the lama, swami,
abbot. Fellow travellers will wish you good luck and success.
The teachings themselves will be presented as a step-ladder to
stages of meditative experience and states of consciousness,
with milestones that have the authority of traditional texts.
Often the path is actually marketed as a stepwise endeavour:
"Training stage 1" of whatever branded spiritual journey it
happens to be. Sometimes the carrot that leads you on is
closeness to the guru; sometimes it is moving up the hierarchy;
sometimes it is a promise of higher levels of realization.

Spiritual striving may be quite helpful in the beginning,
getting us going from our natural tendency to sit in front of
the TV and let life pass us by. But it bears a considerable cost
and, if we continue with it, it may hinder us on the path. We
may become closed in beliefs about the path, the guru, the
further stages, which prevent us from realizing existential truth
arising within us. Such striving may bring us to doubt and
crisis or even psycho-spiritual collapse (spiritual emergency).
So we must ease up, especially as we progress. Desire for
liberation is a wholesome desire, as desires go, and can bring us
to valuable insights and practice. But don't take it too seriously
– it is no more than a good strategy.

If we look closer at the issue of path, we find an inherent
contradiction, because path is a concept in our minds, a
direction that we choose and want, a desire, and a form.

Whereas what we desire to achieve – happiness, awakening and freedom – is quite beyond path, beyond form and concept. Awakening is awakening *from* our habits of wanting, succeeding and achieving. "Truth is a pathless land" said Krishnamurti, and indeed one cannot "get" truth at the end of the journey – it is truth that "gets" us. There is a saying that the truth that we discover at the top of the mountain is actually the truth that we carried up there in the first place. It is just that we did not realize that we had it in our bag all along.

But how can we travel without a path? We feel we would get lost in a pathless land. It would turn into a wandering in the desert. So how are we to solve this apparent contradiction? The Buddha's teaching on this is quite clear: use path as long as you need it, and abandon it when you don't. To illustrate this, the Buddha described a situation in which a man is standing on one shore of a turbulent river and wants to get across to safety and calm on the other shore. And there is no boat. So what does he do? He ties logs together and builds a raft and on his own he crosses to the other shore. Then, the Buddha asks, would it be sensible for the man, thinking that the raft was useful, to hoist it on his head and continue the journey carrying the raft? No. One needs to abandon it when reaching the other shore. So with all goals of inner development, spiritual teachings, step-ladders, paths, hierarchies, and so on.

In other words, we bring to our journey a directed mind, because we do need direction and sometimes determination in order to change habits and patterns and limited ways of thinking. Our practice, whether meditation, body work, yoga, tai ch'i, breathing, music, dance or whatever, directs itself to a place where no direction is needed any more. Even the word practice has this inbuilt contradiction, that if it succeeds it takes us to a place of existential being where the word has no meaning any more. To some extent this happens naturally, by itself. Because even in a most controlled step-by-step teaching, our experience will certainly be mixed. We may be in the midst of hard work getting somewhere, such as trying to concentrate on the breath, when suddenly the breath itself just invites us in to explore the territory hidden there. We are counting how long we can maintain a yoga posture, when we forget to measure, and just enjoy the moment. We may be trying to get the ch'i kung postures right, when we find ourselves letting go and the whole movement and the mind that directs it seems to be happening by itself. We get up from a very achievement-oriented striving exercise, and just feel the sense of being alive, the sense of the morning, the mood of lightness, and moments of not caring where exactly we are.

As we practise, we become more and more friendly with the wild and wonderful surprises of the present moment. The landscape tends to take us over. As we progress, our consciousness and heart themselves learn to love the freedom of the open road, of going nowhere. A perfection appears that was covered over by habits of striving, based on the pain of wanting to be somewhere other than where we were. We may realize that there is nowhere to go other than where we already are, and where we are is complete just as it is because the universe cannot be anything else other than what it is at that moment. From that place the milestones on the road are just another interesting pile of stones.

This is not to say that we cannot get stuck on a path. It can happen quite easily, often because we believe in the authority of teachers, books, traditional prescriptions or our peers. The answer at those times is to stop, breathe and look around. What is really happening right now in this existential moment? It may be as simple as connecting with body sensations, sounds, and feeling life within. It may need us to look directly at those thoughts that tell us we want to be somewhere else as just simple thoughts that pass by in this moment. We can gradually build an autonomy and an independence in which we are like islands in the stormy seas (see chapter 28).

But we can also be stuck off-path, which could mean that we are simply lost. We are not sure where to go, what to do next, how to practise, how to choose the next step, what we need to learn and what not, and who to listen to. Sometimes this can energize a new search, a sense that we need to set out on a kind of mythic hero's journey, leave the comfort of home that is no longer comfortable, and seek our own path in life. But often the answer in this case is to relax into the no-path feeling, lose ourselves in being lost, and discover a deeper security that lies behind all of that. Many years ago at a retreat on Krishnamurti's teachings in Switzerland that I was co-leading, someone came to me and joked: "Do you know how to travel the pathless path? Get lost!"

Another place of being stuck off-path could be if we have too much attachment to a non-dual pathless world of practice before we are ready. We hold the idea of "nowhere to go, nothing to do, nothing to be practised" as a belief rather than an experience. In fact all the great non-dual teachers, whether Ramana Maharshi, Krishnamurti or the Tibetan Dzogchen teachers, all said that while there may not be a path, one needs to be dedicated to awakening. The non-dual teachings tell us that there is no need to strive to get somewhere since this is following a delusion that there is another place to go and time to get there, and somewhere else is better. There is no path because in the totality there is nowhere to go and the beginning is also the end. Nonetheless, we need to be serious and consistent and committed.

From the earliest age, we want to get somewhere and yet at the same time are also in the pathless world of the flow of experience. As children we have an inner drive to learn, develop and discover the world, which is unstoppable, but are also full of timeless play. Ancient tendencies drive us forward to grow and know and become somebody. Yet at the same time we freely explore pathless territory and are somewhere on the boundary of the known and unknown. Let us be like children in our spiritual journey, making use of the path trodden by many before, but playfully jumping off into the unknown at any time, and eventually making that our real home.

CHAPTER 27

WHEN IS AN ACTION NOT AN ACTION?

Sorry, dear reader, you will have to wait until the end of the chapter for the answer. The fact is that we are acting, doing, from the moment we get up in the morning until the moment we go to sleep. Even when we take a rest it can feel that we are still doing something, namely recovering from previous activity and getting ready for what's next. Our dreams too can seem extremely busy and intensive, except that the body is not involved. It is hard to imagine what it is like just to *be*, without doing anything. We may need to imagine a non-human life, such as a cat that can sit quietly in an armchair all day, or an olive tree that grows in silent dignity for 100 years. We can honestly say that we are *human doings* not *human beings*.

One of the most important discoveries of the spiritual life is a reappraisal of what it means to act. Action here means almost anything that we do purposefully, including speech, movement, working and so on. From doing the dishes to meeting others, to sitting in front of the computer. We act because we want to change something, to get something, to get somewhere, to achieve a goal, to prevent or avoid something. If we are too demanding or intense about these goals, we put ourselves and others around us under stress and pressure, and this has some noticeable pathological results on the health of mind and body. But even if we act without any pressure at all, we are usually completely identified with the ends we want to achieve by this busyness, and as such often feel a slave to our goals and intentions.

Of course, goals, directions and intentions in our life are important, and the energy and positivity of engagement can be of great benefit to ourselves and others. There is a need for wisdom in navigating ourselves through the challenges of life with actions that are wholesome, beneficial to ourselves and others, that do not harm ourselves or others, that have moral sensitivity, and that are like a mother who feeds her children. We have discussed this before in the context of both karma and *dana* (see chapters 2 and 7) in which we become aware that the kind of seeds we sow in our lives will tend to bear similar kinds of fruit. However, here I am talking about something a little different. That is, the nature and quality of an action, not just its purpose and results. A Biblical example of the fine-tuning of the quality of an action is the story of Moses when he was advised by his divine inner voice to talk to the rock to draw water from it, instead of which he struck it. He demonstrated a crudity and lack of trust with his action, which brought him highly painful consequences. The Jewish mystical sources say that he was punished because he forgot the language of rocks, meaning the language of nature and being.

There is a great secret in the balance between means and ends – the way we do things and what we do. If we are obsessed by goals, the action is full of pressure, friction, stress, exhaustion and so on. We do not walk our talk. If we are obsessed by means, we are walking, but to nowhere, lost and wandering aimlessly. Means and goals reflect and mirror each other. We actually do not need to separate them. If we pay attention to the means as well as the goals, the actions become more harmonious and bear better fruit. This is so often lacking in peacemaking. Most wars are fought in the name of peace, or for the sake of an ideal of peace. If we just talk about peace and try and get it, it seems unreachable like the rainbow. If we are peaceful and embody peace, it is already there. If we balance peace as an intention or goal with real steps toward healing and inducing trust, all the doors to peace open. There is "peace in every step", as the Zen master Thich Nhat Hanh put it.

Good musicians, practitioners of ch'i kung, tai ch'i and aikido, athletes and sportsmen, all gradually learn this secret of the power that is released when we let go of attachment to goals. They don't lose direction when means and ends are in balance. This was expressed well in the book *Zen in the Art of Archery*. In the moment of a perfectly balanced shot, the way and the goal come together in a moment of pure being, or flow and release. Teachers of the Alexander Technique use a similar method in guiding the body to relearn actions that heal rather than causing structural damage to the body. They talk about movement coming from its source rather than "end-gaining" – trying to get somewhere. The *Tao Te Ching*, the ancient Chinese classic, likens beneficial action to the flow of water: soft, fluid, translucent yet immensely powerful. Therefore the sage "keeps to the deed that consists in taking no action and practises the teaching that uses no words".[1]

When we look at our actions carefully, from a spiritual point of view, we find something quite startling – that we never actually get anywhere with any action that we do. It is simply impossible, an illusion, a habit of the mind that is always running to get somewhere else, to run away from what is to what is not. When clearly seen, the reality is that we are constantly arriving, not leaving. We are again and again arriving in this surprising present moment that unfolds itself in front of us like a red carpet. There is nowhere else we can be other than this moment in which our actions happen, whether we are aware of it or not. And if our minds are full of future plans, intentions and goals, we simply don't notice the truth staring us in the face. We can only live in the present whatever sandcastles our minds are building somewhere else. Our minds are used to restlessness, but when we stop and look at where we really are we notice that we have never left. As T S Eliot said in *Little Gidding*, the end of our explorations will be "to arrive where we started and know the place for the first time".[2]

I once asked my aunt, at the sprightly age of 93, how she explained her ripe old age. "Very simple," she replied, "I practise masterful inactivity!"

When we are aware of the nature of action, then actions become non-actions. As the Tibetan teacher Nyoshul Khenpo Rinpoche writes: "Activities are endless, like ripples on a stream. They end only when we drop them. All activities are like games children play. Like castles made of sand. View them with delight and equanimity, like grandparents overseeing their grandchildren or a shepherd resting on a grassy knoll watching over his grazing flock."[3]

So is this relevant to us as we sit in front of the computer, answer the telephone, catch a bus, heal a client, or read these words right now? It certainly is, since the truth of non-action breaks through and makes us feel joyful and free when we notice it. It happens when we are more playful and less goal directed. It happens when we relax deeply in the midst of activity and find ourselves easily accommodating whatever happens as we go along. It happens when we go with the flow, not just as a new-age slogan, but in a profound experience of acting without resistance and without friction. It happens when we feel everything is just right. It happens when the barriers between us and the world soften and we feel a sublime merging or togetherness. An action becomes a non-action when we feel that it is just happening by itself. We are a witness of action but not its owner or controller. In those wonderful moments we feel that we are not only alive, but that we are being lived.

CHAPTER 28

COPING WITH CONCERNS: ARRIVING BACK HOME

"We have no reason to mistrust our world, for it is not against us."

(Rainer Maria Rilke)

As the Buddha neared his end, disciples from all parts of northern India gathered around him expressing their fear of being left without a teacher. So he offered them his last teaching: "Be an island unto yourself." These words point to themes of insecurity, confidence and autonomy.

At some level, we are continually haunted by existential anxiety. Primal angst is present in the experience of every sentient being. It finds its expression in every aspect of our lives, such as the everyday feelings of concern, worry, agitation, irritation, suspicion, aversion and so on. Or perhaps in habitual safety behaviours such as TV, busyness, money, alcohol. Angst appears endlessly in the field of personal relations, in defensiveness, argumentation, conflict, the need to control the other, fear of being challenged or put down, pride, aggressiveness, withdrawal, being judgemental. Its foundation lies in our instinct to survive, but its tentacles reach into all aspects of our physical, mental and emotional life, and these are largely automatic reactions that are triggered even without genuine threats to our well-being. The experience of constant watchfulness can be monitored scientifically and researchers confirm that the background state of our brain is mild anxiety.

When the Buddha said, "Be an island unto yourself," he didn't mean to encourage isolation and detachment but rather a sense of stability. Islands are connected to each other under the sea. The sense of autonomy goes together with a feeling of connectedness, of being at home. When stable and grounded we feel free to face the unknown and the uncontrollable without insecurity. The sense of autonomy is very important. It enables us to face experiences we would otherwise naturally fear and avoid. Because we are at home, we can invite them in.

It is worth taking our existential fears seriously, as they will dominate and control us both consciously and unconsciously. They can sap our basic joy of life and our freedom of thought and action. Often they are not visible in daily life – we are not talking about the fear of going out at night in a rough part of town, but rather the more diffuse concern that something may or may not happen, or worries about politics, the future, the planet, our income, our neighbours. Where I live, Israel, anxiety is a cultural emotion, waving like the national flag, embedded so deep in the national consciousness that it is assumed to be the way people naturally are. But it has disastrous consequences for the region and for the children that grow up in such an emotional climate.

Most of our primal insecurity is hidden beneath the surface, and we may not have obvious fears; we may be settled, confident, not worried or concerned. All the same, it can catch us unawares, below the belt. For example, it may be that we have done quite a lot of spiritual and psychological work on ourselves and we feel generally happy. But then we keep getting furious at the behaviour or words of others around us, such as close family members or those we work with, and we don't understand where that keeps coming from. Quite often people come to me who have been through years of spiritual practice and with their voice cracking under feelings of doubt and pain they complain that they still seem to get angry at small things. They are irritated with their partners, or worried about what may happen, and they don't understand how that is possible after so much practice. Perhaps, they say, the practice isn't working? When I ask them how many times they experience this anger or concern, and how long it lasts, it is of course far less than before. It needs to be clearly understood that this anger springs from a fundamental, biological and deep sense of protection that nests deep in the unconscious even after years of practice. It need not be a source of blame, but a source of wonder. However hard we try to build walls, life has no protection or protector, said the Buddha, and the feelings of existential angst we share with all sentient beings in the world.

Whether the fears and concerns are heavy or light, there is much we can do to work with them. The first step is always to recognize them, bring them out into the light, and meet them as they are, welcoming them as they arise usually triggered by circumstances, without blame or shame, but just knowing that they are there. In a moment of concern, in the midst of a challenging situation in our own kitchen, stop there, breathe and let it arise into awareness. This noticing can go along with a shift in our relationship to our fears, honouring them, not blaming ourselves for them. There is even something breathtaking and grand in the way we look after ourselves; the character armour is built over our lives because we love and care for ourselves. It is constructed elegantly and is strong and full of the colours of our responses. The shell of a tortoise is beautiful.

Both in the rough and tumble of daily life, and in the quietness of reflection or meditation, we need to go to the next step, which is to put our attention fully where it is helpful. One place is sensory awareness in the body that has nothing to do with the fear. If a sense of anxiety or concern arises, just the contact with our feet on the ground, the breath moving our belly, our hands on our knees is enough to drain away its potency. It becomes just another phenomenon in the field of mind and body.

In the past I suffered from fear of heights. I decided to build a roof with a friend as a way to overcome this. Every time I felt dizzy, I connected completely to the physical sensation of the present moment by giving all of my attention to the touch of the hammer and nails. Every time I used this method the dizziness dissipated and, after a month, I felt that I had overcome the fear entirely.

A second location for attention or mindfulness is in the phenomena arising with the fear itself. It may be that our belly is indeed contracted, or our muscles tense or our breathing constrained. These are handles by which we can get a grasp of the fear. What is often difficult with mindfulness of fear or anxiety is that it is all over us, in mind, body, emotion, memory, hormones, self and so on. But reducing it down to a single phenomenon, just the contracted belly for example, is like pressing the minimize button on our computer. The whole complex of fears is collapsed down to a rather insignificant body movement. Observing it mindfully again and again, as a relatively uninteresting phenomenon that arises, changes and disappears, and disidentifying with it, it will gradually dissolve.

However, some seeds of it may be lurking around for a long time in the subconscious. Years after the time when I thought I had dealt with the fear of heights, I was in the Swiss Alps and one day toward the end of a long hike the trail led us along the edge of steep drop. I could see tiny houses and trees a kilometre below. Fortunately the abyss was open only to one side and so long as I was able to keep my focus on the other side, I was fine. But as we continued walking, the other side of the path also dropped away and I found myself standing on a narrow path on a narrow ridge, between two steep chasms on either side. Suddenly, unexpectedly, I was utterly flooded by the old fear. I collapsed flat on my face and could not go one step further. The fear had almost driven me to jump off the edge in order to end the panic. Dizzy, I sat down, unable to move. I realized with surprise that clearly these kinds of fears never really disappear. I stood up slowly gathering my breath and asked myself: "How can the dharma help me now?" I understood that to be able to walk on I would have to avoid any conscious interpretation of the basic sensory input from seeing and hearing. And it worked: as long as I did not let my mind process what was going on, I was able to keep on walking. The houses and trees down below were nothing other than uninteresting small splashes of red and green. When the concentration on pure sense data lapsed, and the implications of walking on a narrow ridge flooded back in, I collapsed again with paralysing fear. But then with two breaths I came back to awareness and could continue walking and this is how finally I made it back. This incident taught me that these primordial fears run deep and we should not underestimate them. Yet it also showed that when in touch with the present moment, with minimum mental construction about what may happen, mindfulness in itself is enough to assuage our primordial fears.

For many, strong beliefs represent their main shield against life's threats and challenges. Belief in God, in the priest, rabbi or guru, in the Messiah or the Buddha or the saints, or in inclusive cultural concepts such as democracy or science, provide some kind of inner confidence. However, these are fragile defences, because they are dependent. When the Messiah doesn't come, the guru doesn't pay attention, democracy fails – our constructed world collapses. If things get difficult we often blame these icons for betraying us, when actually we should be questioning our beliefs and assumptions and dependence on them. Faith is a deeper and more sustainable place to keep us steady. It is softer than belief, and less dependent on promises. Faith gives us a sense of being held, or covered. It is more an inner state of mind. In the dharma there is the key practice of taking refuge, or finding a deep home, which is much more sustainable and less dependent than the usual habit of feeling at home only when conditions are favourable and comfortable (enough money, good relationships, no conflict, a good house and job). The first refuge is in the Buddha, which is not the Buddha as a person or icon, but the Buddha-like qualities within us. The second is the dharma, the spiritual journey and the truth that emerges as a result, a way of seeing more deeply. The third is the sangha, the community of like-minded souls who are with us on this journey.

But trust is an even more reliable and sustainable quality. Trust is the antidote to fear. It is a basic and powerful psycho-spiritual power, which helps us to stride like an elephant not scuttle fearfully like a mouse. We practise it by the active intention to trust whatever experience we meet, whether it is pleasant or unpleasant. Whatever is happening right now is good enough, it is just what is happening. We act and change things but from trust not fear. We trust our stomach to tell us we need to eat and we trust the eating. We practise taking firm steps, one after another, even if the path is to the unknown, even within experiences that we don't understand. And we trust the path wherever it may lead us. As the song of the Jewish mystic Rabbi Nahman of Bretslev put it: "The entire world is a very narrow bridge ... the main thing is not to be afraid." It is the habits built by our survivor's mind that creates fear. But, in fact, the world is neither for us nor against us. The world is just with us and we with it. Trust is not trust in specific outcomes that we need, it is not trust that things will be ok – they may not be, we are not in control of life. Instead it is a wise and beneficial state of mind with which we approach situations that are constantly coming at us. Even in difficult situations, when we feel that life is scary, threatening or challenging, we can choose to trust it; this may actually help us to choose strategies of action and responses that are wiser and more helpful to us than fear. It is a basic shift in attitude. Instead of blaming the world or others for all the problems, we ought to be asking ourselves what is our inner climate like, and what are we going to do about it.

Mindfulness works with trust – they help each other. Trusting our nature to respond to life in just the way it is, accepting it and allowing ourselves to be as we are, is a great aid to mindfulness, and being aware can be felt as a softness and lightness that spreads through our being. It can mature into a feeling that we belong, a feeling we're at home in this moment and whatever it may bring.

The Buddhist teachings take a radical position, recognizing the deep and subtle hold that primal fear has on us. They say that in the end the only remedy for our existential anxiety is awakening. This is because the most fundamental source of our fears is that we seek to defend ourselves from the changing and unpredictable world. Awakening releases us from the fixation that we are an entity, separate from the world, that needs to seek safety from it. Our existential insecurity dissolves when we know that the world and us are so deeply interconnected that seeking protection from it no longer makes sense. The Buddha related to this topic in response to a question from a young deva (spirit):

"This mind is always frightened, this mind is always agitated about problems that have not yet occurred or that have already arisen. If there is a way to be released from fear, please tell me what it is." He replied: "Only by enlightenment and austerity, only through restraining the senses, only through letting go of everything, do I see any safety for living beings."[1]

The Buddha on another occasion said:

Monks, live with yourself as your island, yourself as your refuge, with nothing else as your refuge. Live with the Dhamma as your island, the Dhamma as your refuge, with nothing else as your refuge. How? ... by staying focused on the body in and of itself – ardent, alert, and mindful – putting aside greed and distress with reference to the world. Staying focused on feelings in and of themselves ... on mind in and of itself ... on mental qualities in and of themselves – ardent, alert, and mindful – putting aside greed and distress with reference to the world. This is how a monk lives with himself as his island, himself as his refuge, with nothing else as his refuge; with the Dhamma as his island, the Dhamma as his refuge, with nothing else as his refuge.[2]

The Sufi tradition uses three beautiful similes to describe ways of dealing with insecurity and fear:

1. **The straw basket.** When the wind blows, the basket tumbles and rolls over and over but remains intact. When we relate to life's challenges lightly, they will still affect us; we may be tossed around, yet we cannot break. It is like the old Taoist image of bamboo, which can bend but not break.

2. **The rock.** Water flows over and around the rock in the river, but it remains in its place, steady, unmoved, connected to the earth. We can remain steady even when storms gather around us. This can be something we learn during the practice of meditation. We can sit like a rock for a long period of time and learn how to keep still and quiet and let the flow of thoughts, feelings, sensations and even pains move through us like water flowing past.

3. **The glass.** When our mind is empty and clear like glass, and we do not hold onto anything, experiences arise and vanish like rays of light that do not stick inside but pass through us. We remain transparent.

Facing, befriending and dissolving our insecurity, undoing the armours, walls and protections, invites other capacities and powers on our journey. An honest sense of natural vulnerability arises. We feel the strength of the grasses that wave in even the slightest breeze but are not brittle and cannot break. We become more open, allowing life to touch us and pass through. Another advantage of autonomy is in our capacity to encounter the unknown. To a great extent, the unknown is that which we wish and yearn for on our spiritual journey, but it is frightening. Mindfulness confronts us with this fear and at the same time shows us the way to cope with it. In melting down our armour, we are exposed to experiences we might otherwise have avoided.

We can go much further: to die all the time – to die to the past, to what was, to what we want or fear things to be, to who we think we are – and with it go all our fears and expectations and even our hopes. It is the deepest form of letting go of our attachments. We can practise dying through different forms of meditation and guided imagery in which we intentionally imagine the ultimate vulnerability, stay with it, and gradually allow it to transform and liberate us. We don't need a skeleton in the cupboard. We need it there dangling in our living room. This way we can fully and completely realize the fragility and impermanence of the body and lessen our identification with it as well as our illusions of ownership of it. If we are able to be free in the places where the most difficult emotions and feelings arise, we know that we have truly become an island in the stormy seas, not only for ourselves but for all others. We have truly come back home.

PART THREE
HOW TO AWAKEN

(*PANNYA*)

CHAPTER 29

THE EYE OF WISDOM AND THE MAGIC OF THE MOMENT

"And now here is my secret, a very simple secret: It is only with the heart that one can see rightly; what is essential is invisible to the eye."

(Antoine de Saint-Exupéry, *The Little Prince*)

"You are the world"; "The world is looking out of your eyes". From a logical point of view such statements make no sense. And more than that, they tend to turn the brain around. From the wisdom point of view they make a lot of sense, and turning the brain around is joyful. These ideas represent a kind of knowing that is global, inclusive and relational. Any authentic spiritual journey that is genuine and deep will move from the dualistic and automatic assumptions about reality based on our thoughts, our interests, and our views, to a non-dual awareness. From separation to inclusiveness. This is not easy, because all our life we've been growing a thinking brain that appears to confirm a given real world, and this seems to be more or less hard-wired in the brain.

For example, in our internal world we may have a constant nagging self-critical and judgemental voice that convinces us that we are small, we can't do this or that, we are failing. But with clarity and wisdom we would see that it's just one of the endless possible narratives that are passing through the consciousness. It's just a painful view, with no reality, although of course there will be a tendency to look for, and so to find, daily proof of it in the world. Another example would be the certainty we feel that we need ambition and desire to succeed and get on in life. It's a view that life is a battleground, and stress is a necessary byproduct. The wisdom view would see that life is just unfolding moment by moment, and in a natural spontaneous way we will respond and align ourselves with what seems right and appropriate. It's a much bigger freer view that could be just as successful in the real world of daily challenges, such as in the workplace, but with far less of a struggle against events. Another example is physical pain. We view it as a fact – solid, real and unpleasant – and so tend to be exclusively concerned with stopping it, taking medicines to shut it up, measuring it, complaining about it and giving it the power to turn us into a victim. There is a closed relationship between me as the sufferer and this external nuisance called the pain. A wisdom view would be to hold such an unpleasant experience with kindness, mindfulness and a readiness to meet it directly. It would be clear that there are uncomfortable pain sensations, but we can drop all the projections and identifications and constructions we make from them. They will lose their dominance. In actual fact the entire world seems to be real, something known and a fact. Yet here too the wisdom view, backed indeed by modern brain sciences, understands that this is somewhat of a delusion, expressed by the Sanskrit word *maya*, and that actually the world that we think we know is a consensus assumption, based on learned responses and conclusions, impressed deeply into the brain and consciousness by conditioning. The world we apparently perceive is a representation engraved in neural networks, an appearance that arises as a result of internal processing. What's really out there without processing is pure mystery. The things we take for granted as facts, such as the body or the tree in the garden, are more unknown than known entities. There is a Theravada Buddhist quote that says: "Whatever we conceive it to be, the reality is other than that." In other words – if it's not mysterious, it's not true.

Buddhist practice to realize this wisdom has three broad avenues: *sila, samadhi, pannya*. *Sila* is essentially ethical behaviour. But it's much more than that. It's the practice of maintaining a beneficial relationship with the world, and purifying our consciousness by living in harmony with all of life. In particular, it means reducing suffering by not harming, not taking, and being kind to ourselves and all beings. As most of the harm that we cause is not the result of ill-will, but rather inattention, *sila* is the practice of awareness of how we talk, think and act toward ourselves and others. This already brings us to a place of awareness and sensitivity as we look carefully at ourselves and other creatures and understand how not to hurt them. *Samadhi* is meditation and presence, gathering ourselves together and settling in the present moment of experience. It is about concentrating and steadying the mind. *Pannya* is wisdom. A transcendental, immediate and global kind of knowing. *Pannya* emphasizes the interconnection of things with each other rather than their separation and definition. It is not a neutral or analytical academic knowing, but the insight that frees us. It liberates and expands consciousness and so has juice and the power to change your life. It is not merely what we know but the elevating *Ah-ha!* moments that change the way we live. It is also not something that I can "have" – wisdom cannot be owned by anybody or belong to anybody. Wisdom also joins together the heart, which is expansive and inclusive, and the mind, which tends to discriminate and separate. When we see and understand the frightened eyes of another person, it is both heart and mind that understand the situation and then *sila* follows with an appropriate word or action. In Sanskrit this wisdom or knowledge is called *vidya*, and *rigpa* in Tibetan. Jiddu Krishnamurti once said: "There is no path to truth and there are not two truths. Truth is not of the past nor of the present. It is timeless. Truth is a state of being which arises when the mind which seeks to divide, to be exclusive, which can think only in terms of results of achieving things, has come to an end." What does that mean? When he refers to the dividing mind he means the conventional mind. It is possible to see things totally differently.

We may think that wisdom is a luxury, which can be left to the spiritual astronauts. Not so, it is a necessity. We can't live without it. It is almost a Buddhist dogma that suffering is rooted in ignorance; not in the circumstances of life but how we view them. Ignorance is the way we construct our world and then forget how we have done so; we take the construction to be the reality. We just need to think for a moment about how the immense suffering and inconceivable death and destruction in armed conflicts are sustained through delusory views of a righteous us and an evil them that we regard as true.

There is an old folk tale of a simple-minded man who ordered a suit from a tailor. The tailor measured him and told him to come back in two weeks and it would be ready. He came back and tried on the jacket. It didn't fit. One sleeve was longer than the other. The buttons were not aligned. However, the tailor said if you bend your body and tilt your shoulders all will be fine. Then he tried on the trousers and the length of the legs was unequal. Never mind, said the tailor, just bend to one side. And the crotch wasn't comfortable. But the tailor said it'll be ok, you just twist your walk and walk with unequal steps. The customer believed the tailor, and limped and stumbled in his new suit into the park. Two men were sitting on a bench. They looked at him. "Poor cripple," one said. "But he has a beautiful suit," said the other.

We limp through life inside our coverings. The suit we wear is the set of conditions that we struggle to adapt to. We depend on so many things: love and acceptance, money, food, health, comforts, entertainment. It makes us feel that we are on automatic pilot, that life is just about coping, functioning, working, having children, getting old and then it is over. The good news is that we do have the wisdom eye inside every one of us, from childhood. It's the source of our search for meaning, for release and a way out. It's the source of our natural longing for freedom and joy. It's inside our hopes and prayers. We can find it in the sense of freedom on an early morning walk by the sea, the breathtaking beauty of the mountains, the total absorption of falling madly in love, the understanding and reflection on why we suffer, and where there is meaningfulness in our lives.

The age-old Biblical myth of the Garden of Eden expresses it powerfully. Original man, meaning us, ate, meaning internalized, the fruit of the tree of knowing good and bad. Knowing, that is our mind, becomes occupied with good and bad *for me*. The fruit of this tree is dualism, interests, separation. When we consume it we find ourselves exiled from paradise. Once I'm out of Eden, it is hard to get back in. As the Bible relates, there is a guardian that protects Eden who wields a twirling sword that cuts things into pieces. We need to avoid this sword of separation, division and distinction, to get back to perfection. But there is another tree at the centre of the Garden of Eden: the tree of life. This is beyond our interests, preferences and dualities. It's not personal. The minute I say I want the tree of life, I've lost it. When we have a point of view of life and not a point of view of what is good for me or bad for me, we'll find ourselves back in Eden, basking under the tree of life.

What kind of inner practice and experiences can take us on the journey past the sword to re-enter paradise? What can we do to go from ordinary limited knowing to *pannya*, universal unlimited knowing? There are many ways to uncover this wisdom. One of them is to realize the dynamic and vital nature of what we previously thought was fixed and solid and uninteresting, something that we never paid attention to. For example, when we look at a breath deeply, with a caring investigative mind, we see that it is a whole universe that is constantly in movement. There are no two breaths the same. The journey of the life-giving air into and out of the body is a river of sensations and experiences. It has a constantly changing texture – short, long, contracted, expanded, rough, smooth, deep, shallow. It has mind and body in it; we can influence it and yet it happens by itself. We have an intimate relationship with the breath – it tells us about ourselves. We see the beauty and mystery of the flow of life in our bodies.

The same is true with pain. Indeed it is unpleasant, but when closely observed it unpacks itself to reveal a rich resource for insight, and a path to free ourselves from its control. What is the changing field of sensations that make up the experience that we usually label as a nasty and unwanted "thing"?

What are its boundaries, centre, texture, movements, waves, beginnings and endings, sharpness, strength and influence on us? What are our responses, our actions, thoughts and feelings that arise along with the sensations? What narratives do we use to explain it? What patterns are elicited by it? Can we embrace it with kindness instead of trying to shut it up and get rid of it? How do we regard ourselves because of it, as victim or as disempowered? In one of my evening classes some time ago, in the middle of the meditation, a woman suddenly burst into floods of tears. At the end of the meditation everyone said: "What happened, why are you crying?" And she said: "I am 55 years old, I have five children at home and I am in constant pain with my hip, which I cannot do anything about except take pills. All my life I've been a victim. I've just done what people told me, what my doctors told me, what my children and husband told me; serving everybody. I thought that was what I was meant to do. But during meditation I began to explore the pain in my hip and it actually started to move and change and come and go. And all of a sudden I realized that I actually had power to influence my body that I never thought I had. I felt more empowered than I have for years. If I can change my pain myself, I'm not a victim any more!"

Another path that reveals wisdom is to challenge boundaries. The mind is only interested in differences and changes, as that is the way it pieces together an apparent world and calls it reality. We can actually see things only because our eyes are in constant movement. The sound of traffic or white noise of distant cities vanish as experiences because they are constant and background. But more deeply, every interaction through the senses and the mind just reveals connections and relationships, otherwise nothing would be knowable. The shape-shifting clouds above, the touch of the leaves as we prepare a salad, the concerts of the birds in our ears, the body that responds and the mind that knows all this – they are all participators in the dance. They do not define boundaries, they dissolve them. If we look carefully, it is not at all clear where I end and the world begins, what the difference is between the world outside and that inside. Boundaries are protective walls built and maintained by an unconscious and often left-brained mental effort. They are unreal constructions. It is a social and individual agreement that we live in a country, it has a boundary called a border, and we have a national identity. But if you look at the planet from space, where is the boundary? It doesn't exist. It's a mental construction that is believed to be a fact. When we walk on the grass under our feet, with the tree in front of us, the birds singing, and the sky hanging above – where are we separate and where are we together? Where do we end and where does the rest of the world begin? If we see that and even live it, it is a radical transformation. It opens the wisdom mind right there. As Thich Nhat Hanh said, the miracle is not to walk on water, it is to walk on this green earth.

The wisdom eye does need us to step out of the usual habits of seeing and knowing. It invites us to look with fresh eyes, and be prepared to live with much more uncertainty, to be friends with the unknown and the mysterious. As in the quote from *The Little Prince*, what is important may not be what is usually visible – but what is invisible may not be readily apparent. To look at the moon is easy, to know what joins us and the moon is more subtle. But we need to look at the moon to sense what is happening between us and the moon. In other words, the invisible is inside the visible, it just needs the wisdom eye. The kind of seeing that will open the door to the mystery needs a persistent and penetrating gaze. But it also needs trust, perhaps a bit of faith and some courage, because we cannot hunt for the invisible, we need to surrender into it. And even if it is difficult and unfamiliar to begin with, our dedication to uncover the truth works steadily, and we slowly come to realize that "if it is not mysterious, it is not true".

We sometimes feel that there is something missing in our life. There is. Us. We need to be less occupied with being this somebody, and feel instead the timeless direct connection with the air we breathe, and the grass under our feet. When our heart is lifted by the singing of the birds, we and they are joined together in that moment, a magical moment of completeness in which nothing is missing and everything is present. This is the sign of the wisdom mind. And it is available at all moments. We may be doing the washing up in the kitchen and thinking that we need to go and read a very important spiritual book about Buddhism. But what the Buddha actually said is: be the water, the touch of the plates, the movement of our hands, the sense of the space around, two feet on the ground, the whole cosmos right there with me and the washing up.

The good news about *pannya* is it's not all or nothing. There is a common view that we are down here in ordinary misery, and we have to work intensely to reach a celestial nirvana up there, which happens to very few lucky ones who leap into bliss with a kind of explosive transformation. So let's forget views about nirvana and just let the wisdom eye constantly expand its insight. And a little bit goes a long way. It gives us a taste of the fruit of the tree of life. Right now.

CHAPTER 30

THOUGHTS: FOAM ON THE WAVES

How can a story
Float up from nothing?
Or are stories always born
From other stories?
What are thoughts?
Orphaned noisy children?
Angels bearing gifts?
Demons wielding swords?
Thoughts are radiant ions
Weaving illusion
Out of pure light
Arising from nothing
Returning to nothing
And in between
Signifying the world.
So raid the unknown
Love the womb
Not just the baby
And let the power of nothing
Reveal everything.

CHAPTER 31
EQUANIMITY: SURFING THE WAVES OF CHANGE

There is no doubt that we are living in times of unprecedented anxiety. Besides the personal narratives of conflict, disease, pain and loss, there are global concerns, for example we may not be sure if the world itself can go on supporting us and our children as it has done up until now. Often we forget what ease, inner peace and complete joy really feel like. I am reminded of the joke about a telegram sent by a perennially anxious mother to her son on holiday: "Start worrying, details to follow." We often turn for help to pills or diversions such as the computer screen or shopping.

Clearly we cannot expect life to endlessly provide us with comfort and security. Nor can we rely on others to provide it. Faced with the constant uncertainty and concern about what is happening or may happen we have no option but to find the resources of trust and steadiness from within. And of course they are there inside, waiting to be invited. Think of the way we started life – the complete trust we had in our mothers, in the world we explored without hesitation. I have watched amazed as my two-year-old granddaughter allows herself to fall asleep in almost anyone's arms, and how if she falls down off a step, she will feel pain, cry, and get right back on it again. Of course, fear accumulates in life as we learn to be watchful of ourselves. But trust is there in equal measure.

As discussed in chapter 28, trust can be developed and is a major spiritual force. It is worth repeating here that trust as a profound and powerful attitude of the heart and mind is not a trust that things will be good or better, because we cannot control the future, and such a trust would lead to expectation and disappointment. But it is a shift toward an active trusting of the world to be what it is, to feel a sense of belonging and intimacy with life whatever it throws at us. After all, it is in the end up to us how we receive the "slings and arrows of outrageous fortune". Trust is developed by being mindful of the fact that the world is not against us and that we can change our inner climate. Mindfulness also shows us the joy of openness and relationships with nature and people, versus the pain of shutting ourselves inside a prison of our fears.

Equanimity is this trust combined with insight and non-attachment. In order to trust the world to be what it is, we need to be less wrapped up in ourselves, less protected by armour, we need to be engaged, open, light and free. It is to be vulnerable and sensitive, yet never knocked down; ready to welcome whatever comes our way. It is about surfing the waves of change, not running away from them, or shutting ourselves in some apparently safe haven or in a comfort zone such as social media. Equanimity is not indifference, although sometimes the two are confused. While equanimity is getting wet and riding the waves, indifference is shutting ourselves in the air-conditioned hotel room nearby. Equanimity is letting the world in. The door is open. Indifference is keeping the world out. The door is kept shut.

How can we develop equanimity? Partly it is the result of all the spiritual practice that we have ever done, which involves seeing things more clearly. Sitting silently in meditation for extended periods automatically leads to equanimity as we learn to stay steady and receive whatever comes. In addition there are directions of practice that can specifically develop this resilience. "Let our meditation be like the earth," said the Buddha, "for then satisfying and unsatisfying contacts with the world through the senses will not invade the mind." We may be in the most problematic situation – whether in the midst of a family crisis, under overwhelming pressure to achieve something, in pain or sickness, or simply caught in the overstimulating honey trap of the shopping mall – a bigger, more universal, and less personal awareness will bring another perspective to it all. We will feel every nuance of the situation but will not be knocked over by it, since there is a much vaster world holding it all. Indeed the experience of the great mother earth under our feet does ground us and we feel more ballast like a great ship instead of a little boat rocked by huge waves. It gives us a sense of taking our place on this earth, without wobbling.

Equanimity is always helped by the big view. That is, a sense that conditions and conditionality create results accordingly, and though we can chart a wise course and navigate toward harmony, we also need to surrender. There is a Tibetan story that illustrates this. Two men were walking in a crowded marketplace. All of a sudden one of them was hit by a stick. He began to shout at the stick. His friend said to him: "Why are you shouting at the stick? Wouldn't it be more sensible to shout at the hand holding the stick?" He agreed, and began shouting at the hand. "But why are you shouting at the hand? Maybe you should shout at the person whose hand it is?" said his friend. So he began shouting at the unknown person who hit him. "But why are you shouting at the person?" his friend asked him. "Maybe that person has had a really hard time, and can't help expressing some of his frustration. Maybe he hasn't had anything to eat for a while. Maybe you should shout at the conditions that caused that person to behave like that." The man who was hit was just about to shout at the conditions, but then he stopped. "But that means there is nothing to shout at – I would need to shout at the whole universe!" he exclaimed. "Exactly!" said his friend. Once we see that everything is caused by endless conditions, there is nothing left to shout about.

We cannot be hurt if we are light and free within ourselves. The doors are open, the windows are open, cold winds do blow in, but they just blow through us. When faced with the rage of someone, for example, we may feel the energy, heat and vibration in the body-mind, but it doesn't stick. Like the grasses, we may bend but we cannot break.

CHAPTER 32

EMPTINESS: "THE MORE POOH LOOKED, THE MORE PIGLET WASN'T THERE"

Soon after the Buddha's awakening during that long night under the banyan tree, he turned to his five companions, now his disciples, and offered some powerful arguments that deconstruct the view that there is an inherent permanent self that dwells within us like the operating system of the computer. Though it seems to be obvious that we exist, the Buddha pointed out that this was a belief and not a fact. Existence exists but is there a need for an "I" that seems to own it? How can there be a "me" as a "thing" or entity, if everything I experience as me is in constant flux and change, and if everything I experience as me is a conglomerate, or aggregate, of impressions, memories, consciousness, shapes, bodily forms, needs, beliefs, labels and so on? Further, I can't control these phenomena that arise and pass on their own, so if I can't control them they can't be mine, even though they seem to be in me. There is a deep riddle in all this. Maybe my "self" is less of an object or entity that I own and more of a kaleidoscope of constantly shifting colours?[1]

There is no doubt that every waking moment I seem to experience myself as a centre of operations, a boundary, a biography, a huge collection of memories, an identity different from others, and a sense of coherence or control, without which I wouldn't be able to survive for a moment – how could I cross a busy street without getting run over if I wasn't an entity that looked after itself? It seems to be a continuous sense that is running the show during all waking hours and even in sleep: an unquestioned fact. But the fact of self is an illusion, a fiction. The only fact is the experience of self, not its inherent existence. As Winnie the Pooh said, if we look for "it" we never find it. In the Pali language, belief in the existence of a self is called *atta,* and the discovery of its illusory nature or transparency is *anatta.*

Does this matter? Isn't all this discussion and exploration and thinking about whether there is or is not a self a conceptual entertainment? Is it important? It is actually vital, and not at all theoretical. First, because this belief in myself is the origin of most of the pain and suffering in my life. It is me (not my body) that gets depressed and bored, me that day and night needs its desires fed and its dislikes avoided. It is me that is terrified of dying, getting lost, being put down by others, being helpless and irrelevant, all of which are kinds of ego death. It is me that is running, busy, unbalanced, angry, disappointed, lonely, failing and feeling ill. All conflict is based on the self, which starts off as a mechanism to protect the body and ends up mostly in protecting itself. Every potential threat to my views, ideas and boundaries, every possible challenge not only to the personal me, but to my family, my nation, my skin colour, my religion, my political system, my resources, is enough for the collective me to spiral into spasms of violence. Clearly every human suffering is experienced by and often caused by an individual and collective me, so all in all it seems a huge burden to believe in one. As Wei Wu Wei wrote: "Why are you unhappy? Because 99.9 per cent of everything you think, and of everything you do, is for yourself – and there isn't one."

The second issue is that an attachment to self leads to a life of illusion. For example, though we do feel some kind of consistent thread on which the beads of our daily experiences are strung, can I really be the same as in the photograph of when I was three years old? Am I the same me as I was even yesterday? Am I the same me if I forget who I am because of Alzheimer's? What kind of me am I when I am asleep? Or drunk? Or in love? Indeed where is this major entity that is controlling and often ruining our lives? Can we point to it? Can we see it? Hold it? Can we even identify the identity? Both Buddhist and Western psychological and philosophical reflections on the self come to the conclusion that it is not a thing but a process. The sense of identity is a dynamic response in the brain that is constantly being recreated. I am not a Stephen, I am "Stephening" myself every moment. But as this is unconscious or automatic we don't see this process happening, so we assume or believe in an apparently solid and consistent me.

A further issue is quite vital, or quite irrelevant, depending on how far we are ready to go in spiritual development. It is that if we see life exclusively from the point of view of me, the person, we are blinkered. It creates a kind of mask or veil through which we can hardly catch a glimpse of a spiritual vision. It is as if we walk about with our hand covering our eyes, and can't see more than tiny glimpses of the light through the fingers. Spiritual realization is seeing from an ultimate and universal point of view. Enlightenment is impersonal – it cannot be owned by anyone. It is true that there is a great deal of positive change that can happen to "us" through inner growth, and there are beautiful qualities that we can develop, such as trust and joy, and kindness, and they mostly do feel they belong to us and are manifested by us. Yet there is the transpersonal, and then the universal, beyond them.

How did this self grow to be such a giant control freak inside us? Where did it come from? It is obvious that babies start out without a sense of self. The child and the world are one. Even though they can cry when the milk isn't there, they don't take it personally! And when they are at the breast, deep quiet, satisfaction and peace quickly returns and wraps both baby and mother. But as the child grows, he or she becomes a self and the world becomes other, "out there". The process is one of withdrawal and separation, of "othering". You cannot tell the child: "Stop! Beware! Don't withdraw into a self!" It's impossible. And most unwise. A healthy self is a necessity, like a healthy body. Indeed, all beings down to the tiniest amoeba are in some way creating and protecting themselves. In Sanskrit this is called *ahamkara*, which means I-making activity. We need to be comfortable with functioning as somebody, which is a necessary response in order to survive as a living being. It is a kind of operating system of the mental computer. But it is still not a thing. It is a convenient fiction.

There appears to be a "me" and a "you", an "us" the collective identity and "them" who are unfortunately mostly regarded as a threat. A wall of protection is built. And we live behind it and experience it as fear, anxiety and insecurity, the primary emotions of defence, as the self wants to persist as somebody and not disappear back into the world again. We hang onto the self as if our lives depended on it, because we indeed believe that is the case. But defending the self in the illusion that we are defending life can have disastrous consequences for life. Think of World War I in which millions died often horrible deaths and which was fought because of honour and pride.

As we withdraw from the world we make the world – it too becomes an apparent entity that can be named, described, conceived and interpreted. Becoming someone creates a here and a there, an inside and an outside, and indeed all the boundaries that are relative to a sense of self. For example, we are all absolutely sure that our body finishes with its skin. But we forget that it is something learned not an absolute truth. I have recently been engaged in research in which the researchers asked me to repeatedly experience and describe boundaries and then boundless awareness without self. They analysed these experiences deeply and also measured with delicate equipment where this happens in the brain. Indeed there does appear to be a part of the brain that is mainly concerned with self and boundaries.[2] The body is actually experienced nowhere else other than in the mind, and boundary-making is deeply ingrained in the mind. Boundaries and borders are in the mind, not in reality. It is like countries – they are concepts not realities and therefore an experience not a fact.

I was teaching in a Krishnamurti school in Varanasi in India for a year in 1991. The school was next to the Varuna river. There was bridge from the school to a poor Indian village on the other side. I asked what the name of the village was and was told: *Ispa*. When I asked the villagers what that meant they said "The Other Side", as opposed to the Krishnamurti Centre that was called "This Side" (*Uspa*). Over time the disparaging name for their own place had become the common usage.

The senses are gateways to let the world in, but then it is processed into facts by the mind. As we listen to the barking of a dog, or gaze at a tree, the senses could actually show us that we and the world are one, merged together, but the mind comes in with its own habits and defines the sound as a bark and places the dog far away and defines the tree as a tree and puts it over there. This creates an apparently known world, but we are ignorant of the way we build the world through perceptions. Here is one of my short poems that hints at this process:

> A new bird arrives
> Calls a strange cry
> In the stillness
> Sound cuts silence
> Is that the way the world is made?
> Is that the way the world is known?

This powerful "selfing" tendency of all of us and indeed of all living beings is driven, supported and maintained by grasping and attachment. This is most obvious when we grasp onto who we would like to become – we want to be more successful, richer, happier, or we may want to be in a loving relationship, to be a parent, more contented at work, to own a car or a house. It is less obvious but still the same process if we would not like to become something, such as bored, depressed or lonely. Any kind of holding on or grasping to any desire will confirm the sense of me, even if, or especially if, we get what we want. The clearest example of this is the desire to be liked and respected, to have a role and to belong to a group. I remember as a child I knew nothing about football as we did not have a television. I felt excluded as all the other kids seemed to support a team except me. So I randomly chose one (Wolverhampton Wanderers actually, about which I knew nothing except that I liked the name) and then began to shout for them as if I knew what they were, and suddenly felt somebody again. When we grasp something we give it existence. Our wanting to be makes us be. It makes us the main actor in our own play.

If we closely examine how this happens in the mind, it starts with the direct sense experience of seeing, tasting and so on. Messages are picked up that cause an immediate felt response, a turning toward or away from, a first seed of desire or aversion. For example, a new car that we like, a person that we admire, an advert that promises something, a smell or taste or unpleasant feeling that we want to avoid, a thought of inadequacy or judgement. These needs – grasping, holding on, or wanting more – follow well-worn tracks in the mind and heart and dig them in deeper. They affirm narratives and stories that make up our stream of consciousness, which supports and strengthens our identity and sense of self and boundary. It all happens quickly and the arrival of a sense of ownership, that it is happening to me, seems hard-wired. There seems something inevitable about the way these tracks (in the Pali language *sankhara*) are laid down – the mind has a kind of thirst for defining the world and making an identity.

A poignant example is the never-ending drive for more comfort, improvement, wealth, happiness and control. It seems natural that we want to fulfil our potential, to achieve something, and to succeed. It is obvious that we have problems we need to solve, painful patterns (*sankharas*) engraved in both body and mind that we need to mend. And working on ourselves is not a bad thing in itself and can bring great benefits, to others as well. But there may be hidden costs too. We derive security from developing and improving, but if we reached a state of perfection such that we didn't need to develop and improve any more, wouldn't all motivation just cease? Many may ask: "How can I get up in the morning if I feel life is ok just as it is and nothing needs to be changed?" But it is worth remembering that the planet is being destroyed through the addiction to economic growth and my own satisfaction is dependent on its good health.

I was asked recently why I constantly travel to teach dharma if I feel the world is fine as it is. I responded that if I had to teach as a way of fixing the world I would be exhausted in a year, and I would have to stop. I teach it from love, I teach it from relationship, I teach it from being. Dharma comes from the look in the eyes of the audience as we share the truth, not from any feeling that the world needs me to change it. When I teach, language is emerging and there is a space of listening together in the present moment. As long as there is no pressure to become something, to take on and fit a role, then I don't feel that I have to be perfect, or perform well, or expect rewards. When we don't dance according to the tune of the Pied Piper of the self, the question of what motivates us to get up in the morning is turned on its head. How can I get up in the morning if I feel constantly driven by a sense that there is something wrong with me and I need to be fixed. I would get up out of bed only to head to the nearest pub or psychologist!

But surely, you may ask, how can I learn dharma and grow spiritually without "becoming" a practitioner or student, how can I develop without the desire to go beyond what I am now? It is true, there is effort needed to practise especially at the beginning of the journey, and this is a form of becoming, a role, but slowly we can use becoming to undo becoming. A lot of energy is needed to launch a rocket against the resistance of gravity, but as it gets higher there is less pulling back and so less effort is needed. This is why the dharma teachings are called a raft that you let go of when you reach the other shore. The teaching has to be applied until it can be abandoned as no longer needed. It gets subtle and paradoxical when we develop an awareness that sees through and lightens this heavy me and mine. As G K Chesterton once said:

"Angels can fly because they take themselves lightly."[3] But here too we can be wise and be careful of a subtle drive for non-existence, which is no different from running after existence. Not liking ourselves, feeling guilt, denial, or cloudy states of disconnection and alienation, may seem like not-self but they are actually drives for non-existence. When becoming ceases, you don't run after anything. When the self arises it arises, and when it doesn't – it disappears. Everything is perfect. No problem. You don't need to construct self, and you don't need to construct not-self.

Instead of trying to stop our compulsions, the wisdom of the dharma invites us to see the pain of them – they turn into our teachers instead of our problems. Our struggle to deal with this shifting unreliable world by means of needs, desires, aversions, conflicts, craving and attachments is fundamentally unsatisfying, even painful. Then we have a possibility of letting it all go, of untying ourselves from it. The Buddha talked about it as a tangle. How do you untangle the tangle? It is mainly about freeing ourselves to fully experience the present moment just as it unfolds, which is spontaneous, quiet and doesn't carry the need to fix or change or add anything. It is not about being Alexander the Great and heroically cutting the Gordian knot with our sword, but just not giving it a lot of interest or belief. This striving to become free and spiritual can be helpful initially, but it can just replace one solid identity with another, and also there may be no end to it: "I'm not spiritual enough"; "I first have to deal with these fears, these problems, these issues, and then …"; "I need a better technique, a more effective teacher, a quicker path". But one of the most powerful and beautiful aspects of the dharma practice is its emphasis on the realization of the essential freedom that exists in the moment. This moment cannot be other than free. It's only the grasping that makes it appear to be bound. So if we drop the grasping and the present moment is revealed, as it is, arising and passing, then we cut through the whole thing. We unbind the chain.

Thanissaro Bikkhu, in *The Paradox of Becoming*, writes:

Right view contains the tools to help dismantle both the sense of self and the concepts of existence and non-existence, thus undercutting any question of whether a self exists. Thus it is the only form of view that can be used ultimately to undercut all types of clinging and the types of becoming that might form around it.

It's useful to examine in detail how this happens. In its purest form, right view forces the mind to view the aggregates and sense media simply as events arising and passing away – as they have come to be. As the mind stays in this mode of perception, it abandons the most basic assumptions that underlie becoming and non-becoming – the idea of "my self" as well as the ideas of the existence and non-existence of the world. This leaves the mind free to focus exclusively on events simply as they have come to be, thus avoiding issues of becoming and non-becoming altogether.

The mind arrives at this point not through the force of logic or sheer will power, but through the simple fact that these assumptions don't even occur to the mind as it stays in this mode. With these assumptions abandoned, one cannot fashion any views around the existence or non-existence of a self in any world at all. Thus there is no place in the content of views for clinging to land.[4]

Take the mindfulness exercise of eating a raisin. When the raisin enters the mouth and there arises a moment of tasting, feeling its texture, and knowing all our responses, there is no hint of "raisinlessness". The raisin world is simply arising as it is. It doesn't occur to you that you should shut it down and try and stop this experience. When the experience of the raisin disappears, in this moment, with right understanding, the raisin and its taste no longer exist and there is no need to resurrect them. Their existence doesn't occur to you. In the spontaneous present moment, it doesn't occur to you to make a story out of being and non-being. Just like the total lack of interest in cigarettes after the addiction to them has completely finished. It doesn't interest you any more to create a stronger "me" out of experiences that come and go.

As the Buddha said to the monk Kaccayana:

> In general, this world is supported by and depends
> on a polarity of notions of existence or non-existence.
> However, when one sees the arising of things as they
> appear, as they really are, with a right understanding,
> then notions of non-existence, not-being, don't occur
> to you. And when one sees the passing of things as
> they really are with right understanding, then notions
> of existence do not occur to you … By and large,
> Kaccayana, this world is in slavery to attachments, to
> clinging, and to bias. But one who has this view doesn't
> get involved with, or cling to these attachments, or
> fixations of awareness, or biases, or obsessions, and
> nor is he determined to be a self … He's not depending
> on anything.[5]

All this can be quite scary. We are attached to being ourselves, which is familiar safe territory that we are afraid will disappear. One time during a retreat in India I had the feeling that I was on the edge of an abyss – wanting but unable to leap into a frightening but compelling place of emptiness, way beyond the known me. Something deep stopped me. I shared this with a teacher there and he recommended that if I visited the edge again and again, and even just abided there, the fear would go. I never jumped. Because I realized there was no abyss. The fear of the unknown and some projections about non-self itself created the abyss and the longing to jump. But truth is not an abyss and there is no need to jump into it – you can just let the truth reveal itself to you. It is more like dropping than jumping, similar to the metaphor that the mindfulness teacher Joseph Goldstein once shared of jumping out of a plane without a parachute. It is so frightening at first. But then you realize, in this case, that there's no ground below. So you can relax and let go and fly free.

Being with the passing moment rather than the strain of controlling life and constant "home improvements" of our fictional selves is joyful, it is the bliss of floating in the ocean instead of being helplessly whirled around in the whirlpool. Everything gets easier if you do not consider yourself to be the lead actor in your life. The full lived experience in the moment does not need anything more. Life is dance. And this is not an invitation to passivity or withdrawal back into the cave – you can have a very active life, and be dancing right in the middle of a full working day. If you take yourself more lightly, everything else lightens up around you, and you can also infect those around you with that cheerful sense of freedom too.

This change is quite hard to describe in words, which are descriptions, distinctions and conceptual forms based on an agreed world and a self. Nirvana is the quenching of the fires that burn us up, but in a traditional Buddhist image, when the fire goes out, no one can tell you where it has gone, in which direction it has gone, or what it looks like when it's gone. We live in the world of concepts including concepts about dharma. So when we ourselves cool down, it can be a subtle experience, it may not be definable or understandable, or it may be experienced as not knowing, as paradox, or as spaces that the world of concepts doesn't like very much. This is the real meaning of emptiness. And this why emptiness is not at all a good word to describe it and leads us back into concepts that don't work. Remaining in silence is better there.

The Buddha was asked once how you can recognize an awakened person. He answered that you can recognize them because they are unfindable. The questioner was understandably confused by this and asked for an explanation. The Buddha replied: "When a person has gone beyond, then there is nothing by which you can measure them. All that can be said about them is no longer relevant, yet you cannot say that they no longer exist. When all ways of being, all phenomena are removed, then all ways of description have also been removed."[6]

Buddhist teaching does not give truth or solidity to the world, but regards it as a conditioned reality, a mutual agreement. The only things we can really know are what is arising through the senses and via the mind. And this is in constant flow and change. But the mind itself is just a centre of knowing, it doesn't go anywhere or have its own agendas or boundaries. It is still. Coming and going is received by a still mind, including the coming and going of a sense of me, and of time, place and movement. The dialogue between stillness and movement was expressed beautifully by the great Thai teacher Ajahn Chah who said that if your mind is peaceful it will be like "still, flowing water".[7]

CHAPTER 33

NOT THIS NOT THAT: THE MIDDLE WAY

A basic objection to any kind of extremism or radicalism is a corner stone of Buddhist teachings. In fact The Middle Way has become a commonly used title for the whole path. Defining the middle way as a place of the middle, we may see it wrongly as a weak compromise, but according to the Buddha it is not a compromise but the best and wisest place to be. A beautiful story about the life of the Buddha illustrates this unique place (see also the story of the Buddha's extreme asceticism told in chapter 24).

Gautama, later to be the Buddha, felt stuck in his practice during his ascetic period in which he virtually starved himself to death in his search for enlightenment. Suddenly, he remembered that once, as a child, he was sitting under a tree on a beautiful sunny day while his father was supervising agricultural workers in the fields. He spontaneously fell into deep concentration, peace and happiness. When recalling this, he said to himself: "If I felt this feeling as a child, perhaps nirvana is already within me, and I shall find it again by ease rather than intense striving."[1]

After the night of his awakening, the Buddha taught that liberation from the control of needs does not require self-torture. In the first sutta that he taught immediately after his awakening, he said he was teaching the middle way, also known as the eightfold path. Each of the eight limbs of the path refers to an aspect of human life and activity: right view/ understanding; right intention/thought; right speech; right action; right livelihood; right effort; right mindfulness; right concentration (quieting and collecting the mind). The word "right" in each case is more "rightness", rather than the dualism of right and wrong. The original word, in the Pali language, is *samma*, which means "what is properly developed".

We may have a bit of antipathy and resistance to middles. The middle way may seem something for the middle classes, for older people that are settled and don't like extremes, the bourgeoisie who are scared of wildness, or those who live with moderation. We may think it is a kind of average. Pushing our limits is exciting, adrenalin is addictive when young, and going to extremes made life interesting. I remember that feeling when I was young during the crazy times of the 1960s. Going to extremes, living beyond boundaries and conventional restrictions felt sacred. Religious fundamentalism, which is rearing its ugly head again today, draws its attraction from an intoxication with extremes, which are justified as God-given.

But the Buddhist middle way goes in a different direction – not limitation but liberation! It is by no means a compromise or a golden mean, nor is it a neutral and rather boring mediocre grey between a strong black and white. It holds a deeper meaning. White is the opposite of black and black implies the absence of white, but grey, despite the limits of the word, expresses innumerable shades and possibilities. Just as between black and white there is an infinite number of greys, so a myriad of possibilities exists between two ends, poles or opposites. And all these shades are not easily describable in language or thought that usually conceive things in terms of this opposite that. After all, we cannot really explain the shades of grey; it is a large and changing space. Black and white are the extremes, they are static and defined, but between them is a great river whose essence is paradoxical. A huge literature can be held by two book-ends.

The great Indian philosopher Nagarjuna, who wrote the *Mulamadyamakakarika* in the third century CE, translated by Stephen Batchelor as *Verses from the Center*,[2] was instrumental in making the term "middle way" into a central concept throughout the Buddhist world. Indeed after Nagarjuna, the middle way became a name for the whole Buddhist path. Like the Buddha, Nagarjuna showed us how life is controlled by apparent dualities such as birth and death, existence and non-existence, self and other, come and go, here and there, past and future, appear and disappear. According to him, this is not a wise way to see the world, and brings with it much discomfort and dissatisfaction. These opposites are not the truth. Truth is neither this nor that or *neti, neti*, which means "not this, not that". This phrase is an ancient Vedic understanding and also a spiritual and analytic practice of the negation of all dualities, which brings on the realization that what is left is just the absolute. For example, it seems to us that birth and death limit our lives, and they occupy us incessantly. But they are real and important only from the point of view of the individual's dramatic preoccupation with survival, not from the point of view of the stream of life. No concept is absolute, no duality exists in itself. They all depend on our point of view. What is "here"? Where is it? Here is where someone says "here" but others will say "here" somewhere else.

The middle way is actually a space of presence, of here and now. The mind tends to wander into the future or to the past and to deal with what happened or did not happen and what may happen, or what we want to happen. The middle way between past and future opens out into the great garden of the present. The vastness of possibilities in the now. The balance between the extremes can be found only when we are here and now. When one of the monks asked the Buddha how he crossed the ocean of samsara, the Buddha replied that he crossed it by not struggling and not stopping. He explained that if he struggled, he would be swept away, and if he stopped he would sink. Only by not fighting and not stopping can we reach the other shore.[3]

"The Buddha-dharma is not to be found in moving forwards, nor in moving backwards, nor in standing still. This, Sumedho, is your place of non-abiding."[4] This is what the Thai teacher Ajahn Chah wrote in his last letter to his student, Ajahn Sumedho, now one of the leading teachers of Theravada in the West. The place where you cannot dwell or get stuck implies that you need to let go, go with the stream, since everything is dynamic, and so is the middle way – a dynamic, unfixed way.

As children we have internalized the meaning of "grey" through the process of conditioned learning, the creation and imprinting of mental constructs through which we perceive the world. But in essence "grey" is not a specific thing, and if we hold onto a defined concept of "grey" we are not in the dynamic space of a freer and unlimited vision. The "grey" is a process space, the result of "dependent origination" (*paticcasamuppada* in Pali), a vast and complex network of relationships, conditions and causality by which we create a known self and a known world as a whole. This view perceives grey as a changing experience; the grey of the present moment is different from the grey of the moment before it, and both are the result of all kinds of causes and conditions. So "grey" is only an abstract concept.

A few years ago when I stayed with my family in Varanasi, where my wife and I taught at a Krishnamurti school, we met a teacher there who liked to walk about with children and watch the birds and we went on a trip with him. During the trip we saw a bright blue bird, and the teacher said: "This bird has a very special blue colour." My daughter Tamarin said: "No, no, it's green." The teacher replied: "No, no, it's blue, don't you see – it's blue?" My daughter was insistent, and this exchange continued for several minutes. In the evening, a few hours after we returned to our house, there was a knock at the door. It was the teacher, penitent, who said to my daughter with tears in his eyes: "If you saw green then it was green, if you saw green it's your truth and that's the colour of the bird."

This story illustrates that we build perceptions and knowledge about the world from sensory inputs. We construct a conditioned picture of the world based on memory, learning, habit and agreements between humans on what is conventionally held to be reality, and then keep confirming it. It is generally a world based on interests, preferences and what we want and what we do not want. But when we become aware of the great cycle of life, which is beyond our personal perspectives and concepts, we understand that it is not possible to define and know completely what is "blue" and what is "green". It is a realm of constant surprise, movement and change. It leaves us stunned and silent, dwelling in wisdom that is beyond ideas and concepts.

This is a deeper level of non-duality. It is a more ultimate understanding, independent of place or time, of concepts or assumptions about reality. It is a dynamic and limitless being where all things are interdependent and relate to each other. What is the ultimate middle way in Buddhist practice? There can be several answers to this question, but one lies in the term "right view", which is part of the eightfold path, and can also be translated as a right vision or right seeing. The heart of right view is recognizing that there is actually no duality in the world. We seem to recognize sound because before that there was silence. We know a thought because it arises and was not there before. We know sky because it is above and tree because it is separate from its surroundings – but all of this is a mental operation based on duality. Only thinking creates the division and differentiation – "there is nothing either good or bad, but thinking makes it so" (Shakespeare, *Hamlet*, Act 2, Scene 2). Right view is wisdom that knows interconnectedness rather than thinking that chops the world into discrete pieces. Thinking dualistically will tell us we "own" our body, which is a thing, separate from the rest of the world. Right view will reveal that the body is made of all the elements of the universe, from carbon to water to air, plus all the influences and impressions that have been received, and all is being returned to the universe in a constant two-way flow. The tree is embedded in, and made from, everything else. All things are like diamonds, which reflect and relate to all other things.

The most fundamental duality of all is existence versus non-existence. Obsession with existence, that things are fixed and permanent, is deterministic philosophy. This tends to put us in a jail of a mechanical unchanging world where we have no role or influence. But the obsession with non-existence is just as bad. It is nihilism, in which we are subject to purposeless chaos and there is no point in goodness or action. The perception of these two opposite ends can also be expressed on the deep psychological plane – the most famous dualistic quotation of all time is probably in *Hamlet* again: "To be or not to be, that is the question." The urge to live, the vitality and the will to live, is "positive psychology" as opposed to the urge not to exist, which is a lack of will, depression, self-negation, escapism and denial. But in actual fact, things exist and then don't exist. They arise and they cease. A car passing, a bird passing, a thought passing. Now it is there, now it is not. Now you see it, now you don't. All of this arising and passing is within a dynamic whole, an ultimate dance. Even the concepts of existing or non-existing are relevant only in the dualist world view.

In the *Nidanasamyutta Sutta* the monk Kaccana asks the Buddha what is right view. The Buddha replies:

> This world, Kaccana, for the most part depends upon a duality – upon the notion of existence and the notion of non-existence. But for one who sees the origin of the world as it really is with correct wisdom, there is no notion of non-existence in regard to the world. And for one who sees the cessation of the world as it really is with correct wisdom, there is no notion of existence in regard to the world.
>
> This world, Kaccana, is for the most part shackled by engagement, clinging, and attachment. But one with the right view does not hold onto or become attached to any mental standpoint, adherence, underlying tendency; he does not take a stand about "my self". He has no perplexity or doubt that what arises is only suffering arising, what ceases is only suffering ceasing. His knowledge about this is independent of others. It is in this way, Kaccana, that there is right view. "All exists": Kaccana, this is one extreme. "All does not exist": this is the second extreme. Without veering toward either of these extremes, the Tathagata teaches the Dhamma of the middle way.[5]

Similarly, when the wandering hermit Vacchagotta asked, "Is there a self?"[6] the Buddha did not answer. "If you do not answer, it means that there is no self," responded Vacchagotta. Again the Buddha remained silent. After a while Ananda, the Buddha's attendant, asked him: "Why didn't you answer?" The Buddha replied that a thunderous silence is the correct answer. Because any answer given would give rise to duality. If he had replied that there was a self, his words would have become a belief, an ideology, a proof that the self does exist. If he had answered that there is no self, this answer would also create an ideology, a concept or a "thing" called "emptiness". This is a subtle and elusive matter, so any answer will only be harmful. Silence is better.

Koans are Zen questions designed to break down the assumptions underlying our ordinary conceptual world and take us beyond the known and conventional. A well-known example is: "What is the sound of one hand clapping?" This is a question that has no real answer. The Zen student was required to spend a long time in a continual internal search for answers to unanswerable questions, designed to dismantle mental patterns. Every answer that arises collapses again faced with the same deconstructive questioning. Sudden realization can happen when the mind is exhausted from fruitlessly churning possibilities. Surrender leads to a place of mystery, in which conceptualization breaks down in the face of absolute truth. This is enlightenment.

Consciousness without dualistic perception can shake the familiar ground on which we stand, which we are used to relying on. In this sense, the middle way is like falling between the cracks into enlightenment, into the abyss of infinity. Letting go of duality is like doing a trapeze jump. Between two ends into the space in the middle. A terrifying and yet awesome space opens underneath us when we let go of one safe trapeze and before we grasp the other one. But then we realize that in this case there is nowhere we can fall. There is actually no abyss. There is, in truth, no ground to land on so we cannot get hurt. We float in space. What there is, is *tathata*, which means "suchness" in Sanskrit, just the space of being.

CHAPTER 34
LOVE IS THE ESSENCE

"She loves me! She loves me not! She loves me! She loves me not!" We used to say this as children as we plucked petals off daisies. This is an image of love that is entirely fickle and uncertain. It either happens or not. And it can go as it came. As adults, love can often seem perverse and unreliable. We can love someone close to us, but if they do something that we interpret as threatening to our ego, such as flirting with someone else, our love seems to vanish and in an instant turns into anger and resentment. Or love seems to die with time as we get bored with a partner. Or love that we have for somebody or something becomes a source of suffering, not joy, when it bears no fruit and is not returned or fulfilled. The love that we have for our children can seem to evaporate and give way to despair and friction as soon as they become rebellious teenagers. Usually it comes back, but we may not know that at the time. We may love a beautiful thing, or place, or person, but only if it is ours or connected to us, not if it belongs to someone else. If this is how most of humanity experiences love, how can we talk about love as the essence of life, or love as a universal quality?

If love makes the world go round, how can it come and go according to our moods and experiences? This touches us in the deepest and often the most painful places. How much we wish we could love more! How much we wish we were loved more! Our parental love may have been limited, budgeted, when we were a child. When we go through the pain of separation, or face coldness and distance from partners or family, or the horrors of war and violence, how much we long for a world in which love stays and cannot be destroyed. If "Love is as strong as death", as it says in the *Song of Songs*, why does it disappear so easily?

We need to look a little closer at the picture and understand that the ordinary love that comes and goes is conditioned. That means it is dependent on conditions. One set of conditions opens our heart, another closes it. The conditions that open the heart are often the conditions that make us feel good, feel wanted, feel supported and important. We love when love is returned, we love somebody or something when it is ours. As things get further from us it is much more difficult to love them. We love ourselves and our things most, we love our family a bit less, our friends even less, associates still less, "our" people less again, other people much less, descending until our love for people as a whole is more or less zero. What that means is that love is held hostage by the needs of the self, bound up with the self process. Watch carefully what happens when our love for someone close to us is gradually contaminated, squeezed and eventually banished when we don't get treated with respect, when there are constant arguments, when we get the cold shoulder. Love is replaced by defensiveness and insecurity. We build walls and love can't get out.

So how can it be undone? How can our love flow more freely, more consistently, and less subject to the whims and caprices of circumstance? How can we open our hearts to a greater love? This is a rich question with many kinds and levels of answers. I can suggest a few directions here.

One thing immediately comes to mind. To be honest about what is really happening. To notice the way love comes and goes is already a way to become intimate with the landscape of love. We can feel more in touch with the language of love. Instead of blaming ourselves when our love turns to anger, we can watch the process within us, and emerge somewhat chastened and humbled, and human. When anger bursts out of us at the impossible behaviour of a family member, it can open a wisdom eye within us, and we can feel our own humility. If we feel exhausted, stressed and our heart is closed, it is natural. Just feel it as it is and know that too is the language of the heart telling us about our true condition at that moment. This is the beginning of a deeper love. Another kind of illusion, so often seen, is pretending to have more love than we actually have. Some people talk a lot about love, even universal love, and behave as if they loved everyone, until that person feels threatened, when out comes loads of unconscious anger. Better indeed to see how we lose it. If there is less illusion, there is more love.

Love needs to be paid for, it is not a kind of ecstatic flavour that we can have when we want. We pay for it by constantly tilling the soil of our relationships so that love can grow. What do I mean by that? The respect that we feel and generate for the other person, the understanding of their needs and their life and their difficulties and pains, the ability to put ourselves in their shoes, is cultivation. When we are challenged, can we look the other person in the eye and understand their needs and hidden stories? If so, love will melt the walls that we erect so quickly and automatically. Can we see and appreciate the depths, the feelings, the longings and the hidden worlds within someone we are relating to in the moment, whether the moment is one of togetherness or one of dispute? If so, love won't need to hide.

We may think that the heart acts spontaneously, that we have no control over it, that it should not be played with and that love cannot be constructed or improved. In fact that is not so. Many of the difficulties we have with conditioned love are the due to the blocks and barriers we place in the way of the free flow of the heart. For example, our fears of not being accepted or appreciated can be a constant check on our love, constricting it all the time, throwing doubt on it, freezing it with our fears. We work psychologically or through meditation or other spiritual practices to let go of some of the fears, the old scars and wounds, the blocks and the self-importance. As we do this we are bound to see our love grow and become stronger.

But underneath it all is the potential of a universal love. It is the ground out of which all feelings grow and blossom, whether positive feelings like affection and enthusiasm, or negative feelings like frustration and anger. They grow in the same soil, but the positive are joyful and connected and the negative are painful and bounded. Nonetheless, in the depths of the heart is an immeasurable power that vibrates with all life in kindness and connection. It is too big to be squeezed into the container of the ego. It is love that is without measure and without boundary. It doesn't belong to us and cannot be destroyed if the objects of love change and go. Can this too be developed? The answer is yes. Or to be more precise, it cannot be developed because it is already there. But we can develop our ability to live, experience and join it. In two ways. One we have already mentioned, which is the reduction of the blocks and patterns that keep our love imprisoned. The second way is to learn to extend our love, to reach out with it. A classical Buddhist technique for this is the cultivation of loving kindness, *metta*. This is a meditation practice in which we radiate love first to people who are close to us, which is quite easy, but then we extend the circle and radiate love to those we do not know and even those we do not like, and eventually to all living beings. By extending the circle all the time we learn to unchain our hearts from self-concern, and spread our care wider and wider like a great mother spreading her arms to invite in more and more beings to find shelter. We can do this by repeatedly practising an enduring kindness toward all we meet during the day, whether it is our meetings with ourselves, with the bus driver, our boss at work, or the pigeon on the roof. We can amplify it by using phrases, much the same as a mantra, to trigger the heart to open its walls, such as "may I love and accept myself just as I am right now" or "may you be happy and peaceful".

Sometimes we don't see boundless love because it is so near and we don't recognize it. We look over the top of it at the problematic world. But it is included in the way we know the world. Indeed our knowing is not dry and mechanical, as if we were computers. A wise understanding of the world as it reveals itself to us moment by moment is always full of juice, full of love. "Doubt thou the stars are fire, Doubt that the sun doth move, Doubt truth to be a liar, But never doubt I love" (*Hamlet*, Act 2, Scene 2).

The heart and the mind are utterly intertwined like two trees that have grown into each other. If we develop a free and wide open heart, it feeds our ability to notice life, to take others into account, to live with more engagement and a rich juicy present-moment awareness. When you fall in love the whole world shines back at you. And the opposite. If we are more aware and awake, it activates and fills the heart. For example, if we pay careful attention to the way someone close to us moves their body, the way their thoughts, concerns, joys and pains arise and are expressed in the world, the way their face expresses their inner life, we are bound, through this devoted interest and attention, to love them more. As we notice that small bright flower by the side of the road, the smile of our best friend, our soul brother or sister, or the curious eyes of a child, we are bound to feel that genuine connection, in which we let ourselves go a bit, and feel for the other. In this knowing there is love. In the Bible the same Hebrew word is used for knowing and for making love! Boundless love is embedded in our connection with the world. We just need to notice it. And give it space.

CHAPTER 35

DYING TO LIVE: THE PARABLE OF JONAH

I feel a personal connection to the story of Jonah in the Bible, a destiny connection that began with my birth, and perhaps even before that. My father used to recite the *Book of Jonah* frequently and from his love of the story he gave me the Hebrew name Jonah. My connection to the story also comes from its message. Unlike most other books of the Bible, the *Book of Jonah* tells an existential story about the journey of an impressive character who is struggling to find his meaning, his purpose and the real inner voice that calls him.

Jonah is a prophet. A prophet in the Biblical sense isn't a perfect person, he isn't Buddha, but he has the capacity to hear or channel the word of God and therefore is given moral authority by the community. The prophet is blessed with an expanded awareness and the ability to listen to voices beyond normal reality, the "still small voice" (I *Kings* 19:12) of the divine. He is different from ordinary people for whom daily life, the clamour and cacophony of the marketplace, and their own needs and interests tend to fill up all the space in their consciousness and they have little room left to listen deeply to the subtle vibrations of the sacred.

Jonah is all too human. He yearns for the truth, as his names hint – Jonah is the son of Amitai (which translates to "the son of truth" in Hebrew). His story is based on his struggle to live his truth, his resistance to it. He receives an inner calling that he must travel to Nineveh, to awaken its people to their moral bankruptcy and corruption, to tell them that they must return to goodness and integrity. But Jonah feels he isn't ready. He is scared, as any of us would be: Nineveh was the capital of the huge, rich and cruel empire of the Assyrians, so his mission would be like a call to us to go to New York and warn the people that they are on a downhill path to disaster. So he flees from his purpose, his deeper sense of what is right. Actually, he is like us, for don't most of us also run away from the intuitions and inner messages that tell us what is most meaningful and what is the challenge that we must face? We are invited to transcend our ordinary selves, but we also run and hide in our comfort zones, turning to television or screens. We say to ourselves: "Tomorrow I will be serious about my life, tomorrow I will make the change I am longing for, tomorrow I will listen to my authentic voice, tomorrow I will make more space for quiet." Or: "I know what I should do but I'm tired, busy, worried, unavailable. I will do it tomorrow."

Jonah runs away in a particular direction – downward – "he goes down" to Jaffa, "he goes down" to the ship, "he goes down" into the hold of the ship (1:3–5). He is in despair, one could say depressed. During the great storm, while the sailors struggle to save the ship, he descends into his cabin and falls asleep. He flees life, he tries to annihilate himself, to disappear, to die. This is deep denial. A desperate attempt to escape from the storm of life – our vulnerability, our failures, our limits, our battles with the uncontrollable and unpredictable. The storm of life is karma. Jonah has made an unwise choice, has screwed up, and karma responds with a veritable tsunami. It happens to us all the time, when we don't pay attention to what is needed and appropriate we find life hits us back where it hurts. And we complain that "it never rains but it pours".

The sailors are good people, full of compassion, they don't want to harm Jonah. Even after they discover that the storm broke out on account of him, they do everything they can not to harm him. At a certain point he says "throw me overboard, and the sea will calm down for you" (1:12) but they continue to struggle with the storm. In the end they realize that it is hopeless. They ask forgiveness from God, and throw Jonah into the sea. The storm ceases.

In the sea he is swallowed by a great fish. The word Jonah in the Aramaic language means fish, by the way. Now he has gone down even deeper – into the depths of the sea in the belly of the fish – in the dark, alone, lost underwater. He cries: "You have thrown me into the depths, into the heart of the sea and the floods have engulfed me … The waters closed over me … I descended to the bottom of the mountains and was locked up by the earth" (2:4–7). His whole life collapses and he arrives at the point of nothingness. He sheds his humanness, his personality and his life story. This is the end, the bottom, a kind of death. Ground zero. Now, when his narratives and stories have disappeared, he is submerged into the elements of which the world is made – water and earth. This is like a shamanistic journey in which we drop down to a deep silent space to meet our death. This is like a deep meditation in which we encounter the zero place within us.

We can imagine this kind of inner journey when we feel overwhelmed by the storms in our life, when there is no escape, when we feel pushed to our limits, and we cannot take it any more. We are ready to be swallowed up in the belly of the great fish – an image of the unconscious – ready to stop all the coping and struggling, and running toward or away from things, and be swallowed by nothingness. The great fish is not external to us, it exists within us. Its belly is a dark, deep, inner place, our source, the power place in us. Perhaps deep rest, perhaps meditation, without stories, memories of the past or yearnings for the future. In order to reach that place we must surrender and let go. Sometimes life does it to us whether we like it or not. For example, it can happen to those who discover that their death is imminent, or after a painful loss. It may create the deepest surrender into their original being.

In this place of nothingness, the searcher for truth (*Ben Amitai*) finds it, the real source of his life, his meaning and purpose. Fear ends. When we have reached our zero point, our connection to the foundations of our world, there is no reason for fear or resistance. A clarity arises in us: "I'm no longer willing to play this game, I'm not willing to carry on as if it is ok, business as usual. I know what I must do."

He prays, he makes promises and vows, and the fish vomits him out onto dry land. Now he is ready to fulfil his mission. He has no reason to refuse. This is a resurrection. He comes to Nineveh, which is a huge city that took three days to cross. Somehow, he manages to persuade the people to change, to repent. Can we imagine doing something like that? But Jonah does, and surprisingly he succeeds. The inhabitants of Nineveh fast "from the great to the small", from the king to the cows. They strip off their fine clothing and wear sackcloth. They mend their ways: "Let everyone turn back from his evil ways and from the injustice of which he is guilty" (3:5–8).

Thus ends Jonah's mission. It seems he succeeded, but he is still not happy. He leaves Nineveh and sits on a hill near the city to see what will happen. He doesn't want God to forgive the people of Nineveh, he wants them to be punished – perhaps because he knows what a huge destruction and suffering the Assyrians had caused to his people and to the whole region. He wants confirmation that there is order in the world: reward and punishment, that the Assyrians pay a price for their heartlessness and cruelty. This is the voice of his ordinary ego that still hangs onto concepts of good and evil. He argues with the divine, with what is beyond such human habits of mind. The disappointed Jonah again wants to die. But then life (God in the Biblical context) arranges a powerful personal experience. It is hot, and Jonah suffers under the sun. But there is a castor-oil plant which gives him shade and Jonah rejoices in this. But then it becomes infected with a worm that kills the plant and the suffering Jonah, under the blazing sun, falls into despair. But he hears the voice of insight: "You care about this *Ricinus* plant that you didn't create, but you are keen to destroy a whole city of thousands of people, children, babies and animals due to your view of justice." Here the story ends.

In addition to this drama of deep transformation, there are other themes in the story that are important. One is forgiveness. The issue of forgiveness appears a number of times:

the sailors forgive Jonah for falling asleep during the storm and
for causing the storm in the first place. God forgives the people
of Nineveh for their behaviour, despite the huge destruction
that they wrought over the entire region. Jonah is forgiven
for his behaviour, for his capitulation to fear. Forgiveness is
greater than us and our personality. It comes from a place that
is beyond the "I". The voice of God speaks continuously, it is
a kind of vibration or music that we must tune into that says
that the true picture, karma, is much vaster than a narrow view
of reward and punishment. And it says: "I forgive you." Repair,
change, the ability to nullify the past and to rewrite the script of
our lives, to change our track, flows from a deep inner knowing.
This is quite beyond the socially acceptable definitions
and judgements of ourselves as good or bad, successful or
unsuccessful in our roles and activities as spiritual practitioners,
partners, parents, professionals or just human beings.

This is another message of the story: our destiny, what life
throws at us, is changeable. We can shift it, in a significant way.
Jonah's destiny changed as a result of his encounter with his
death and rebirth; the people of Nineveh changed when they
faced themselves in the mirror and repented. This is the central
idea of the Jewish fast day of Yom Kippur. On this day, Jews
are invited to descend deep into the belly of the fish, to let go
of their ordinary selves. It is called the Sabbath of Sabbaths,
meaning the ultimate cessation. Although many Jews regard
this day as a day of confession, of prayer or supplication to win
a better destiny and to improve their lives, the real meaning
of this day is a shamanistic process of return to our beginning,
leaving our framework, and a sinking into non-expectation.
This is not an organized and linear process, but rather an
unconscious shift that may occur without us understanding
how, and it creates a corresponding shift in our destiny.

An additional message is about intention. When the Dalai
Lama was asked how to gain more life energy he answered that
we should connect with our highest motivation. Like Jonah,
we too flee again and again from our highest motivation,
despite the fact that this is the source of our energy. What

happens to us day by day is not just external events. We
create it through the quality of our meeting with life and our
response to it. Life is dynamic, unexpected. Nothing is built,
nothing is predictable, nothing is sealed. Our intentions guide
our responses to unpredictable events, which are the seeds that
grow the fruits that we later consume. In every unexpected
moment of life we dance between our fate and our response,
encountering life and creating it. In the end, like Jonah, we are
liberated by our highest motivation.

Finally, there is compassion. The *Book of Jonah* ends with
God asking Jonah a question: "You cared about the plant,
which you did not work for and which you did not grow,
which appeared overnight and perished overnight. And
should not I care about Nineveh, that great city, in which
there are more than a hundred and twenty thousand persons
who do not yet know their right hand from their left, and
many animals as well?" (4:10–11). This is the language of
compassion, which Jonah has trouble grasping. The *Ricinus*
plant is a beautiful image that is intended to bring Jonah into
an encounter with his vulnerability. It shows us our basic
fragility and dependence, the fact that we are exposed to the
storms of life without any real protection. Jonah experiences
this teaching, not as a concept but in his very flesh. When we
deeply experience our own vulnerability in our body we feel
compassion for the vulnerability of all others. Compassion
comes from the deep realization that we and all other beings
in samsara are like the *Ricinus* plant, one day there and the
next gone. The Buddha said that the whole world hangs by
a single thread; our fragility is absolute and however hard we
try to build walls, seek permanence and comfort, ultimately
nothing can protect us. In the end, everything falls apart.
Us, our bodies, the world in which we live, friends, family –
everything is impermanent. Though we are busy throughout
life building and maintaining our protective shields – our
money, our knowledge, our roles, our relationships, our beliefs
– against the unpredictable and uncontrollable, the abyss is
much closer than we think. This vulnerability unifies us with

all life. It creates an affinity and sympathy that is the basis of compassion. Compassion is the ability to open the heart through intimate contact with the vulnerability of every being.

Wisdom and compassion are two sides of the same coin, and are the basis of the spiritual life. Jonah certainly found wisdom – the power and insight that comes from living from our truth, from the awareness of our innate freedom. But the story shows that wisdom is limited without compassion. We need this connection between consciousness and the heart. Does Jonah understand this? It is hard to know. But we can hope that this human prophet, so like us, does understand. With wisdom and compassion we live our lives from the realization of the total interconnection of everything. The ultimate. The story ends in a resounding silence. There is nothing much left to say.

CHAPTER 36

DOES GOD EXIST OR IS EXISTENCE GOD?

One evening I was sitting with my wife and three teenage daughters in an apartment in India at a Krishnamurti school where we were teaching, and we were singing Jewish traditional songs. All of a sudden there was a knock on the door and there stood Didi, an Indian woman we knew. Of course we invited her in. She looked all over the room and listened to us singing with more and more puzzlement. "But where are your gods?" she burst out. "In the Jewish religion God is one and invisible," we said. She considered this for a moment, and then shook her head in pity and said: "Oh! You poor people."

This comment was hilariously unexpected. In Western culture there is usually an assumption that the Judeo-Christian view of one supreme deity is more elevated and sophisticated than the apparently primitive worship of images, icons and multiple deities each with their own divine character. We regard it as an evolutionary development of the intellect, an ability to hold a more abstract and less material concept of the deity. There is also some comfort in having one divine being, instead of a fragmentation of deities sometimes squabbling with each other for power in an uncomfortable mirror image of life on earth. Yet there may be a price to pay, as pointed out by Didi. Namely that in retaining the view that there is a God, yet thinking about God abstractly, as an invisible being or source, we may have locked God up inside our own minds. The deity becomes a mere high thought passing by, and as such is no deity at all. Indeed most people have an image of God in their minds based on their childhood – often a severe father or bearded grandfather in the sky doling out rewards and punishments. In that case, it may indeed be better to have an icon in front of us such as a statue of the dancing Shiva, or suffering Jesus, or a picture of compassionate Kwan Yin or Virgin Mary, or of the vast gaze of Ramana Maharshi. That at least helps to remind us of genuinely divine qualities that we can embody. As Patanjali said, God can start with a concept but after that has to be properly conceived (or born) in us. Forms may help in this process although there is the obvious risk that worship of icons and idols, such as the Ganesha statue on the mantelpiece, stops there. Then we would need an Abraham or a Buddha to shatter the idols and invite the formless back in.

God as an individual or collective thought is so interwoven into our culture, our history, our identity and our language, that it takes on an apparent reality and grows like a great cloud above us. From childhood we are taught that God is creator of the world, the power behind reality, the source of goodness, or basically the universal "other" that we can thank or blame as we go through pleasant or unpleasant experiences. Without any collective sense of what this invisible God may actually be, we still use it conveniently as a jewel box or rubbish bin or safe refuge, or moral authority, or ultimate mystery, to locate there everything that we don't understand, that is beyond, that makes for life's hopes and pains. For example, driven by insecurity, we cannot bear to contemplate the uncertainties of what will happen to us and so, as in the Jewish fast day of Yom Kippur, or in the Christian concept of the Day of Reckoning, we imagine God to be a great clerk writing our fates in a ledger. Of course the sense of a divine being can bring us comfort, relief, and a trust in something greater. But this is often a self-created loop, a deep conviction dependent on personal beliefs.

Belief means investing a mental event with reality; constructing a conviction that it really exists somewhere out there, such as "above". The belief in God is a giant belief, never mind in what form this belief takes. Both theists and atheists are party to this belief. The theists have brought the huge but invisible elephant into the room; the atheists want to kick him out. Truth is laughing at both, and says that the only truth here is that belief has been ignorantly mistaken for reality.

The Buddhist teachings have been described as atheistic. They are far from it. The Buddha, at least according to the early texts, made it very clear that whether or not God exists should be "left undeclared". There were quite a few questions, particularly about ontology, that he refused to answer as he said that both yes and no would lead to confusion and it is better to leave them open as a non-conceptual springboard to an expanded awareness. But in the case of questions concerning the existence of God he was much stronger. He was reported to have said that such a belief that God exists or that God does not exist would actually undermine spiritual life, and would in fact obstruct our ability to know the ultimate reality. He said it would get us lost in what he described as "a thicket of views". Since we know how many wars and massacres have been caused by religious believers, and are still being caused by them, just how much brutality, suffering and pain is down to religious belief, this thicket indeed has sharp thorns.

The Buddhist path of practice is based on inquiry, a ruthless honesty and love of truth. At the very minimum, honesty would invite us to see a belief as a belief, a view as a view, a conviction as a conviction, and nothing more than that. We need to take ownership and responsibility for our beliefs and views, and know them as such. By this, the teachings say, we retain authenticity. We reduce the illusion that our views are of reality, independent of us, that our views are true, and of course that others' views are false.

As soon as God appears in our minds as a thought, it is a limited product of our consciousness and nothing to do with ultimacy. Though belief in God may be helpful in generating devotion, surrender, trust, confidence and other states of mind, it is not in the realm of totality, the universal. Ultimacy is way beyond thought. It may be regarded as the source of thought, and the source of everything else, and as such it cannot be contained by thought. Thoughts about it are like trying to cut gravity with a knife. What we see and know is an interpretation, a learned and conditioned construction. The world as we know it is engraved in our own brains as neural networks. This imprisons us in our own constructions. The God view is one of those constructions. If we hold to it, we have invited God into the prison with us and imprisoned both. This is not the way to liberation.

One way out of this is to collapse the duality that there is a mundane limited ordinary reality "below", and an all-powerful God or creator to whom we pray and supplicate "above". Duality is created by the assumption that there is an apparently solid self-existent external world, including a deity, and a subjective world, or internal self. In actual fact we can't help but have duality as an integral part of ordinary perception, as it is built-in or hard-wired as a mechanism of consciousness. But if we are serious about religious and spiritual practice we will be on a journey to reduce duality and live more in a spontaneous awakened non-dual presence. If we abandon this journey, and duality becomes the one and only direction of our religious life, through the separation of heaven and earth, it may utterly undermine all our efforts and longing for spiritual freedom.

Paradoxically, some traditional formulations and images used to describe God show us this. In Old Testament language along with earthly and dualistic images of father, king, protector and so on are names that point us to life and totality, such as "place", "presence", "source". The only time in the Bible God is asked point-blank who he is, he answers, "I am that I am", which can be translated from the Hebrew simply as "being". Further, the Biblical "home" of God within the Jewish temple was the heart of the temple, the "Holy of Holies". It was an empty room. These mythological pointers are clear. If we want to know the divine, we need to look toward being or existence; and this is empty of the world as we know it. How are we to understand that?

Existence itself is not something we can look at, own or understand. We cannot contain it within our ordinary experience, based on neural networks, and self and world.

At best we can point to it, think about it and give it names
– such as God! But to really see it, we cannot use the
mechanisms of the ordinary mind, which are constructions
born of time, memory and conditioning. It needs a much
deeper process, of meditation, spiritual quest and realization.
If we do not do this, we are left with just the tip of the
iceberg, not the bulk, and this we call God and leave it at that,
as a way to avoid looking under the surface. We are afraid to
do this as we have built ourselves around coping, survival and
functioning, as a toolkit to attempt to control what happens.
To the "me" who is intent on controlling existence the idea
that existence is vast, impersonal and uncontrollable is deeply
threatening. The last thing the self and the mind wants to do
is to be absorbed in existence, lost in the unknown, merged
with the beyond. So God here is a collective escape, and if we
don't want to get stuck there, we have to surrender, renounce
the attachment to the known, the attachment to control and
explore with all the wisdom we can muster the essence of this
moment-by-moment existence.

One way of doing this is to become aware of the
impossibility of thoughts about God, to encourage such
concepts to undo themselves, to explode themselves. Just by
replacing the word God with words such as "the absolute",
"the ultimate reality", "presence" – thought becomes unsure
of itself. It releases a questioning that, like a virus, may run
through the mind and undo assumptions and beliefs. If the
thought of God can be treated as a koan, it will bring us closer
to the divine. "Life is not a problem to be solved but a mystery
to be lived," runs the well-known saying. This can give us the
humbling sense that we are limited and conditioned beings
that are reaching out beyond ourselves. Yet, if considered
carefully, a human being is already a mystery beyond itself.
Do we really exist? In what way can we say so? Descartes
said that he knows he exists because he can have a thought:
"I think, therefore I am." But that tells us only that thought
exists. The mind cannot actually contain the existence of itself,
cannot really understand what is being, cannot understand

of what it is really made, let alone how it appeared as it is. So the question of the existence of God is no different from the question of the existence of a thought. To put it another way, thinking about God does not necessarily reveal God, it just reveals that there is a thought of God, and thinking about a thought likewise reveals only thought. And there we stop.

So can't a thought reach out beyond itself? Yes, surely it can, otherwise there would be no world – a memory of the face of our mother or the sight of an olive tree represents something out there even though we cannot say absolutely what it is. It is quite magical to contemplate the stars at night and to appreciate this mind that has understood the Big Bang. However, when a thought tries to reach out so far beyond itself that it attempts to know the infinite, the source, including the source of itself, all it is left with are some negatives (non-ordinary) or superlatives (the omniscient, the all-knowing, the compassionate). It leaves us feeling that we are sitting at the bottom of a well trying to know the sky we can't see. Clearly we need some wisdom as to what powers and means we have that could take us to the beyond. How can we use thought to make a jump beyond thought? In the world of the known, how can we unleash the power of the unknown, which seems far, far greater than the small territory of the known?

This is actually the very basis and ground of dharma practice. And the way outlined in this practice is vast, rich and sophisticated. One can pick out one or two themes. The first is a consistent direction to release ourselves from attachments and clinging, from all those things that create an automatic life, that tie us to the known world of things, concepts, views and selves. This involves deep practice of seeing things as they really are, and letting them go – seeing our patterns and constructions, and deeply seeing that they are essentially dynamic and free. It is like digging a well, and throwing away everything that is not water. We do not define what is water, it is subtle, hard to see and deep, but we will know it when we reach it. The biggest amount of earth to be discarded is the belief in me and mine. This ego-centred view of reality, the solid subject who automatically sees everything as solid objects, cements an inherent dualism that is applied to all moments of experience, including that of the divine. We discard the God concept along with the self concept along with subjectivity. This involves deep meditative practice and the practice of mindful awareness of the nature of experience. Fortunately, when we do this we find that we do not have to work so hard to get rid of things, they go by themselves. Their essential nature is dynamic and free. The earth vanishes as we start to dig. When we examine carefully any of the constructions that we are conditioned to believe in, such as ownership of my body, these things prove to be unfindable, ephemeral and elusive. We are shown the transparency of so-called solid reality, and we can see through it to the divine.

Put another way, if there is a hint of ownership or identification with what we call the divine or ultimacy, it's gone. "Our" God is no God at all. We cannot claim that being in any way belongs to us, or is even interested in us. Being just is. Owning God is losing God. This also applies more subtly to the issue of divine providence. If we go down that road it leads us to illusions of expectation, illusions that somehow God is there to provide (providence) benefit and not harm, we forget that benefit and harm are descriptions of experiences defined by us the subject. They are not inherent in reality itself. If we believe in divine goodness, then when harm arrives we lose faith, as so many Jews did after the Holocaust. It is unnecessary. The divine is in the essence of the unfolding moment, within the magic of existence itself, never mind whether this unfolding moment is convenient or inconvenient to this body-mind.

Another aspect of spiritual practice is development of powers of mind that then lead us beyond thought. The ability to be tranquil, calm and silent, to be steady and concentrated, and to light the fire of curiosity and interest, are examples. Science has shown that meditation can balance and harmonize the right brain, which is the part of the brain that allows global oceanic experience, with the left brain more involved in creating the boundaries of self and world. Using such a coherent brain, when we look at something so simple as the breath, we can see through it to the immediacy of the experience as well as the dynamic unbounded nature of things. If we look at our weight pressing on the ground we can see through it to the pull of gravity that is not owned by us. Powers of mind include powers of the heart. Based on a happiness and inner freedom – which is felt in our cells – the power of love is in its nature boundless, it is a power that opens worlds and breaks barriers. All of these powers will take us beyond the imprisonment of dualistic thought.

In that place things look different. There is no longer the need to construct some perfect "other" and put him above and us below in some lower place. We ourselves become the field where above and below meet and are then transcended. The lofty idea of being becomes simple beingness. The sacred becomes a verb and not a noun.

To realize the divine, we need to die to the ordinary world of concepts, the consensus reality, the known, the world of thought, the world of identification and analysis, the world that we know and construct through our consciousness. Nisargadatta Maharaj said: "Die now into the now." God in the Bible says: "No man can know me and live." The high priest in the Jewish temple was at risk of dying when he went into the "empty room". He had to undergo intense purification and internal preparation to come out alive. Actually in that place we are more alive than ever. It is a place of pure being. But being is also the nature of the ultimate. In the silence of no concept and no belief, in the quiet of pure presence, God finds us. In that place the word God and the word truth are interchangeable. It's scary. We are afraid to let go of the known. Few are ready to jump into that abyss but, if we are, then when we let go we may realize the movement is not like jumping but more like falling, and as much falling out of as into, and the abyss turns out to be the Garden of Eden. This launch into space is not entirely in our hands. But we can prepare the ground. And be entirely available to hear the call from beyond.

CHAPTER 37
THE GODDESS WITHIN

Shechina, the goddess
Means "presence" in Hebrew
"She who dwells within".
Many mourn her absence
But she is only absent
When we are absent
Which is most of the time.
She is homeless
When we are not at home.
She is left outside
When we shut ourselves inside
Our gates and villas.
But when we welcome the world
In an unconditional embrace
Suddenly she is there
And here and everywhere,
And when we surrender
To this perfect moment
Of appreciation and attention
Then she unfolds herself
In front of our eyes
And we truly know
She never left
But was too close
For us to notice.

CHAPTER 38
KARMA: WELCOMING IT AND CHANGING IT

Karma, in Sanskrit, simply means "action". No more, no less. It is the way of the world: a law of action and reaction. It is about influences; the influence of all things on all things. As this is such a vast network of interactions throughout the universe, it is quite impossible to say what exactly will be the result of any action. Think of the butterfly effect, the idea that networks of interaction are so interconnected that merely the flapping of the wings of a butterfly could create a tornado a few weeks later on the other side of the world. It is only a metaphor, as it could never be proven what caused what, but nonetheless the world does appear to be that way.

The network of influences is not random chaos, in which case there would be no world. Karma refers to the patterns that keep maintaining themselves, and so one can also say that karma is what keeps the world happening, in more or less the way it has been. Karma is what makes an oak tree keep on being an oak, and not switching midway through its life to being a fig tree even if it also wants to grow some figs. It has a strong tendency to "oaking", yet at the same time it goes through huge changes from being an acorn to a great gnarled tree, from the influences of water, wind, and weather, to the woodcutter who cuts it down and the carpenter who turns it into shelves.

There are some traditional Buddhist views that hold that karma is only about human action and not the action of oak trees or molecules; it is what happens when humans act volitionally. However, my own view is that this is anthropocentric, and there is no reason to consider ourselves as so special. Karma is not just about living beings or human actions. But it is of course our human tendencies that are most interesting to us, so from my own perspective of how I can act in the world karma is an operating principle. When we look at how it impacts us, we can see that generally the kinds of seeds we sow in life tend to create similar results. If we sow seeds of health, harmony and goodness, we are likely to reap crops of the same type. If we sow seeds of harm, exploitation and self-centredness, we are likely to face similar things. However, there are no rules here, only tendencies. The puzzle that has occupied people endlessly is why does it so often happen that the good folk suffer and that evil triumphs and the perpetrators enjoy the fruits of evil. This can only be illuminated by wisdom, not by logical thought, and wisdom shows us the panoramic picture in which karma is understood as a network of conditional influences that is vast and it does not obey our human need for cause and effect and rational explanation.

The Biblical *Book of Job* is a first-class example of the journey we need to go on to move from our concepts about fate to this deeper transcendental wisdom. Job prided himself on his goodness, and assumed good things would result from that, and indeed he was happy and smugly comfortable. But this was challenged by fate, in the form of the devil, who brought down on him sickness, suffering and tragedy. The whole book is about Job's intense heroic struggle to understand why good people like himself so often suffer and the bad ones don't. In the book, his friends offered him every possible explanation that religion, society and conventional thinking could offer, but none of them satisfied Job's intensive quest for truth. In the end he gave up the quest. At that moment of total surrender he was granted a revelation from "above", which told him that life is play and change, that there is no rational answer to human suffering, and that he just needs to let go into the unknown with a compassionate and wise heart.

Action and reaction happens, but the system is so big that it also gives us a lot of freedom. It is neither a total nihilistic chaos, which would leave no room for ethics, purpose or meaning in life, nor is it a deterministic world that works like clockwork. Both of those are the concepts of a dualistic mind. The reality is neither this nor that but a dynamic non-dual middle way (see chapter 33). In the ocean of influences and possibilities there is plenty of room for us to change ourselves and our lives. For example, a strong cycle of action and reaction is addiction. The cigarette we smoke now makes the next one more likely. This is how karma operates. We do have the power to change, to break the habits, and change the conditions – to clean up our act. Yet there are no guarantees, and much that happens will happen anyway whatever we do or think.

This is very far away from a common and rather simplistic view of karma, which is "do good otherwise you will pay for it in the next life". In 1999 the England football manager Glenn Hoddle gave an interview in *The Times* newspaper in which he expressed the view of karma that disabled people became that way because of misdeeds that they must have done in a previous life. This caused such a furore in Parliament that he lost his job. But, besides the offence, he was expressing a completely mistaken view of karma. Here are some common misconceptions:

- **Karma is a system of reward and punishment. It is more or less the same as a simple view of fate.** No it is not. It is much less personal and far less interested in us. It is much bigger than that and not as predictable. It is closer to our concept of "nature". We all want a predictable world, and long for some order, and so we imagine that there is a kind of book with our rewards and punishments written in it. But intuitively we know it doesn't work like that. There is indeed an echo from the world that responds in kind to what we say, do and think. But it is not linear or predictable. Good men can and do have terrible fates, and the reverse is also true. Even the Buddha clearly expressed that the network of influences in the world is so vast that no-one, including himself, was able to predict what would be the results of a particular action.

- **Karma is the influence of one life on the next.** No, this is also a great oversimplification. Karma is about the influence of one moment on the next. The quality of one moment influences the quality of the next. As we live and die and perhaps are reborn moment by moment, it operates in our lives, between lives and, mostly, between moments. Belief in reincarnation is just that, a belief, no more. There is no reason to suppose that karma works more between one life and the next, than it does in this very life. We are being reborn constantly into the next moment. The Buddha emphasized that birth and death are integral to the wheel of life, which is constantly creating us and our experience. There is a similar understanding in the Kabbalah, where the idea that the rewards for our actions will happen in "the world to come" is understood as "the world that keeps coming". It is surely wiser and more beneficial to watch it happening in this life where we can learn from the way things influence us and we influence others, than to dump our problems and mistakes into some unknown future.
- **Karma is about actions.** No, it is mostly about intentions behind the actions. For example, a surgeon will cut a body with a knife. This is a healing act creating, hopefully, healing results for his patient. The same cutting action with a knife performed when someone stabs another person in anger has the opposite intentions and the opposite karma.

We may well ask, if karma, properly understood, is not a one-to-one rule of reward and punishment, how does it help us? Does the concept of karma add anything to us? I think it does. Primarily, it helps us understand that our intentions and actions, spread into the world, are not meaningless. All are meaningful. Our actions and efforts are not lost. They spin off into the world, influencing the way things are. Therefore we have to take care of our thoughts, intentions and actions: they make change in the world and we are responsible for them. Karma is a guide to wholesome and harmonious living. It is similar to an ecological way of life. The rubbish or pollutants we throw out into our precious planet do not actually disappear but come back to haunt us and give us diseases. On the other hand, if we care for and purify our environment we live a more pure and healthy life.

If we understand that the quality of our actions influences the quality of life, it can create a radical shift in the way we do things. For example, if we believe in peace and want to end conflict, according to conventional thinking, we need to forcefully convince others of our views. According to karmic understanding, we do it differently – we act peacefully so as to bring peace. A saying I quoted earlier puts it well:

> Sow a thought, reap an act,
> Sow an act, reap a habit,
> Sow a habit, reap a personality,
> Sow a personality, reap a destiny.

We can sow the best seeds, and hopefully reap the best fruit, in this life, if we pay attention to what we are doing. We can watch karma happening as the things we do in the world roll on and on, creating results in the most unexpected places. One lie that we tell can make a big mess and do harm to us or others, can make us feel guilty, uncomfortable and agitated, can boomerang on us, can steal our peace and joy. If we watch this process carefully we can see the wheels of karma rolling, and know that we must be caring, wise and responsible in all our thoughts, our words and deeds.

CHAPTER 39

OUR BUDDHA-NATURE IS A WOMB

We take it for granted that there is a pure soul within us. Woven into all the great spiritual traditions is the confidence that we are somehow made of the same material as the divine, or at least we carry some element of the divine within us. The Judeo-Christian tradition enshrines it in the statement in the *Book of Genesis* that the human being is made in the image of God. What or where this is is left to us as a mystery. In the later Kabbalistic tradition, it is more clearly expressed as "divine sparks", fragments of the infinite light that lodge in the world. In other words, we carry within us a minute element of an original primal consciousness of infinite light. In the Indian spiritual tradition, the pure soul is described as *atman*, an inner self that reflects and manifests the ultimate self ("itself") of existence. Transformation through the multitude of spiritual practices and yogas is the release of the inner self and its merging with the ultimate. The word yoga itself means union or joining, implying this process.

But if we do not frame all this in a religious language or context, in the Judeo-Christian language of God and divinity, or the Hinduistic language of the *atman*, or the Buddhist language of Buddha-nature, can we still entertain such an understanding? Is there a more secular version? The word spirit itself is a common form of secular language and concept in use in today's culture, although it does have roots in Greek, Christian and alchemical traditions. This spirit is somehow connected with consciousness, the uniquely human powers of awareness. The problem for most of us is that this concept is very vague. It is a kind of belief or assumption, collected together out of general East-West, psychological and new-age spirituality. Does spirit really exist or is it a hopeful concept? What is this pure spirit within us? How do we know it? How do we recognize it? Do we know when we are in touch with it? Do we know when we are ignoring it? Can it be said to belong to us in any way? Perhaps we belong to it? The inquiry into the what, where, how and why of the spirit leaves us with a stunned silence. This is probably a good thing, otherwise it too would become a subject for cerebral analysis and scientific research.

In our search for a language of the spirit that fits secular culture, Buddhism can be an immense help. This is because it contains such a sophisticated and refined knowledge of inner space, and, further, it describes our spiritual life more as a quest for truth, for liberation, rather than for God's blessings. Indeed Buddhism itself arose as an agnostic inquiry into existential reality in contrast to the prevailing Brahministic and priestly cults of *atman* that prevailed in India 2,500 years ago. Therefore it would be a good place to look for some clarity on the subject of the pure being within us. What does the Buddha say about pure being? Surprisingly, the teachings are crystal clear. There is no such thing. More than that, the longing for a transcendental reality that is somehow connected to us, somehow ours, can be a stumbling block in our development as much as a blessing that motivates us to search for truth and liberation. It can arise as a longing for something other than life as it is, and is therefore another manifestation and projection of *dukkha*, deep unsatisfactoriness. It implies that life in the body is somehow inadequate, unspiritual and contracted, and that a pure soul is something beyond, something perfect. This splitting is itself a form of suffering, and a hindrance on the path. It is a primary human delusion. Early Buddhism turns all this on its head. There is no need to look for a pure being within us, or infinity above. If we open our eyes, strip away the veils of delusion, then this very living experience itself is infinite. Freedom is in the heart of any experience, not in replacing it with a more spiritual experience. All experience is fundamentally illusory if we identify with it and believe it to be a fact, but can open to a timeless, impersonal and groundless awareness. All reality is ultimate if we learn to see it as it really is. As the poet William Blake wrote: "If the doors of perception were cleansed everything would appear to man as it is, infinite."

However, later developments in Buddhism, particularly in the Mahayana traditions in Tibet and China, brought back the concept of a pure soul within us, but in a highly interesting language of consciousness, rather than the language of gods or *atman*. This inherent Buddha-nature is a power within us to partake of the freedom and liberation of the Buddhas. More specifically, this is described in Sanskrit as *garbha*, meaning "womb". This is a powerful and fleshy image. It is an image of an empty space that is nonetheless full of potential and that is ready and willing to be impregnated. It is an image of an emptiness inside that is available and open to receive the wisdom of liberation. Tibetan Dzogchen teachings call it the *dharmakaya*, a dharma "body" that is a pure, undifferentiated, unconditioned, primal and perfect being. This turns on its head the idea that we "have" something pure within us. We do not. There is no spirit as such, there is just a potential for release. It is the empty space within us that is the purity. It is the mystery, the existential question, the space in which we do not exist, the space in which there is no "me and mine" that is the Buddha-nature. It is something beyond the mind that permits us to question the unknown; it is the power that we have to reflect on the uncomfortable experience of embodiment in life – this is the womb within in which awakening is nurtured.

This image definitely helps us. Because for centuries people have battled with the problem – if we are made "in the image of God" how can we so foolish, helpless, aggressive, and sometimes downright evil? Here is another way of looking at it – the divine within us is a potential. And the place to look for the potential is not within the usual domain of "what I want, what I don't want, what makes me feel good, who I am, how spiritual I am", all of which gives rise to the problematic and small human being, circling around his desires and dislikes from birth to death. It is in the absence of all this self-importance that the first whisper of the divine is heard.

CHAPTER 40
UNITY: CONCEPT OR EXPERIENCE?

In Psalm 133 we read: "See: how good and pleasant it is for brothers to dwell together in unity." The sense of unity is one of the greatest and most lovely of experiences that we can have. Usually it is a moment of grace, a blessing that arises in specific situations, such as the ecstasy of complete togetherness and intimacy with someone we love – an overwhelming sense of awe at the greatness of this world when we reach the top of the mountain or are swimming under the waves of the sea, or the goodness of dwelling together in harmony as the psalm describes. But it is often dependent and fleeting. We may feel it only to the extent that we are free of fear and insecurity, as when there is a sense of unity in "our" group or nation or belief, so long as "the others" are kept safely away. This is an illusion of unity, dependent on certain conditions or boundaries that we set up. It is more of a feeling of comfort than a feeling of unity. But imagine how it would feel if those moments were extended to become part of our daily life? Imagine what life would be like if the sense of unity was not just there with a chosen few but with all life. What if the word "brothers" in the psalm implied all living beings with whom we dwell together in this world? Imagine if the sense of unity was not only with all life but with the basis and ground of life itself, that holds us all. It would be a taste of the divine.

The sense of unity is a wonderful feeling, but why is it so occasional, so dependent on certain conditions? It is because a dominant programme running in our consciousness is that of separation, of being locked in a rather lonely and self-centred ego, or self, from which we look out at the world. This is the human condition that begins more or less at birth. We are born as an integral part of the world, and then gradually learn to survive in it as an independent autonomous unit by functioning and thinking as a separate self, an identity, which is very occupied with looking after itself. The experiences of unity, such as falling in love, come as a strong breakthrough, or chink in the armour, or crack through which we glimpse the light. They are a memory of how things can be without this separation. These breaches in the walls can feel all the more wonderful because of the contrast between those expanded moments of rejoining the world and the regular contracted place that we are used to living in. I remember some sublime moments of unity in the peace dialogues and workshops we facilitated between Israelis and Palestinians. There were moments in which there was a silent joining of hearts and a look of love in the eyes. The joy rose because of the dramatic discovery of the sense of togetherness between people who are usually so tragically separate. Those moments felt like "brothers dwelling together in unity".

We feel these experiences so rarely, and wish for them so much, because it is fundamentally painful to be constantly enclosed in the prison of our limited self-view. It is therefore not surprising that unity is constantly referred to, praised, and elevated in our minds and in our hearts. It is a deep longing for completion or oneness that is channelled into thoughts, poetry, philosophies, art, rituals, worship, and especially prayer. But we have to be aware that the experience of unity is not the same as thoughts about it. When we think or talk about the one, or oneness, or unity, it does feel that there is an ultimate truth in it, though often hard to grasp, but it is still in the territory of concept. Spiritual teachers can talk about it from morning to night but this may never get through as an experience to those that listen. I remember the late Swami Shyam, who led an ashram in Kulu in the Himalayas, trying very hard and not too successfully to convince my 11-year-old daughter about unity. My daughter kept pointing to a nail in the wooden table around which they sat, and said: "How on earth can this nail be in oneness with the wood it nails? They are surely two." All the concepts, arguments and images that he used did not get through. The perception that nail and wood are two was too strong. It needs a direct experiential insight into the bigness, the togetherness and the interrelationship of things to reveal unity.

Indeed, any concept about anything is already dualistic. There is us, the thinker, the subject or the source, and the thought, or picture that arises. Two things: unity gone. More than that, we also feel that any concept that arises in the mind belongs to us; we possess it. We believe in it, we talk about it, we assume it to be true, and we assume that it exists. A concept as high as unity or oneness seems abstract and inclusive, so it is easy to forget that it is still a concept in the mind, and therefore reducing unity not increasing it, especially if it is placed up there above it all, like the concept "creator". The grand concept of unity or oneness is attractive, sexy, spiritual by definition. It is a new-age way of talking about God in non-theological language; it is belief in the new gods instead of the old ones. But it is just as illusory, in that if we talk and think about it it rubs off on us and we ourselves can own the glorious halo that it offers. It expands the "me and mine" instead of dissolving it and as such increases separation and reduces the unity instead of increasing it. For example, new-age believers who talk about unity are just as interested in who is in the "in-group" as the rest of the population.

The Buddha warned about the subtle traps in holding such views and concepts. He warned that there are those who conceive of themselves as all or in all, or who conceive themselves as separate from the all, or created by it, or conceiving it to be "theirs" in order to enjoy it. The Buddha says: "Why is that? Because they have not fully understood it."[1]

So how do we go about seeking a real experience and full understanding of unity? There are of course multitudes of ways to realize the sense of belonging and intimacy with the whole, all of which are ways to uncover and actually experience an impersonal and liberating truth rather than develop a set of views. There is intensive dancing, prayer, music, yoga, meditation, and the thousand ways to open the heart to the world. And there are the non-dual teachings such as Advaita Vedanta in which there is no seeking for unity as something "over there", but a dropping into it right here. But in all these ways, we have to be serious and committed. Prayer is the commonest way, but mostly it is far from unity – we pray to some other (deity or saint) for some benefit to ourselves or our group. Only if the prayer is so intensive that it devours us and we are absorbed in and released into the limitless, and released from our boundaries, would it bring us to unity. In meditation, one of the best ways is to simply pay attention to what is coming into us through the senses. Master Hsuan Hua said:

> Using your inherent wisdom, observe inwardly the mind and body and outwardly the world. Completely understand both as you would look through a pane of glass: from the outside seeing in and from the inside seeing out. Inwardly there is no body and mind and outwardly there is no world. But although there is no body nor mind nor world, the body and mind and the world function in accord with each other.[2]

If continuously present, we become more and more of a participant and less an observer, and gradually grow toward a consistent sense of partnership with everything without any views about it all, and we just know that the world and ourselves are one.

What tends to happen is that we first feel the painful sense of our separation (us from them, us from ourselves, us from the world, us from God). This may seem far from unity, but it is actually the first step. Before we can get out of prison we need to notice that we are in one, and then to see where are the walls, and then where is the door. It needs great humility, and also persistence and patience. Only then may we get hints of its opposite, of what is not separate. There is an ancient Indian riddle that asks: "What is the spiritual journey? It is like ants eating a cube of sugar." We would immediately assume that the sugar is the sweet spiritual experience and the ants are us that consume it. Wrong. It is the other way round. We are the cube of sugar, and the ants are the spiritual experiences that gradually consume our separate self until we are "eaten up" and disappear into the world.

CHAPTER 41

THE SHAMBHALA WARRIOR: THE SWORD OF WISDOM

*"How do you rule an empire? Like you fry a small fish –
lightly."*

(*Tao Te Ching*, chapter 60)

When we grow psychologically and spiritually, when we
develop empathy and awareness, when we meet our inner life
and open our hearts to ourselves and the world, something
changes in our relationship to the world. Compassion develops
as a natural result of seeing clearly ourselves and others, our
shared struggles and shared vulnerability. We are likely to
be filled with motivation and inspiration to help others and
to become active for peace, and a better world. But we may
soon discover to our chagrin that the world will not react like
a puppy rolling over on its back and asking for its tummy to
be stroked; it is possible that our good intentions will not be
received well. We may meet frustration, pessimism, cynicism,
despair, rejection, misunderstanding and much negativity, even
from those people we are trying to help. For example, people
working in social change and peacemaking NGOs are endlessly
frustrated and often burnt out. To cope with this, we need to
develop attitudes and skills that will help to empower us for
kind and effective action in the world. What is enlightened
action in the world and how does it manifest?

The Shambhala warrior, a Tibetan image that has been
with me for many years, is close to my heart. It answers
this question. Shambhala is a Tibetan name for paradise.
The Shambhala warrior fights against suffering, conflict and
ignorance. He or she is endowed with perfections or qualities
from which their powers come forth, and their weaponry is

the sword of wisdom and compassion. They seem to appear from the heavenly Garden of Eden so as to save the world. Such warriors can be found in every corner of the world, and they often appear in unexpected places. I have a Palestinian friend who spent ten years in an Israeli prison. She says that throughout her imprisonment she made sure that not one grain of hatred would accumulate in her heart, only love. After her release she volunteered to establish several clinics for treating children suffering from trauma as a result of the Israel–Palestine conflict, and became a powerful peace leader. There are also women in Israel whose grief for the loss of their children's lives motivated them to become untiringly active for reconciliation. You too, reading this chapter, could be such a warrior. Shambhala warriors are not necessarily devout Buddhists, but they must have a big soul, an open heart and be full human beings. We have a potential to act in the world out of a deep vision of the roots of pain and joy, of human and non-human nature, and of how things arise and pass. This is a universal potential; it is always available to each of us, and its realization depends on us alone.

One of the main ways this potential manifests is in authentic presence. Once I met an old Bedouin sheikh who had struggled against all odds for most of his life in order to provide for the needs and subsistence of his people. I was moved by his gentle, modest and firm presence and the glitter in his eyes. I sensed clearly this was an authentic person to the depths of his soul. Meditation can bring this quality to flower in our lives too; the practice of authentic presence with whatever arises within us allows us to be present authentically in the outside world as well. Authenticity means that we go about our lives without playing games, without hiding anything and without hypocrisy; an authentic person does not surrender to fear or escape to comfort zones, but remains steadfast in the eye of the storms of life.

The Tibetan teacher Chögyam Trungpa once said: "What attitude leads to the most beneficial contribution to society? How can we engage in right and authentic action? Only through being *present*."[1] Aware presence teaches us to see the way things are, a consequence of myriad causes and conditions, and from that place go out and make a difference. We regard whatever happens from our big heart of innate compassion and wisdom, without attaching much importance to our views, opinions, standpoints or reactions.

Non-clinging is a basic way of being that is a cornerstone in all traditions of Buddhism. It releases us from fixations with the way we imagine things ought to happen or the need for things to be one way and not another. It comes with a deep understanding that we cannot control life. This life controls us. Did we choose to be born? Did we choose to be who we are, or even where we are right now? For example, most of us would love to have more balance in our lives, but we forget that life is wild and unpredictable and is not there to supply us with balance. When we relinquish the expectation that life will fulfil our wishes, when we drop our dependence on views that are dressed up as the truth, when we meet this wild life face to face, we become spontaneous and free and our actions in the world arise as a dance and not as a struggle.

The heaviest mental burden is the control of the "I" – who I think I am, what I want to be or don't want to be, my self-importance, my rules, opinions and labels, my ego, my possessions, my views of success or failure, my image in the eyes of others and all the myriad manifestations of me and mine. But Shambhala warriors are not concerned about other people's views of them, which are neither interesting nor helpful. There is a story of the empty boat. Once, someone needed to cross the river, so he called the boatman, got into the boat and they started to cross. In midstream, their boat was hit by another boat and the boatman stood up and furiously shouted curses at the other boatman. They carried on, and further across they were hit by another boat, an empty one. The boatman sat quietly. "Why didn't you shout this time?" asked the passenger. "Because there was no-one to shout at," answered the boatman. If you are empty, you cannot be hurt, but if you have an ego to defend you are brittle. An attitude like that gives us enormous freedom, especially in challenging situations where you are likely to encounter opposition. The hard truths that authentic persons express may well give rise to discomfort, fear and guilt in others, and make them feel defensive. It is never easy to listen to the voice of our heart and speak out clearly against corruption and injustice, especially against powerful people, regimes or institutions.

The Mahayana Buddhist teaching talks about bodhisattvas – men or women who put off entering nirvana in order to act with dedication for the welfare and awakening of all sentient beings. Their lack of sense of self is so profound that were their goal to be accomplished, and they managed to bring about the awakening of all the beings in the world, it is said that if we asked them who did this they would answer: "I have no idea, it just happened!" We do indeed have the capacity to do wonderful things in our lives. The ego likes to shout: "I did that! It's my project! I want the credit! I want to hold onto it!" Or sometimes: "I failed again. It never works for me. I am always messing up!" But if we don't allow these beguiling voices of the self to interfere, we are filled with vibrant and selfless energy. Deep personal spiritual practice gives me a sustainable energy that has allowed me for over 35 years to act for the sake of others with joy and without burnout. Throughout the course of my life I founded many organizations: alternative medicine organizations in England in the late 1970s, environmental organizations in the Galilee, peace projects and initiatives in Israel-Palestine, and also Tovana – a society of thousands of people who practise the dharma in Israel. And when I am "no-one" at the back of the hall during a Tovana activity, I feel greater satisfaction and calm than when I think that somehow it all started in me. When we are not centred on ourselves, the compassionate action we take wells up naturally, joyfully and spontaneously from inside us, and indeed we can feel that it is happening by itself.

I can illustrate this process of melting the ego by some reflections from my own life. I live in the village of Clil, which I helped establish, an ideological community based

on Mahatma Gandhi's ecology principles. One of the most
powerful experiences of my life was during the years 1981–4
which I mostly spent clearing rocks from the land by hand.
I, an academic, a doctor of molecular biology from England,
found myself clearing stones day after day, year after year,
bent over and surrendering to the earth. After that I built my
house with my own hands, stone by stone. It was a beautiful
purifying experience, and I felt as if all that I had gone
through in my life until that moment had not really taken
place and all that I was at that moment was not relevant. All
my history was like a dream from last night. I don't mean to
suggest that in order to be a Shambhala warrior the reader
must now go off and pick stones from the nearest field!
It's just an example of how, when there is no sense of self-
importance, we are "no-one" and at the very same time part
of everyone and everything.

Losing our attachment to our roles and self-images, we take
ourselves more lightly and freely. A characteristic of Shambhala
warriors is that they cannot be labelled. They are not amenable
to definition. In one of Carlos Castaneda's books there is a
scene where the narrator meets the great Yaqui spiritual guide
Don Juan Matus and discovers that he is a short and ordinary-
looking old man sitting on a bench in a park in Mexico,
wearing a three-piece suit and looking like a businessman.
One would never imagine that this man is a wild and powerful
shaman. The Buddha once said that the appearance of
enlightened persons is not strong charisma but transparent
emptiness; their eyes reflect the entire world and not their
personality. When the Buddha was asked how one might
identify an awakened person, he answered that we would not
be able to find him or her even if they were actually standing
in front of us. None of the conventional classifications, labels
and descriptions apply to such a person.

Shambhala warriors also allow their emotions to arise
and pass. We cannot rely upon emotions to give the right
motivation for acting in the world. In actual fact, they cause
tremendous suffering. Emotions are extremely powerful and

at times they control us. We cannot act clearly and effectively without acknowledging them and giving them space. In daily life, as in meditation, we need to be intimate with the emotions that arise within us, to allow the emotions to arise and sing within us and be fully present when they appear and disappear. We do not need to encourage their expression nor suppression, but see them and feel them in the space between both. Instead of their becoming a huge dramatic story, and taking them to therapy, often all that is needed is to allow them to be themselves and let them pass. I once saw an interview with the Dalai Lama, who was asked about the situation of women in the Tibetan community. He started to cry, and then laughed and said: "Tradition is a great force. Even I cannot change the society radically." His tears were a beautiful response of a free person. Sadness is an important emotion that expresses our nobility. When we witness the suffering that exists in the world without anger, the sadness that can arise is like pathos, the most significant emotion in ancient Greece drama, and which is very close to compassion and engagement with all the suffering in the world.

When we wish to make a change in the world, there are two key dualities that we need to be aware of, and between which we need to find a dynamic balance, a golden mean. One is the balance between ends and means. If we are too much attached to ends, outcomes, we are always running after results like a donkey after the carrot on a stick. It leads to burnout, stress and pressure, and an obsessive missionary mind that annoys everyone. On the other hand, if we are too stuck with means, we will be busy trying to get things right and prepare ourselves, and endlessly sharpen the tools but never use them to build the house. Activities sow seeds that do not necessarily bring about measurable results. Measuring the effects of our action can create tension and pressure that are rooted in perceptions of success and failure. Sometimes organizations measure results compulsively and this puts everyone under stress and burnout. In the late 1990s we ran a programme in Nablus called "The Transformation of Suffering", within which groups of Israelis and Palestinians would meet for weekends of dialogue workshops. We encouraged participants to listen to each other's personal pain arising from the conflict, and this opened hearts and minds and the participants formed deep connections. After a few years the Palestinian Authority wanted to know what we were doing and asked us whether our workshops have led to the dismantling of a single Israeli settlement in the occupied territories. "No," we said. "If so," they asked, "what good is it for us?" We answered that we were doing education, not politics, training people to be peace leaders in their communities. I told them about one Palestinian boy who said: "The only Israelis I ever saw until now were the soldiers in the streets, and I felt that people were bad. Now I understand that there is also real goodness in the human heart. This will stay with me all my life." The representatives were fairly impressed, but eventually we were required to obey the wider political reality and the programme had to end.

Activities that come out of the goodness of our hearts are like seeds – they need water, food and appropriate conditions, and we also need to let go and allow them to grow so that life can pick the fruit. There is nothing wrong in thinking about the connection between circumstances and results, but we must do so wisely, with the understanding that they are interdependent and that change occurs within a much larger web of conditions and circumstances. In other words, we need to act with an understanding of the way the law of karma operates. The quality of our actions is the nutriment of karmic seeds that will give growth to a new reality. We may get caught up in the illusion that our actions can bring about huge change, such as when writing a successful report, but when we look at the larger picture we see that everything changes by itself and we cannot foresee anything. It is better to relax and allow life to carry us in its wake; we can rest.

Another fine balance is between inner and outer experience. We need to express what's in our hearts, to act decisively and speak out in situations where others are silent. But this needs to be balanced by inner qualities such as brightness, clarity, peacefulness and joy. If we are too dominated by the outer, we are a busy bee, constantly active, often agitated, sometimes mechanical and frustrated. If we are too much in the inner life we can get paralysed and psychologically constipated. Maybe we sit at home passively, in front of screens and media, bemoaning what's going on in the world. Or, alternatively, perhaps we work on ourselves with a view that we need to be perfectly peaceful before we can go out and make peace, and then we will feel we are never ready to go out there and give voice. A dynamic balance between inner and outer releases amazing power and potential where heart and mind, voice and body, are in sync. We strive for realization of a vision but at the same time manifest peacefulness, harmony, compassion and a broad and inclusive wise heart.

This is expressed in the name of the peacemaking organization that several of us established some time ago – Middleway – and it was embodied in many kinds of activities that we did. One example of the balance between inner and outer are the silent peace walks that took place for several years. These walks brought together Israeli Jews and Palestinians who walked together in single file at a slow and uniform pace, manifesting stability, unity and friendliness – the forces that can heal conflict. One inspiration for these walks was the Cambodian Buddhist monk Maha Ghosananda who walked endlessly around his country at a time of the terrible slaughters, saying repeatedly to the combatants: "Do not kill each other, kill the hatred in your hearts." A phrase that we used to characterize this balance of inner and outer, expressing well the understanding that real peace depends on peacefulness, was that pioneered by A J Muste, a prominent protestor against the Vietnam war: "There is no way to peace; peace itself is the way." One of these walks included 300 Palestinians and Israelis and started at the village of Barta'a and ended at the separation wall that divides the territories of Israel and the Palestinian Authority. At one point some Palestinian young men started waving flags of Palestine, so I told them that peace does not need flags. After that we continued in silence step by step toward the dividing fence, where we all sang and danced!

Social activism that is informed by the dharma does not preach. It encourages us to walk our talk and to "be the change you wish to see in the world" as Mahatma Gandhi put it. Social and political activists often deal with this issue; the meeting rooms of their organizations are sometimes noisy with friction between views, hopes, arguments and egos of their colleagues. These arguments lead to confusion and despair, because the activists who want to make the world a better place cannot understand why it is so difficult. It is because of the dominance of the outer over the inner. As the saying goes: "The road to hell is paved with good intentions." This can lead to catastrophe. For example, during the Vietnam war in the 1960s three million people were killed "in the name of freedom", as the Americans put it. Most wars break out in the name of peace, just as innumerable massacres are carried out in the name of God. We have to be really careful of the view that the world's problems will be solved only if "they" change, not "us".

Activists may object that a broad view and joyful peaceful heart are unhelpful foundations for action, arguing that they couldn't do anything without motivation based on a burning need for change and a righteous anger over injustice. These personal motives are indeed sources of energy, and sometimes they are also needed, but if they take centre stage they can create all the problems described above. Whereas if these drives are softened a larger inner space opens that in most instances is a space of love, and this is a more powerful and sustainable motivation. Love grows with a minimizing of subjectivity and clinging to personal stories, and the quietening of anger and frustration. In fact love can be found behind all our actions, often camouflaged as a desire to fix the world. In its essence, love is an expression of our sense of belonging to the world, and in a certain way love and belonging are one and the same. We want to help a blind person cross the road because we know how she feels, we have empathy, and in a way both of us share the same human vulnerability. This feeling of love is a powerful force that underlies all our actions. We may lose touch with it, forget it and fail to notice it, yet nonetheless love, empathy and compassion have formidable power.

Love and compassion are joyful, complete, reconciling and sustainable elements in all our actions in the world. Acting in the spirit of the dharma is an act of love.

CHAPTER 42

ENLIGHTENMENT AND AWAKENING

Awakening isn't any thing
Even though we run after it.
But as we stumble
From knowing to being,
We accidentally fall into it
While falling out
Of everything else.

The word enlightenment is enticing. It conjures up a radical and ecstatic transformation, a filling up with light, more or less turning a human being into an angel. We think of the Buddha, of Moses on Mount Sinai, of Jesus, and of enlightened beings throughout the ages, and we may sense awe or sacredness. It may trigger faith. However, as we are not entirely sure what enlightenment actually is, we cannot actually say who is or is not enlightened.

Enlightenment is a rather bad word. It is an English translation of various terms in Sanskrit or Pali or Japanese, such as nirvana or satori. This translation became popular some time ago, when it was assumed that this ultimate transformation was a breakthrough event, some kind of intellectual and ecstatic insight, a seeing of light, an eureka moment. It harked back to the Enlightenment period in European history, which was a period of intellectual and cultural creativity, coming out of the dark ages of religious authority. However, there are much better words to describe it. The word awakening is an important one. Of the 108 words indicating liberation in the Buddhist canon, awakening is the one the Buddha used to describe his own state. A villager once met the Buddha walking in the street and was impressed with his presence. "Who are you?" asked the villager. "Are you a god, a prince, a demon, an angel?" The Buddha answered: "No, I am not a god, a prince, a demon or an angel. I am awake. Just like a red, blue, or white lotus – born in the water, grown in the water, rising up above the water – stands untainted by the water, in the same way I – born in the world, grown in the world, having overcome the world – live untainted by the world. Remember me, brahmin, as 'awakened'."[1] Awakening is a better term, more faithful to the nature of the transformation. It has more to do with waking up from a dream of ordinary mundane reality, than lighting up this reality with transcendental light.

We believe totally in this ordinary reality, the dream of seeing the world as a given, a fact. A tree is a tree, a rock is a rock, a person is a person and an enemy is an enemy. My anger is real and the cause of my anger, another person, is to blame. I am a separate me and I spend my life looking after myself and those I am close to, and I am afraid to die. Time exists and I don't have enough of it. I must manifest myself in life and be successful like others, and I need to spend my life doing what others seem to be doing all the time: surviving, consuming, fighting, thinking, building, watching TV, working, and believing in the consensus as the reality. This is a kind of sleepwalking through our life. Waking up is waking up out of this dream – each moment is seen as a fresh, original and alive moment, that arises and passes like a line written in water, or a bird passing in the sky. These living moments are timeless and don't belong to me or to anyone. Jiddu Krishnamurti wrote in his journal:

On a still night when the stars are clear and close, you would be aware of expanding space and the mysterious order of all things, of the immeasurable and of nothing, of the movement of the dark hills and the hoot of an owl. In that utter silence of the mind this mystery expands without time and space. [...] This is love.[2]

Awakening is a shift to another way of viewing the world, a sense of perfection, completion, totality and interconnectedness. As such it need not be obvious or dramatic, as Elijah says in the Bible, the voice of God is not in thunder but in the "hidden voice of stillness". It does not need ecstasy. It may be wrapped inside ordinary reality, like a diamond covered in mud. It is about stillness with intensity. Nirvana, for example, is translated as "quenching the fires" – the fires are the fires that keep us burning up with activity and need. They are the fires of restless busyness, running toward what we want and what would be better, and away from what we do not want, what is threatening or disturbing. They are the fires of compulsively seeing things as we are conditioned to see them, especially seeing and busily maintaining ourselves as a person separate from the universe. Nirvana implies a deep peace in which we merge with the world so there is no longer any friction. There is nothing to be fixed. It is not a cold deadness – the fire isn't dead, it simply goes back home to become part of the universe. The Buddha used the image to explain that enlightenment is not a particular state of a person that we "get to". There is no address – it is a return to everything. He said that it is impossible to say where the fire went when it goes out. It does not go out to the east, west, or any other direction. Nirvana is also a word that illustrates the process. The fire goes out when all its fuel is used up. When we no longer feed the illusions of conditioned ordinary reality – samsara – nirvana is what is left.

This can be rather scary. If the apparent conventional reality of me and the world doesn't hold together when deeply investigated, what can I hang on to? If my mind is making my world – where is the ground? Where is the reality? If we get up in the morning without the security of the known, in a space in which "me" and "other" are no longer assumed and all seeming boundaries are just concepts, at the very least we would dive back under the bedclothes. Indeed, the spiritual journey is not always a stroll along a pleasant boulevard, and we can get lost. Indeed, we may have to get lost to get out of the matrix, because it is our belief in a known and constructed world that holds us tight. But we soon discover that we are inhabiting a vast new territory, and, once we taste it, there is no going back, we would not exchange it for anything, and it is nothing if not natural to live with this universal wisdom rather than the previous limited awareness.

All of us have moments of awakening, moments when we look at things more clearly, with insight and with a big heart. Usually they last a moment and are forgotten. True spiritual awakening occurs when these moments are more intense and prolonged, when they become our state, or way of being. Then one can say a person is awakened or enlightened. Here is a description of one moment of awakening, among many, in my own life:

I had just been digging in the vegetable garden, preparing another bed for the summer vegetables. I stood in the middle of the garden and relaxed. I took in the whole picture and it suddenly felt overwhelming. The garden exploded with richness: the multiple varieties of green, the red roses, the healing and sacred orange calendula, the tantalizing tastes and aromas, the intoxicating smell of deep wet earth. It was the work of my hands and yet it was making me as much as I was making it – I was only one part of everything else in the world that all together made this garden and this moment. This joyful cycle had no purpose, no end, just the beauty of engagement with life. It made me weep. What is the awakening? It is the participation. It is melting into the moment. The garden needed me to know it, so we could exist together. As the knower of it, I was just one more necessary part of the picture. Along with each radish.

Such experiences create an irreversible change in the way the person regards themselves and the world. If you are consistently interested in, directed toward and surrendered to liberation, it unfolds itself; the belief that ordinary experience is reality falls away – that fire has no more fuel and goes out. Then awakening itself becomes less special and unusual, and is the only way things can be seen and known. From that place, "looking back", the world of descriptions, definitions, separations and identities becomes merely a functional fiction. Stephen, this being writing these words, is a convenient construction of a mind that is used to doing that, but it has no real interest or reality. When the mind meets the world through the senses and makes contact, a natural construction appears to happen, driven by karma, but it arises and falls back into the totality and actually nothing really happened, because the mind and the world were never separate in the first place.

From this wisdom it is absurd to describe a person as enlightened. An enlightened person is an oxymoron. Enlightenment cannot be owned by anyone or contained in any frame or identity of a person or a mind. It is more faithful to its essence to say that it happens to itself.

The journey to awakening is written into the instruction manuals of all the great spiritual traditions. Whether Christian mystics, Muslim Sufis, Jewish Hasidim, or Buddhist meditators, the guidelines are there. Although I must admit a personal preference for the Buddhist teachings as they are so well developed, so clear and accessible, with so little mystification and so much wisdom and expertise on navigating the inner journey. The way always starts with a base of deep morality, deep purity, what Don Juan in the Castaneda books called "impeccability". We have all seen that abuse or harming of self or other doesn't go together with awakening. From that base, the path involves familiar components: meditation and spiritual exercises, a balanced mind and body, development of trust, faith, concentration, joy, peace and letting go. All held together by a deep commitment to the journey. The journey could be long or short. It could and often does involve extremely difficult periods of doubt, fear, weakness or pain – the dark night of the soul. It is generally not a one-off revelation, more of a gradual peeling away of attachments and blindness, like a snake shedding skins. Awakening is beyond our mental processes, beyond thought and beyond concept. As such we can never measure it, expect it, design it or plan it. The more we push for it, the more it runs away. It is both up to our efforts and quite beyond our efforts. There is a Zen quote: "Enlightenment is an accident. All we can do is become more accident-prone."

The Buddha awakened in the teeth of a multipronged onslaught by the demon Mara, representing the voice of doubt, temptation and resistance. This was the last gasp of the ordinary mind, trying to tempt the Buddha back to attachments to the known, to conventional conditioned reality. Mara's final ploy was to question the authenticity of his awakening. He asked who is a witness, who can validate his awakening. The Buddha didn't answer and just pointed to the earth. Our interconnection with the world – the tweets of love we receive from the wind and the rain and the earth and the sky – are an anchor. If we get lost it is only in relation to the maps of the world that we constructed inside ourselves that are no longer relevant. Therefore we have to lose ourselves to find the world – and the world is always waiting to welcome us home again. It may be the greatest task we can do with our one precious life. And it is the journey itself that makes it so, not just the destination.

CHAPTER 43

NOT THE BIG BANG?

The rest is silence, rest in silence
Not a dead suppression
But a living stillness, the source of whispered secrets
A white page which permits these words
Not an absence but a presence
That invites everything to speak
In the voice of its being
That needs no language.
Friction screams, but harmony is quiet,
For nothing needs to be done or undone
As it all happens by itself.
It is the silence of the womb
Before it gave birth to noise
Or the question that knows no answer
Or whatever is not the Big Bang
And the stillness where words have disappeared
As all descriptions no longer function.
It is part of all of us
Do you remember?

APPENDICES

APPENDIX I

SPIRITUAL TEACHING – HOW IT WORKS

Amir Freimann interview with Stephen Fulder on 20 October 2015[1]

Amir: Let's start with Stephen as a student – who were your teachers and who do you still consider as your teachers today?

Stephen: In the Theravada tradition that I've been practising and involved with, the principle of a single primary teacher (root guru, or *satguru*) is not relevant, and so I've had plenty of teachers. My first teacher was S N Goenka, but the relationship with him was impersonal, as he was teaching thousands of students. In Goenka's tradition, based on a Burmese lineage, the teachers teach the practice rather technically and don't really relate to you as an individual and to your issues or your life. They are masters at passing on to you a technique and motivating and encouraging you to practise intensively.

Amir: But even though you say there was no personal relationship with Goenka and he was just communicating the teaching in a technical way, there was something about him that made him a better vehicle for the teaching than many others in that tradition. There was a reason why you went to see him and not hundreds of other teachers. There must have been something about the person that is an important factor in the transmission of the teaching.

Stephen: Yes, I only did one retreat with Goenka himself, who is charismatic and inspiring, and after that I did about a dozen with Sayama. She came from the same tradition as Goenka and they both had the same teacher. Why I kept going back to *her* is an interesting question. I think it's because she embodied a very finely tuned and subtle understanding of practice. I really respected her extraordinary power of mind, her *samadhi*, and how she brought this into the practice. There was something about her that was crystal clear, as if she was coming from a subtle awareness and a space that I could trust, that did not embody a lot of belief or tradition or control. She radiated a present-moment awareness that was very big, free, unbounded, powerful and deserved respect. Also, Sayama was one of the few teachers I met in my life that clearly had extraordinary powers. She would often answer my questions before I asked them. I would come into her room with a question in my mind and she would immediately start to answer it and so I didn't need to say anything. So in terms of a student–teacher relationship there was definitely more content, flow and dynamism than the relationship with Goenka.

Amir: Could you say that in your relationship with Sayama there was spiritual intimacy or a deep connection? Because what you described of her ability to know what's in your mind and respond must surely have something to do with knowing each other very well or communicating on a deep level.

Stephen: Not exactly. There was deep communication but it was not at all personal. It was technique oriented. She didn't know me nor was interested in me as Stephen, with a certain character and personality. I don't think she really cared about me that much … (laughing). She was dedicated to understanding and guiding my experiences, on a specific well-trodden path within the frame of reference of the practice. There is a benefit in this dedication, but also a cost, since it is a bit like a parent only relating to their child according to how well they do at school. A lot will be missing, for example the ability to know the gifts and inner life of each person and so guide the practice more holistically and individually.

Since then I met many teachers who I sat with and talked to and though I wouldn't say they were major teachers in my life they certainly helped me on the road. Some of those really did have a much more personal relationship with me, such that in a way we never forgot each other. There are a few who I would say have been more significant guides, friends and co-travellers along the way, including Fred von Allman, Joseph Goldstein and particularly Christopher Titmuss, whom I have been close to for more than 30 years, and for whom I have enormous respect and appreciation as a friend, a teacher and a colleague.

I want to stress that teaching happens at several levels at once, not all of which may be consciously known by the student. There is the guiding in which the teacher as a kind of tour guide defines the path and the way and supports the student along it. There is the imparting of verbal knowledge, inspiration and hints of what is beyond. There is the modelling, in which the teacher radiates a more invisible way of being. Teaching can also happen when the teacher mirrors or reflects back to you something you asked or did, offering a larger, freer and wiser perspective, and in that moment they become teachers of yours, although it's not consciously a teacher–student relationship in any way. Once I was in India on a six-week self-retreat, in a small room in an ashram, and there was a spiritual teacher teaching in a nearby ashram. He used to come to my room 5:30 in the morning every couple of days and we would sit and talk. He would first of all kiss my feet, which is of course an Indian way of expressing his appreciation for my practice, and I bowed to his feet as well because the appreciation was mutual. Then we would talk and I felt that any question I threw out was answered from a huge space, as if throwing a pebble into a great clay jar and listening to the unlimited resonances. You could feel that space behind his eyes, from which I was seen and understood. The words could be about rice and beans or about the most subtle and delicate movements in consciousness. Everything that was put in there came back out spontaneously, immediately, with no obvious thought behind it, emerging like an echo from this expanded awareness.

He's not my teacher and I did not see him before or after that, but we had something very powerful, intimate and unforgettable that went on between us. I was clearly in the role of student and he was in the role of teacher. Maybe in another time it could have been reversed, where I might've helped him, but that was the framework we chose and kind of agreed on without words, and we were both happy with that.

Amir: You're really giving a few very different examples or different models of the teacher–student relationship.

Stephen: Yes, teaching can be much more existential than sitting on a stage and giving talks. It can be with the eyes, with body language, with the way you are with people, with how you sing to a baby or how you relate to a dog or a cat in the street – and that's teaching. On a subtle level it is teaching because it's coming from that expanded awareness and clarity and wisdom that I was talking about, manifesting naturally within ordinary life. I feel that people who are quite developed teach that way. They don't always teach as intentionally and consistently, it might be quite spontaneous and actually they can't do anything else. This doesn't need a label – but it is teaching.

Amir: Are you saying that for some people the formality of a defined teacher–student interrelation can enhance their ability, and draw them toward greater depth, responsibility, care, and freedom, while for others it may do the opposite and actually be an obstacle?

Stephen: That's right. In many cases it is really needed to start off, as it sets the scene, defines the territory of teaching, and is familiar to students, a bit like going back to school. Thus it is an agreement that reduces the concerns and insecurities of the unknown. But indeed there are some students who don't really need this theatre and for whom the projections and roles of teacher and student are just a nuisance. More than that it may trigger psychological resistance and friction, perhaps because of some previous pain connected with their relationship with "father". In any case, the formality and the separation and the roles gradually break down along the way, and then the word "teacher" becomes irrelevant. When you talk about a deeper level, the roles, concepts and words tend to break down and cease to function as a medium of teaching. One should be aware of that. The teaching then happens naturally because nothing else can happen, and it is expressed in speech, body and mind. There isn't anything that a teacher needs to do, he or she is manifesting their spirituality through themselves. The role vanishes and there is no thought that says: "I'm going to teach now. Look at the way I'm walking down the corridor."

Amir: And yet you seem ok with being called a teacher, you seem comfortable being in that position and fulfilling that function – why is that? Are there any benefits, psychological or spiritual, that you get from being a teacher?

Stephen: For sure. The importance is in the doing of it, not in the label, which is not interesting. If I am called a teacher or not called a teacher, it doesn't turn a hair. One benefit for me is that the expression or teaching of the dharma releases more of the stream. Teaching moves through me and out, so I feel the flow and that's joyful, and that's one reason why I keep teaching. Another reason is that there is nothing more interesting for me to do in life. What else is there? Go to the office every day and do an ordinary job? It's so joyful to be in the environment of the teaching situation and to be creative, and playful. It brings out of me qualities that are needed in this struggling world, so I think it's what I can do to help the world. Another benefit I feel is that teaching simply opens the heart in the present-moment meetings with an individual or even a group. In the last year I have been going round pubs and bars, under the title "Buddha at the Bar", giving talks and meditations to large numbers of people, and it warms the heart to bring a different message to young people who are often so much in need of a more hopeful and meaningful view beyond the usual diet of conflict, materialism, competitiveness, pressure and agitation.

Amir: Are you saying that to have the right relationship to what comes out of you as a teacher you have to let go of any sense of possessing the teaching or identifying yourself with it?

Stephen: Yes, definitely. You let go of possessing the teaching, of owning the role, and in the same way you let go of you possessing yourself – the self that's on stage. You have to let go of that. The Dalai Lama expresses this very beautifully before giving teachings by symbolically bowing down to the seat before sitting on it. It's a ritual that says: "I'm going to sit on that seat and honour the role given to me, but I wear the role like clothes, and then come down and take the clothes off." Someone once told me that being a dharma teacher is not about giving the most charismatic and wonderful talk you can give, but if you give the worst talk ever, you get up from your seat and have no more thoughts about it.

Amir: Do you think that, as the Dalai Lama sits on his seat and puts on those clothes, he also activates in himself certain human qualities, that are required of somebody in that role? Is that something you experience when you sit on the stage in front of people asking you questions; that certain human qualities manifest in you that don't manifest in other situations?

Stephen: No, I don't think there are qualities I don't have in other situations too, but certainly conditions will pull out of you and emphasize particular qualities that are needed and fitting to that situation. For example, the condition of running – I run every couple of days – pulls out of me qualities of perseverance. Teaching enhances sensitivity in a few dimensions. It invites me to be particularly caring and very watchful, and not to talk unkindly or unwisely; more watchful or mindful than perhaps I am with my grandchildren. Then, it encourages me to develop qualities of steadiness and confidence as well as fine-tuned ethics and care, clarity of mind, kindness, confidence, and a little bit of authority. I'm given the authority and I am aware of that and appreciate it so I hold it with tenderness and some respect. Maybe there's also a lift in energy that comes from being on the stage. A lift of the heart I would say.

Amir: Would you say that you are spiritually elevated as you step into that position?

Stephen: In a way yes, but there are many other situations in life when I also feel that. So it's definitely not the only one. I might feel that also in the deep silence of early morning before sunrise, when everything is quiet and I can only hear the jackals far away. So it's not only in the teacher role, but the conditions of the teaching do tend to elevate you to the best you can be. Yes, I do feel that.

Amir: How do you feel or respond when people say to you that you are their teacher, or ask you to be their teacher?

Stephen: I don't prevent it, I don't tell people they must not say that about me – I can't. But I don't at all encourage it. I don't support exclusivity in today's modern culture, and I suggest to students to learn from many teachers. Sometimes when people say to me, "I want you to be my teacher," I say to them, ok, I don't mind you regarding me as being the main teacher for the moment, but I don't really like the label, and eventually you should have other teachers as well. I tend to discourage exclusivity whether in relation to myself or other teachers because I think it reduces the autonomy, the independence of mind and the authenticity and confidence of the student.

The other thing is that I don't want to be constantly available for those who expect me to be in that role all the time. The role of personal teacher would carry with it an obligation. I just don't want to be disturbed when I'm not teaching, like when I'm in my vegetable garden. I actually don't want people calling me with questions like "Should I go to India?", "Should I get married?", "Should I change jobs?" etc. I am fine if they ask me those questions in the context of retreats and teaching, and then I'd relate to them, but that's it and then I go home and I take off that role like peeling off well-worn clothes.

Amir: This is solving quite a few problems that are inherent in other models of teacher–student relationship. But after guiding a lot of people along the path, don't you think that for some people the process of surrender to or via a teacher, of trusting somebody else very deeply, more than they trust themselves, is an important catalyst on their journey?

Stephen: It can indeed be helpful but only if it's light. If it's too intense and total it can undo their spiritual journey, because they're replacing themselves with someone else. But of all the questions you have asked so far, this is the most problematic and nuanced. Because on the one hand you can say, what's wrong with praying to the Buddha, as a larger-than-life figure, identifying with and respecting his qualities and so letting the prayer to the Buddha remind you of your own Buddha qualities? But it only works if it is quite light. If there is a strong sense of supplication, worship, glorification, and deification of a teacher or an icon, it can disempower our practice and disconnect us from our spiritual sources. Where I feel it's too much I would tend to question it and bring it back down to size. I would tend to say to the person: "You're going too far making the teacher unrealistically dominant, using projection onto the teacher to avoid meeting your own existential pain and joy, and I suggest you go back to yourself a little bit." I think it's the scale; when trust and dependence on a teacher goes over the top it almost begins to be pathological.

In our Theravada tradition we would tend to constantly shift the focus from the teacher to the teaching, the dharma itself. I would tend to say: "Take refuge in the dharma, not in Stephen." This is different from the guru tradition, where the guru would be happy to hold that place of dependence for longer, to allow more intensity of transference. But it's a good question and not black-and-white.

Amir: It seems that in the tradition of the guru–disciple relationship there is more love and personal bonding.

Stephen: Yes, I agree, and I'm not saying it's necessarily a bad thing. It can sometimes be a great heart-opening friendship and appreciation. A teacher can take a student under his wing and he or she might blossom there. But it is not the primary way of our practice-oriented tradition, in which the teacher can be a spiritual friend and encourage the students to be the highest that they can be, but is one stage removed.

There are also of course many dangers and possible abuses in the guru–disciple relationship and I think it's better to play it safe and be careful. It's worth remembering that the higher the teacher's status and the more students surrender to them, the more perfect they need to be. When they overstep the boundaries of ethical sensitivity, or they get tempted by all kinds of desires and needs, or they become narcissistic and controlling, or they don't walk their talk, they can crash down from the high place that the students have placed them. I've met many people who have gone through really difficult situations with gurus, and eventually they came to the dharma and said: "What a relief! Thank goodness I'm out of that mess, of believing totally in a person and doing what he says."

Amir: After one interview in particular, I recently started thinking about a distinction I make between what I call "therapeutic relationships" and "transformative relationships". A few weeks ago I interviewed in New York the founder of the New York Zen Dojo, a Zen master and a psychotherapist by the name of Barry Magid, and he said that all those who come to the spiritual path do so because they have a psychological

problem. He explained that the most common problems
are self-hatred and difficulty to deal with the complexity of
life, and whether they come to him as a therapist or as a Zen
teacher, it's basically the same for him. What do you think of
that approach?

Stephen: It is very cloudy issue, I'm afraid, and a complex
question to answer. I am going to try to answer it in various
ways that are not linearly related. It is true that everybody
that comes to the spiritual journey has psychological issues.
There's nobody without them. And they do need to be
addressed otherwise they will weigh you down and you will
feel imprisoned by your issues and stories. But you can't
afford to spend all your life fixing yourself. The statement of
Barry Magid reflects a very widespread view in American and
Western culture, of not being good enough, and having to
constantly repair oneself – "First I've got to fix my fears, then
I've got to fix my addictions, my relationship issues, my money
problems, my miserable childhood …" – and on and on. The
whole spiritual journey gets reduced to busy house cleaning
and repairing bits and pieces of yourself. But it is perfectly
possible to go through very deep transformative experiences
and wrap up the psychological issues later. Instead of endlessly
repairing your psychology you can put yourself entirely in
another place, of freedom and "being". Then, although the
psychological issues haven't disappeared, in that context they do
not have the same power to cause suffering. So in my view the
transformative dimension can be experienced right from the
start along with the therapeutic, and very slowly the territory of
the therapeutic is reduced and the transformative grows.

Some people will be more dominated by psychological
issues and then the teacher and the teaching can help them
to allow, receive and view the psychological issues with more
equanimity, detachment and inner peace. Yet the practice
must move on to reveal the basic emptiness of these patterns,
something of the "me" that is burdened with them and the
nature of the suffering itself that they cause. Yes, you've got

psychological issues but what is your connection to deep silence? What about the freedom which is not connected to psychological issues? What is the consciousness of the ocean, from which a wave called, for example, self-esteem, rises? The self-esteem is a form in consciousness that gives you trouble, but there is the consciousness itself, that gives rise to the form. I'm always trying to integrate the psychological and the spiritual and I think we can go much further and deeper than the statement of the Zen teacher implies.

Amir: So are we talking about two different motivations – a motivation to heal and a motivation to transcend – or is it the same motivation and some people interpret it as psychological and others as spiritual?

Stephen: That's an interesting question. They are not really two, more of a continuum which starts as healing and continues as transcendence with a big overlap in the middle. I'd say it's up to me as a teacher to constantly take the motivation one step forward from wherever it is. Indeed lots of people come to meditation at the beginning because they've got migraines or insomnia or things like that. I regard that as completely legitimate and I say ok, let's practise. Then as the practice continues I encourage the discovery of deeper intentions, and refinement of the motivations. When you climb a mountain, the reasons why you're climbing can change on the way up. Maybe at the bottom of the mountain you say: "I'm going to climb that mountain because I have to cure my childhood issues. I had a terrible childhood, I have a lot of anxieties, and I need to climb this mountain and deal with them." I would respond: "Let's start. I'll help you, we'll climb together." We would start steadily climbing, and after a few hundred metres up the mountain I'd call out: "Hey, did you notice the small blue flowers next to the path?" "Yeah. They are really nice." I'd suggest: "Let's pay more attention to the flowers." Then, after another two hundred metres I'd say: "What an amazing sunset." "Yes, it is really inspiring."

After some time, I might throw out: "What about the flowers and the beautiful sunset inside you? Do you see them as you walk?" And you go: "Wow, oh, yes, of course, I have flowers in me …" The whole psychological motivation that was at the beginning has really been purified and transformed. It becomes the longing for total freedom. Eventually that too dissolves, and there is no real need for any motivation based on the wish to be somewhere else other than where you really are and who you really are. The mountain vanishes and climbing is the same as being.

APPENDIX 2
BASIC MEDITATION INSTRUCTIONS

- Choose a quiet corner or room in the house or a shaded protected spot in nature, which will become your favourite and regular place for practice.
- Sit upright and steady, without strain but with an energetic and relaxed dignity, like a king. If on the ground, sit on the edge of a cushion or two to bring your knees closer to the ground and reduce the tendency to roll backwards. Your legs can be crossed in any way that is easy. If on a chair let your two feet touch the ground and sit erect.
- Close your eyes and gather yourself together, mind and body present in this moment. It is like arriving home, or landing in the here and now. Feel the luxury of simply being. Drop into presence.
- Remind yourself that meditation is about being, not doing: there is nothing to be fixed, nothing to be gained or obtained, nothing wrong and no struggle. The only effort needed is to be present as consistently as possible, and interested in what is actually going on.
- After some time choose the breath as a primary object of mindfulness, and a natural place to consistently rest the attention. Notice how each breath feels, track it as it enters and travels through the body, expanding the stomach, and then its journey out with the stomach contracting again. Let each breath be natural and soft, just as it is, closely embraced by your attention, as if the breath is breathing you. You can explore the subtle journey of the breath through all the body and the cells.
- Notice and appreciate any calmness and sense of ok-ness that arises.

- Notice how breath and bodily awareness are experienced together. Sometimes move the attention to this sense of embodiment, the sensations of aliveness that move and change in the body, such as the touch of the hands.
- Meditative attention does not need to hunt for a particular "right" experience. It is a direct knowing of what is actually going on, with a radical acceptance.
- When thoughts, commenting, memories, pictures, stories about the past or future or any other mental content or pattern arises, let them appear and pass by like clouds in the sky, in the background. If the mental content is insistent and dominant it can be helpful to step back and give it a label such as "judgemental thought". If you identify with the thought and it carries you away with it to the past or future, step out of the train of thinking onto the platform, and return to the breath.
- All kinds of experiences and impressions can arise naturally. They can be at the level of the body, such as stress, tension, pain, ease or peace. They can be at the level of feelings, such as tiredness, boredom, agitation, sadness, enthusiasm, blankness, irritation, or any other. They are not disturbances or problems that stop meditation, they are the raw material for meditation. Leave the breath and turn your attention to these experience as simple phenomena that arise, stay for a while and pass. Try to identify them but not identify with them. Be aware of the actual experience as it is and what if any is the reaction to it. Be aware if it is pleasant or unpleasant.
- Be kind to yourself. No need to judge yourself as a success or failure. No need to measure progress. No need to label any psychological or physical experience as problematic. Allow whatever arises to be just as it is, even if it is difficult, let it be, and let it go. Be aware that everything passes by.
- Gradually get a sense that you are not on automatic pilot, but are able to hold your changing inner life with kindness, appreciation and interest.

NOTES

Introduction

1 Booth, Robert. "Way ahead of the curve: UK hosts first summit on mindful politics." *The Guardian*, 13 October 2017.

Chapter 2

1 Carter, J R, and Palihawadana, M. *The Dhammapada*. Oxford: Oxford University Press, 2008.

Chapter 8

1 Wilbur, Ken. *Grace and Grit: Spirituality and Healing in the Life and Death of Treya Killam Wilbur.* Colorado: Shambhala, 2000.

2 Bar Lev, Liora. *We Better Remember the Good.* Jerusalem: Carmel Publishers (forthcoming: in press).

Chapter 11

1 Eliot, T S. *Four Quartets.* London: Faber & Faber, 1960.

2 Palmer, Martin, trans. *The Book of Chuang Tzu.* London: Penguin, 2006.

Chapter 13

1 St Pierre, L S, and Persinger, M A. "Experimental facilitation of the sensed presence is predicted by the specific patterns of the applied magnetic fields, not by suggestibility: re-analyses of 19 experiments." *International Journal of Neurosciences* 116: 1079–96 (2006).

2 Cade, M, and Coxhead, N. *The Awakened Mind.* Toronto: Delacorte Press, 1979.

Chapter 15

1 *Ambalatthikarahulavada Sutta, Majjhima Nikaya* 61.
2 *Canki Sutta, Majjhima Nikaya* 95.

Chapter 16

1 See, for example: Chiesa, A, and Serretti, A. "Mindfulness-based interventions for chronic pain: a systematic review of the evidence." *Journal of Alternative and Complementary Medicine* 17: 83–93 (2011).

Chapter 17

1 Baer, R A, ed. *Mindfulness-Based Treatment Approaches: Clinician's Guide to Evidence Base and Applications.* New York: Academic Press, 2005.
2 Teasedale, J D, et al. "Prevention of relapse/recurrence in depression by Mindfulness-Based Cognitive Therapy." *Journal of Consulting and Clinical Psychology* 68: 615–23 (2000).
3 Report by the Mindfulness All-Party Parliamentary Group (MAPPG). *Mindful Nation UK*, 2015. Available from: www.themindfulnessinitiative.org.uk.
4 Rapgay, L, and Bystrisky, A. "Classical mindfulness: an introduction to its theory and practice for clinical application." *Annals of the New York Academy of Sciences* 1172: 148–62 (2009).
5 Chiesa, A, and Serretti, A. "Mindfulness-based interventions for chronic pain: a systematic review of the evidence." *Journal of Alternative and Complementary Medicine* 17: 83–93 (2011).
6 Didonna, F, ed. *Clinical Handbook of Mindfulness.* New York: Springer, 2008.
7 Hofmann S G, and Gómez A F. "Mindfulness-based interventions for anxiety and depression." *Psychiatric Clinics of North America* 40.4: 739–49 (2017).
8 Haller H, et al. "Mindfulness-based interventions for women with breast cancer: an updated systematic review and meta-analysis." *Acta Oncologica* 56.12: 1665–76 (2017).

9   Garland S N, et al. "The quest for mindful sleep: a critical synthesis of the impact of mindfulness-based interventions for insomnia." *Current Sleep Medicine Reports* 2.3: 142–51 (2016).

10 Sutcliffe K M, et al. "Mindfulness in organisations: a cross level review." *Annual Review of Organizational Psychology and Organizational Behavior* 3: 55–81 (2016).

11 Thich Nhat Hanh. *Peace Is Every Step: The Path of Mindfulness in Everyday Life.* New York: Bantam, 1992.

12 Thich Nhat Hanh. *The Miracle of Mindfulness: An Introduction to the Practice of Meditation.* Boston: Beacon Press, 1999.

Chapter 19

1   Dowman, Keith, trans. *The Flight of the Garuda.* Boston: Wisdom Publications, 1994.

Chapter 20

1   Hillesum, Etty. *An Interrupted Life: The Diaries and Letters of Etty Hillesum 1941–43.* London: Persephone Books, 1999.

Chapter 23

1   Fronsdal, Gil, trans. *The Dhammpada.* Boston: Shambhala, 2005.

Chapter 24

1   *Maha-Saccaka Sutta, Majjhima Nikaya* 36:85, 36:100.
2   *Sagaathaa Vagga, Samyutta Nikaya* 1:1.

Chapter 27

1   Lau, D C, trans. *Lao Tzu: Tao Te Ching.* Harmondsworth: Penguin Books, 1963.
2   Eliot, T S. *Four Quartets.* London: Faber & Faber, 1960.
3   Khenpo, Nyoshul. *Natural Great Perfection.* Ithaca: Snow Lion Publications, 1995.

Chapter 28

1 *Devaputta Samyutta Sutta, Samyutta Nikaya* 17.
2 *Cakkavatti-Sihananda Sutta, Digha Nikaya* 26.

Chapter 32

1 *Anatta-Lakkhana Sutta, Samyutta Nikaya* 22:59.
2 Dor-Ziderman, Y, et al. "Self-specific processing in the meditating brain: a MEG neurophenomenology study." *Neuroscience of Consciousness* 1.1: 1–13 (2016).
3 Chesterton, G K. *Orthodoxy.* Mineola, Dover Publications, 2004.
4 Thanissaro Bikkhu. *The Paradox of Becoming.* 2008. Available online at: www.accesstoinsight.org/lib/authors/ thanissaro/paradoxofbecoming.pdf.
5 *Kaccayanagotta Sutta, Samyutta Nikaya* 12:15.
6 *Upasiva-manava-puccha, Sutta Nipata* 1074–6.
7 Online at: www.ajahnchah.org/book/Still_Flowing_Water1. php.

Chapter 33

1 *Maha-Saccaka Sutta, Majjhima Nikaya* 36:85, 36:100.
2 Batchelor, Stephen. *Verses from the Center: A Buddhist Vision of the Sublime.* New York: Riverhead Books, 2000. (A free poetic translation of Nagarjuna's *Mulamadyamakakarika.*)
3 *Sagaathaa Vagga, Samyutta Nikaya* 1:1.
4 Passano, A, and Amaro, A. *The Island.* Redwood: Abhayagiri Monastic Foundation, 2009.
5 *Nidanasamyutta Sutta, Samyutta Nikaya* 12:15.
6 *Abyakatasamyutta Sutta, Samyutta Nikaya* 44:10.

Chapter 40

1 *Mulapariyaya Sutta, Majjhima Nikaya* 1:25.
2 Hsuan Hua. *The Sixth Patriach's Dharma Jewel Platform Sutra.* Burlingame: Buddhist Text Translation Society, 2001.

Chapter 41

1 Gimian, C R, ed. *The Essential Chögyam Trungpa.*
Shambhala: Boston, 1999.

Chapter 42

1 *Dona Sutta, Anguttara Nikaya* 4:36.
2 Krishnamurti's Journal, Ojai, 10 April 1975.

Appendix I

1 This interview with Stephen Fulder, carried out by Amir
Freimann, is one of many with spiritual teachers and
students from various paths and traditions. Reprinted here
by kind permission from *Spiritual Transmission: Paradoxes
and Dilemmas* (2018) by Amir Freimann, published by
Monkfish Book Publishing Company, Rhinebeck, New
York. The interview has been edited.

GLOSSARY

Ahamkara (Sanskrit)
The I-making tendency: the process in which living beings develop a sense of self and centre and control.

Anatta
The key Buddhist dogma and liberating insight that there is no fixed, permanent and independent self or ego (*atta*) that runs things. Though we assume there is one, when sought it is transparent and unfindable.

Atman (Sanskrit)
The Vedic belief in a universal and ultimate "self" or soul that is beyond all phenomena or individuality.

Avidya
Lack of wisdom or clarity, ignorance. It implies living on automatic pilot without seeing the way we construct the experience of ourselves and the world.

Brahmaviharas
Literally "celestial mansions" or "kingdoms of heaven". Immeasurable states of an expanded and inclusive heart. There are classically four of them: *metta, karuna, mudita, upekkha* (loving kindness, compassion, shared joy and equanimity).

Dana
An attitude and way of life based on generosity of heart. Living according to the flow of giving and receiving instead of greed or grasping.

Dhamma (Sanskrit: Dharma)

The nature of things and the cosmic order, and the seeing of it. The Buddhist teachings and path to liberation.

Dukkha

The basic unsatisfactoriness and the pain, suffering and struggle that is an inherent part of the ordinary experience of all living beings.

Karma (Sanskrit)

Web of interactions, habits, patterns and influences that create the world and us as we appear to be. The seeds sown in the world and in the future by our actions and intentions. Fate or destiny.

Karuna

Compassion, empathy, and the way we are touched by, and resonate with, all suffering.

Kilesa

Blocks, contaminations, psychological habit patterns, or obstacles that obscure, steal and obstruct our wisdom and freedom.

Kusala

Wholesome, helpful and healthy. Practice or actions of mind, body and speech that helps us on the road to liberation.

Maya (Sanskrit)

The illusory nature of the world as seen through the conventional conditioned mind. Belief in the way things seem to be.

Metta

Practising and living with a big heart that radiates kindness and friendliness unconditionally to ourselves and all living beings.

Mudita
Sympathetic joy. The way we resonate with and participate in the joy of others.

Nirvana (Sanskrit)
Literally: cooling the fire. States of awakening and liberation. Total and irreversible release.

Pannya
Wisdom and insight. A seeing and knowing that cuts through appearances and reveals what is deeper, authentic and liberating.

Parami
Refined, pure and sublime qualities that develop during a life of spiritual practice. These qualities take the place of ordinary personality attributes.

Paticcasamuppada
12 steps of dependent origination or the wheel of life. The basic Buddhist teaching that shows how samsara and nirvana, experience and suffering, ourselves and the world, including our birth and death, are created through conditioning and interdependence.

Sacca
Honesty, authenticity, love of truth and rejection of pretence and delusion.

Samadhi (Sanskrit)
Focus and concentration. The ability to settle into and stay with an object of meditation. Serenity and steadiness of mind.

Samma
The fruition, perfection or development of basic human functions and practices, such as speech, intention or meditation. It is particularly applied to the eightfold path.

Samsara (Sanskrit)
Ordinary reality characterized by struggle and the survival instinct. Often described as life going round and round, or the "daily round".

Sankhara
Constructions, beliefs, assumptions, explanations and mental patterns that appear to be facts. They can be about ourselves and the world.

Sati
Mindfulness. Being awake, aware and present, and the capacity to return to presence from distraction.

Sattva (Sanskrit)
A range of qualities including goodness, positivity, truth, wholesomeness, serenity, balance, subtlety, peacefulness and virtuousness. These draw us toward dharma.

Sila
Ethics and morality. Harmonious and beneficial action of body speech and mind.

Tathata
Base or ground reality which is indescribable and undefinable, often translated as "suchness" or "that". It is sublime and known only by profound wisdom.

Upadana
Attachment or clinging. It also means feeding, in the sense that what we feed, for example our desires or fears, grows and takes root.

Upekkha
Equanimity, steadiness, and inner balance. External events fail to destroy, disturb or overwhelm us because of an inner emptiness and freedom.

Vedana
The immediate sense of pleasant, unpleasant or neutral that accompanies all sensory input.

Vidya
Wisdom, clarity, the ability to see under the surface and explore the actual nature of experience. The opposite of *avidya*, *vidya* cuts through our conditioning.

Vipassana
Clear seeing or insight, especially liberating insights into the real nature of our experience as being dynamic and passing conditioned phenomena.

USEFUL WEBSITES

www.stephenfulder.com

www.accesstoinsight.org

www.insightmeditation.org

www.gaiahouse.co.uk

www.worldwideinsight.org

www.dharma.org

www.buddhanet.net

www.dharmaseed.org

ACKNOWLEDGEMENTS

Concerning the original version of this book, I would firstly like to acknowledge the great help I have received from Muli Glazer who contributed his skill in putting the dharma into language, which is no easy task, as well as the many students and colleagues who helped with individual articles.

I would like to acknowledge the help of Dr. Carmel Shalev, Jonathan Harrison, Ilan Luttenberg, Chanan Kubitsky, Dr. Assaf Federman, Rabbi James Jacobsen-Maisels, and Harriet Lewis, for the translation of articles from Hebrew to English.

I wish to express my great appreciation to my wife Rachel, for her deep understanding, support and encouragement all along the way.